Computer Networks and Communications

COMPUTER NETWORKS AND COMMUNICATIONS

Ritu Choudhary

CENTRUM PRESS
NEW DELHI-110002 (INDIA)

CENTRUM PRESS

H.O.: 4360/4, Ansari Road, Daryaganj,
New Delhi-110002 (India)
Tel: 23278000, 23261597, 23255577, 23286875

B.O.: No. 1015, Ist Main Road, BSK IIIrd Stage,
IIIrd Phase, IIIrd Block, Bangalore-560085 (INDIA)
Tel: 080-41723429

Email: centrumpress@gmail.com
Visit us at: www.centrumpress.com

Computer Networks and Communications

First Edition, 2011

PRINTED IN INDIA

Printed at Tarun Offset Printers, Delhi-110053

Contents

Preface *vii*

1. Computer Network 1
2. Medium Access Controlling of Sub Layer 90
3. OSI Network Layer 127
4. Mobile Communication 252
5. Network Operating Systems 267

Bibliography 285
Index 287

Preface

Today computer is available in many offices and homes and there is a need to share data and programs among various computers with the advancement of data communication facilities. The communication between computers has increased and it thus it has extended the power of computer beyond the computer room. Now a user sitting at one place can communicate computers of any remote sites through communication channel. We all are acquainted with some sorts of communication in our day-to-day life. For communication of information and messages we use telephone and postal communication systems. Similarly data and information from one computer system can be transmitted to other systems across geographical areas. Thus data transmission is the movement of information using some standard methods. These methods include electrical signals carried along a conductor, optical signals along an optical fibers and electromagnetic areas.

Suppose a manager has to write several letters to various clients. First, he/she has to use his/her PC and Word Processing package to prepare his/her letter. If the PC is connected to the entire client's PCs through networking, he/she can send the letters to all the clients within minutes. Thus irrespective of geographical areas, if PCs are connected through communication channel, the data and information, computer files and any other program can be transmitted to other computer systems within seconds. The modern form of communication like e-mail and Internet is possible only because of computer networking. The aim of this book is to introduce you the various aspects of computer network and communication.

Author

1

Computer Network

NETWORKING

A *computer network* is an interconnection of various computer systems located at the same or different places. The interconnection is done through a communication link also known as the physical layer of the network and this link is such that it is totally transparent to the users of the network. The transparency of the communication link is brought about by the interfacing software known as protocols which enables a user in one location to freely access a computer system/database/process/software in another location.

For such an extensive and involved subject, which includes so many different technologies, hardware devices and protocols, the definition of networking is actually quite simple. A network is simply a collection of computers or other hardware devices that are connected together, either physically or logically, using special hardware and software to allow them to exchange information and cooperate. Networking is the term that describes the processes involved in designing, implementing, upgrading, managing and otherwise working with networks and network technologies.

Networks are used for an incredible array of different purposes. In fact, the definitions above are so simple for the specific reason that networks can be used so broadly, and can allow such a wide variety of tasks to be accomplished. While most people learning about networking focus on the interconnection of PCs and other "true" computers, you use various types of networks every day. Each time you pick up a phone, use a credit card at a store, get cash from an ATM machine, or even plug in an electrical appliance, you are using some type of network.

In fact, the definition can even be expanded beyond the world of technology altogether: I'm sure you've heard the term "networking" used to describe the process of finding an employer or employee by talking to friends and associates. In this case too, the idea is that independent units are connected together to share information and cooperate all devices represents, in a way, a return to the "good old days" of mainframe computers. Before computers were small and personal, they were large and centralized machines that were shared by many users operating remote terminals. While having all of the computer power in one place had many disadvantages, one benefit was that all users were connected because they shared the central computer.

Individualized PCs took away that advantage, in favour of the benefits of independence. Networking attempts to move computing into the middle ground, providing PC users with the best of both worlds: the independence and flexibility of personal computers, and the connectivity and resource sharing of mainframes. in fact, networking is today considered so vital that it's hard to conceive of an organization with two or more computers that would not want to connect them together!

TYPES OF NETWORKING

The word "networking" strikes fear into legions of otherwise intrepid job hunters. It conjures up one of three images: calling everyone in your address book to see whether anyone knows anyone who may know anyone who may give you an informational interview, attending club meetings with other job hunters or having your friends come up with ideas and contacts instead of advising you to get out there and network. But there is no need to fear because there are many different types of networking techniques you can use to help with your job search and references.

Obviously number three doesn't always work. But the other two aren't so appealing either. Who enjoys calling total strangers and asking them to meet with you when there's nothing in it for them? If they're successful in what they do – and why else would you want to meet with them? – they're likely to be busy doing it.

- *Strong-Contact Networks*: Structured explicitly to pass business referrals among members, they allow only one member per profession. Strong-contact networks are particularly good for developing in-depth relationships because you see the same members week after week and pass referrals as a part of each meeting.
- *Casual-contact Networks*: Bring business people together in a less-structured context than strong-contact networks, but for many they are a primary source of referrals; membership is not limited by profession. These groups are good for developing breadth in your network, but deep, long-lasting relationships can be formed as well.
- *Service Organizations:* Associations that exist to provide and support humanitarian efforts and good works in the community and larger venues. They also bring people together in settings that facilitate referral and knowledge networking. Like casual-contact groups, they help you add breadth and diversity to your network.
- *Professional Associations*: Established to exchange information and ideas among those in a given industry, as well as to promote and support that industry. These networks often include direct competitors, but they also provide contacts in related, non-competing businesses as well.
- *Social/business Organizations:* Combine social activities with business networking and can provide a variety of networking opportunities; many tend to resemble singles bars.
- *Women's Networking groups:* Still important networking organizations, but are slowly disappearing as women enter the business

mainstream, especially as professionals, entrepreneurs, and small-business owners.
- *On line Networks*: A new phenomenon covering a wide range of interests.

ARCHITECTURE

In communications, data is transferred wither on parallel or serial mode. Parallel communication is faster but requires more wires. Serial communications is much slower but requires fewer wires. Serial is more practical for communication with remote sites, and the existing telephone networks use serial communications for linking computers.

LOCAL AREA NETWORK

LAN is normally transmit data in a digital form with typical transmission speeds of up to several megabytes per second. These speeds can be achieved using parallel transmission where a cable with multiple core is used, or serial transmission, making use of high frequency carriers, using coaxial cables, fibre optics or even a simple pair of wires because distances are short. Modems are not normally required although some mechanism for converting from parallel to serial transmission and back again may be needed. The terminals and workstations are able to connect to either one of the two host computers at will. The network also has a file server and a print server. The former is a special computer which provides a form of auxiliary storage which can be used by any other computer on the network and the latter is a special computer which can receive data from other computers on the network and print it. There is also an external communication server on the LAN, which enables communication between equipment on the network and system elsewhere.

Local Area Network link computers in the same area for the purpose of sharing information and hardware. Usually the computers are within 300 metres of each other, because they must be connected by a cable hookup, which can be expensive. People at the work stations in a LAN gain more capabilities in work processing, data processing, information retrieval and communication without duplication of equipment, databases and activities. LAN has become popular. Many businesses are installing LAN in order to improve the efficiency of office functions and to facilitate office automation. The configuration of the LAN can be a star or a ring topology or simply devises attached along a length of cable.

Description

LAN or Local Area Network is the most common kind of network set up. There are two ways to connect a LAN network. The simplest and easiest way is the peer-to-peer connection network. This is when two or more computers are directly connected to each other. For example if there were four computers in the network, computer 1 would be connected to computer 2, computer 2 would be connected to computer 3 and computer 3 would be connected to computer 4. This means each computer is dependent on the other. And if there were a network problem with any one computer, all of them would be affected. The other type if the client server connection.

A local area network, or LAN, is a network of connected computers in a room, building, or set of buildings. Local area networks have been around since the beginning of computer use. A LAN is defined as a user network whereby data is sent at high rates between people located relatively close to each other. LANs do not usually make use of leased communication lines, but only means of communication that are provided by the installer of the network.

The Internet is a wide area network, or WAN, which is distinct from a LAN. In contrast to the term *Internet,* local area networks are often called *intranets,* though sometimes this term refers to a cluster of LANs associated with a particular company or organization but not connected to the larger Internet. A local area network uses a hub or router to connect computers together. The means of communication is the omnipresent Ethernet cable or wireless wi-fi technology. These technologies offer data transfer rates running between 10 to 10000 Mbit/s.

Perhaps the most frequently employed use of a LAN is to connect users to the Internet with only one connected router. In modern times, we use broadband cable or DSL modems to connect to the Internet, and it would be clumsy to have a modem associated with every computer, so we simply plug the modem into a router and link the router to computers with Ethernet cables. Configuring a LAN can be intimidating at first, but contemporary operating systems have programmes that do most of the necessary configurations automatically, so setting up a local area network is pretty easy.

A local area network (LAN) supplies networking capability to a group of computers in close proximity to each other such as in an office building, a school, or a home. A LAN is useful for sharing resources like files, printers, games or other applications. A LAN in turn often connects to other LANs, and to the Internet or other WAN.

ADVANTAGES OF LAN

To Facilitate Communication

Where key personnel are scattered on offices on several floors and perhaps in several buildings, conferences may be inconvenient. Telephone calls may also prove frustrating if the participants cannot express their difficulties accurately. One solution may be the use of electronics mail, in which individuals use a LAN a leave, written messages to a number of subordinate for example a memo ?V it may also be possible to keep a computerized distribution line and use electronic mail and a LAN for this purpose.

To Improve Communications, Speed and Accuracy

It is uncommon for the inter-office mail of even fairly small companies to take several days for delivery. In contrast, sending messages through LAN is virtually instantaneous and there is also less chance of the message being lost. Communications may also be more accurate because no ambiguous messages are taken by the other and because word processors can be used to compose the message.

To Share Computer Equipment

Letter-quality printers and large hard-disk drives can be expensive. Local area networks enable users to share equipment by networking microcomputers or workstations together. For example, a company with twenty microcomputer users, each requiring only limited hard-disk space and occasional printing, might save substantial amount in equipment costs through networking. Savings may also be achieved by buying less expensive terminals or disk-less microcomputer, rather than fully configured stand-alone equipment.

To Share Computer Files

LAN enables the users to share files with each other. This advantage is invaluable (for example, to word-processing personnel who need access to filed documents or to managers using electronic mail). Corporate databases, important policy or procedure statements and even local classified advertisements can call be stored on shared computer files.

To Save Software Costs

The purchase or lease of most software products includes a licensing agreement that restricts copying software's. Whereas some software companies require buyers to purchase separate copies for each computer or microcomputer, others offer ? Site-licensing agreement that permits purchasers to pay a single one time fee per LAN. Since many commercial software packages are costly, the savings for companies with local area networks can be considerable.

WIDE AREA NETWORK (WAN)

The term wide area network (WAN) is used to describe a computer spanning a region or global area. A large company may use the WAN to connect its regional computers, manufacturing centres, distribution centres and regional accounting centres. They are connected to national headquarters, and therefore to each other for communication purposes.

The wide area network, often referred to as a WAN, is a communications network that makes use of existing technology to connect local computer networks into a larger working network that may cover both national and international locations. This is in contrast to both the local area network and the metropolitan area network, which provides communication within a restricted geographic area. Here is how the wide area network functions, and why it is so important to communications today.

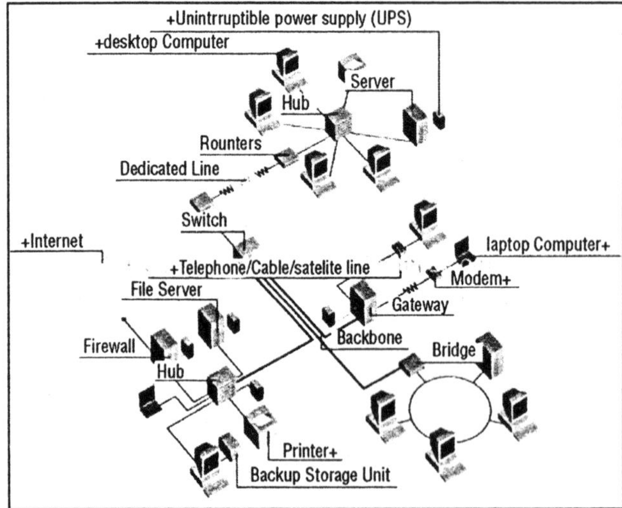

The concept of linking one computer network with another is often desirable, especially for businesses that operate a number of facilities. Beginning with the local area network and going up to the wide area network, this is most easily accomplished by using existing telephony technology. Essentially, fibre optics are used to create the link between networks located in different facilities. Often, this means using standard phone lines, referred to as POTS, or employing PSTN (public switched telephone network) technology. During the 1990s, a third option, that of ISDN (integrated services digital network) solutions for creation a wide area network gained a great deal of popularity, mainly because the concept made it more cost effective to extend the network beyond national boundaries. With coverage in a broad area, a wide area network allows companies to make use of common resources in order to operate. For example, many retail drugstores make use of a wide area network as part of their support to customers who fill prescriptions with one of their stores. Once in the common customer database for the pharmacy, the client is free to fill a prescription at any of the company's locations, even while vacationing in another state.

Overview

WAN or Wide Area Network is when several LANs or independent computers are connected to a single, wider network. The Internet is the perfect example of WAN. E-mails, Chat Rooms and IMs all connect to the WAN of the Internet. WAN is much more complex and requires connecting devices or hubs from all over the world.

The term Wide Area Network (WAN) usually refers to a network which covers a large geographical area, and use communications circuits to connect the intermediate nodes. A major factor impacting WAN design and performance is a requirement that they lease communications circuits from telephone companies or other communications carriers. Transmission rates are typically 2 Mbps, 34 Mbps, 45 Mbps, 155 Mbps, 625 Mbps (or sometimes considerably more).

Numerous WANs have been constructed, including public packet networks, large corporate networks, military networks, banking networks, stock brokerage networks, and airline reservation networks. Some WANs are very extensive, spanning the globe, but most do not provide true global coverage. Organizations supporting WANs using the Internet Protocol are known as Network Service Providers (NSPs). These form the core of the Internet.

Wide Area Networks, or WANs, connect a geographically diverse group of computers within a state, country, or even across several states or countries. WANs typically are connected by telephone lines, other types of communication lines, or radio waves. Quite often, smaller local area networks (LANs) are linked together to form a WAN. This is accomplished via dedicated private lines, leased from telecommunications firms like Sprint and AT&T, or by Switched Multi-Megabit Data Services (SMDS) technology, developed in 1995 to eliminate the need for a leased line.

WAN technology has been refined over a period of several decades. It first emerged in the mid-twentieth century with the advent of networks like ARPAnet. Developed in 1969 by the Department of Defence, ARPAnet and several other networks eventually evolved into the Internet, the largest WAN in the world.

The packet switching technology most commonly used with WANs surfaced in the 1960s, and standard packet switching protocol, known as X.25, was developed in 1976. To increase network speed, packet switching allows for the parceling of data into smaller chunks, known as packets, prior to transmission. These packets can travel independently via alternate routes, and they are reassembled once they reach their target. Although X.25 remained the most popular WAN packet switching protocol for years, other packet switching protocols used with increasing frequency by WAN developers and administrators include the Internet standard, Transmission Control Protocol/Internet Protocol (TCP/IP), and Frame Relay, used most often by WANs connected via high speed T–1 and T–3 lines.

WANs are used for a variety of purposes. A corporation with offices in several locations may use a WAN to form an intranet. Quite often, the individual offices will use their own LANs for things like internal messaging, data processing functions, and hardware and software sharing. When these LANs are joined together to form a WAN, similar data sharing and messaging capabilities become possible across a much broader geographic area.

Businesses wanting to link up with their suppliers or distributors may create a WAN as a means of establishing an extranet. For example, an extranet could provide a sales representative with electronic access to information in about the time it might take to deliver a product, or the availability of a product. Some WANs bring together various types of communications, such as data, video, and voice. Some organizations, including companies, universities, research centres, hospitals, and libraries, use WANs to connect to the Internet.

The characteristics of the transmission facilities lead to an emphasis on efficiency of communications techniques in the design of WANs. Controlling the volume of traffic and avoiding excessive delays is important. Since the topologies of WANs are likely to be more complex than those of LANs, routing algorithms also receive more emphasis. Many WANs also implement sophisticated monitoring procedures to account for which users consume the network resources. This is, in some cases, used to generate billing information to charge individual users.

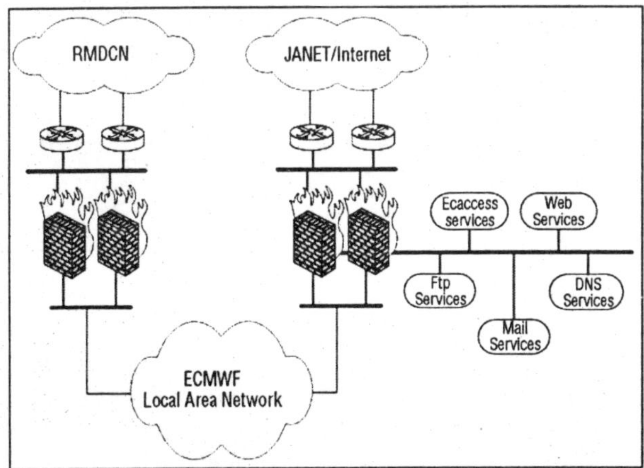

The size of a network is limited due to size and distance constraints. However networks may be connected over a high-speed communications link (called a WAN link) to link them together and thus becomes a WAN. WAN links are usually:

- Dial up connection
- *Dedicated connection*: It is a permanent full time connection. When a dedicated connection is used, the cable is leased rather than a part of the cable bandwidth and the user has exclusive use.
- *Switched network*: Several users share the same line or the bandwidth of the line. There are two types of switched networks:

- *Circuit switching:* This is a temporary connection between two points such as dial-up or ISDN.
- *Packet switching*: This is a connection between multiple points. It breaks data down into small packets to be sent across the network. A virtual circuit can improve performance by establishing a set path for data transmission. This will shave some overhead of a packet switching network. A variant of packet switching is called cell-switching where the data is broken into small cells with a fixed length.

WAN TECHNOLOGY COMPARISONS

Terms

- *Circuit switching:* Physical switched connection.
- *Message switching:* A store and forward mechanism where messages are treated as individual units.
- *Packet switching:* Messages are broken down into smaller packets with individual destination information. Independent routing is used which allows the packets to use any route between the source send destination. Much RAM and processing power is required to support this switching type.
- *Data gram packet switching:* Uses independent paths.
- *Virtual circuit packet switching:* This is used for audio and video streaming. A set path is established between the source and destination and a connection-oriented service is made.

LAN AND WAN

- A LAN is restricted to a limited geographical coverage of few kilometres, but a WAN spans greater distance and many operate nationwide or even worldwide.
- The cost to transmit data in a LAN is negligible since the transmission medium is usually owned by user organization. However, in case of a WAN, this cost may be very high because the transmission medium used are leased lines or public systems such as

telephone lines, microwave and satellite links.

- In a LAN, the computer terminals and peripherals devices are usually physically connected with wired and coaxial cables. Whereas, in a WAN there may not be a direct physical connection between various computers.
- Data transmission speed is much higher in LAN than in a WAN. Typical transmission speeds in LAN are 0.1 to 100 bits per second. On the other hand, in a WAN the data transmission speed is normally of the order of 1800 to 9600 bits per second.
- Fewer data transmission error occurs in case of LAN as compared to a WAN. This is mainly because in the case of a LAN, the distance covered by the data is negligible as compared to WAN.

METROPOLITAN AREA NETWORKS (MAN)

As implied by their names, Metropolitan and Wide area networks have wider geographical reaches than Local area networks. While MAN usually spans over a city, the reach of a WAN extends over one or more computers and possibly the whole world. Despite the differences in their geographical reach, MAN??s and WAN??s of today generally use the same technology. For example if the computers of an Insurance Company spread all over the country are connected together and information/data travels from operating offices to controlling office and vice versa then we can say that WAN is implemented in the company.

GOALS AND APPLICATIONS OF NETWORKS

NETWORK GOALS

- The main goal of networking is "Resource sharing", and it is to make all programmes, data and equipment available to anyone on the network with out the regard to the physical location of the resource and the user.
- A second goal is to provide high reliablity by having alternative sources of supply. For example, all files

could be replicatied on two or three machines, so if one of them is unavailable, the other copies could be available.

- Another goal is saving money. Small computers have a much better price/performance ratio than larger ones. Mainframes are roughly a factor of ten times faster than the fastest single chip micro-processors, but they cost thousand times more. This imbalance has caused many system designers to build systems consisting of powerful personal computers, one per user, with data kept on one or more shared file server machines. This goal leads to networks with many computers located in the same building. Such a network is called a LAN(local area network).
- Another closely related goal is to increase the systems perfomance as the work load increases by just adding more processors. With central mainframes, when the system is full, it must be replaced by a larger one, usually at great expense and with even greater disruption to the users.
- Computer networks provide a powerful communication medium. A file that was updated/modified on a network, can be seen by the other users on the network immediately.

NETWORK APPLICATIONS

- Access to remote programmes.
- Access to remote databases.
- Value-added communication facilities.

Calling up a distant computer via a network is cheaper than calling it directly. The lower rate is possible because in a normal telephone call ties up an expensive, dedicated circuit for the duration of the call, whereas access via a network ties up long-distance lines only while data are actually being transmitted.

MOTIVATION

Sophisticated multi-party applications will use many traffic streams with very different characteristics and will be network-aware so they can perform well on a variety of networks. At the same time, we see the emergence of an electronic service industry that is eager to deliver a wide variety of services to end-users.

Services will range from low-level "bearer" services that transport bit streams over the network infrastructure to value-added services such as video conferencing, computing services, and data mining. Complex applications will support cooperation among multiple parties by combining video conferencing with access to large amounts of archived data, real time data streams, and distributed computing tasks. Supporting this service model and this emerging class of complex services requires innovation in a number of areas.

- First, the requirements on how the network should handle traffic streams will be very diverse, both in terms of the ability to share resources between cooperating traffic streams and the quality of service for individual streams.
- Second, conditions in the network and at the endpoints will change continuously, and mechanisms are needed that allow the network, services and application to adjust quickly.
- Third, in many cases, applications and services have advance knowledge of changes in resource requirements, and mechanisms are needed to make use of this information to optimize performance.
- Fourth, we have to develop systematic methods for balancing the constraints and priorities of services competing for network resources.

NETWORK MODEL

We view network entities as playing one of three roles, as is illustrated in the figure above:

- A bearer provides links and switching points that move bits among endpoints according to certain simple agreements about resource allocation.
- A service provider packages bearer functions and its

own computing resources to provide services ranging from simple services such as CBR ATM connections to complex value added services such as multimedia conferencing services that adapt media rates and formats among heterogeneous endpoints, or distributed computing and storage capabilities. Services can be hierarchical, *i.e.* a complex service might be built on top of simpler services. We will distinguish between services that require handling the data and those that don't. The latter can be handled directly in the switching points, while the former might be implemented on service nodes. Service nodes are outside of the core network and are represented in our model by "virtual endpoints".

- An application runs on a set of computational endpoints and operates by invoking services in the network. Applications can be very simple, (*e.g.* dialing a number on a phone to get directory assistance) or more complex (*e.g.* a distributed computing application that uses a collective communication service).

Let us illustrate the model using a video conferencing scenario. The application provides information on participants, connectivity, limits on simultaneous activity on the connections, etc. If the conference is dynamic, the information has to include a characterization of the dynamic behaviour. The video conferencing service will combine the application information with a requirements specification specific to video conferencing.

This results in a session specification that is used to contract for bearer resources and computation capability to satisfy the session requirements. The service mesh thus constructed provides an abstracted view of the underlying bearer resources, in which only those links and switching points at the periphery of the bearers' meshes are visible; this is illustrated in the figure below. The service layer will also provide the bearer layer with information on how the traffic belonging to the new application should be handled. These instructions will be translated into specific switch schedules, buffer allocations, etc. by the bearer.

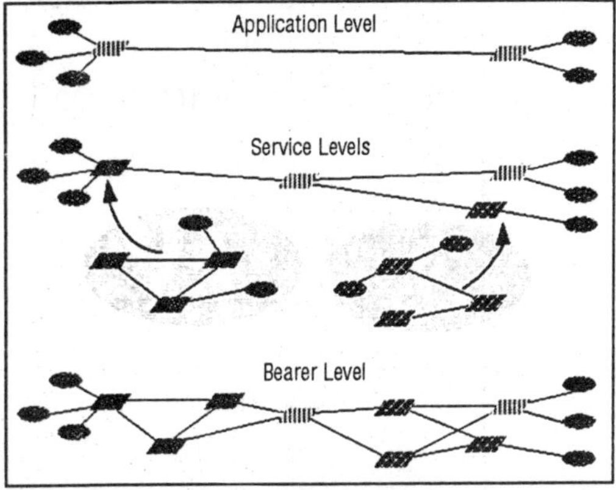

Throughout the video conference resource allocation will be adjusted. These adjustments can be triggered by the application (*e.g.* a receiver changes the video source it wants to see), by the service layer (*e.g.* reallocating resources in the service mesh) or by the bearer layer (*e.g.* changes in available bandwidth). The adjustments will be very different: the simplest changes will require only local changes on one or a small number of nodes, while others, like rerouting, will require a global view. Ideally, many changes can be accommodated through local adjustments, since this will result in more responsive and efficient service.

A useful view of this functionality is provided by the "active network" concept under discussion among a group of ARPA-supported researchers. In this view, the network conveys objects that may carry methods to be invoked at different points, and may "programme" switching and processing entities in application-specific ways. Our research fits well into this model. The resource allocation capabilities we envision are needed to allow the network to host the customised computations envisioned for active networks. At the same time, active network mechanisms will be used in support of the customization of resource management to meet application needs. We call this type of network "application-aware" since it directly cooperates with applications and services to maximize network responsiveness to application requirements. In the following section, we elucidate the research issues that we plan to pursue in developing the underpinnings of such an "application-aware" network.

ALLOCATING A VIRTUAL APPLICATION MESH

A virtual application mesh represents the resources allocated for the application, *e.g.* bandwidth on links, "capacity" on switch nodes, and virtual end-point resources. Virtual meshes differ from traditional routes in two fundamental ways. First, resources are associated with an application session, and not with individual connections. Second, while switches traditionally make resource allocation decisions fairly independently, switch nodes coordinate resource allocation both at startup and runtime. These features make it possible to optimize resource allocation using global goals and constraints (*e.g.* limit total resource utilization) instead of local ones (*e.g.* fairness on a per-link and per-connection basis).

The virtual application mesh also supports application awareness: the application has considerable flexibility over how resource inside the virtual mesh are allocated initially and reallocated, for example in response to changes in the conditions in the network or in the application requirements. These changes must be handled quickly and efficiently. How the virtual application mesh is laid out will impact the cost of these adjustments, so the initial mesh allocation problem has a planning component. However, allocating a virtual application mesh is considerably more complex than to traditional point-to-point or point-to- multipoint routing. It requires allocating more diverse resources, and also the simultaneous allocation of resources for a large number of application streams.

SWITCH POINT MANAGEMENT

Service-related activities in networks take place on a wide range of time scales. However, resource allocation decisions are typically limited, *e.g.* per-packet scheduling inside the network combined with a transport protocol executing on the endpoint. Responsive application-aware networking will require coordinated resource allocation at many time scales. Coordination can take the form of exchanging information regarding status and present and future requirements, coordination of resource allocation activities, and the specification (using a language or programme) of actions to be taken under certain conditions. These interactions will pay off in several areas. Examples include application- and service-specific dynamic sharing of resources between streams under changing network conditions; the implementation of services models that sit in between best effort and guaranteed services, for example using application provided hints; application- and service-specific flow control; and the extension of the time horizon of schedulers, for example by considering application frame boundaries during scheduling.

Critical to the implementation of this network model is the ability to safely inject application and service state and code into the network. This enables application and service specific actions on switching points without the need for expensive and time consuming interactions with endpoints. Interactions between switching points and the application running on the endpoints will of course still be required, but they can be done in a service-specific instead of a generic fashion. The application and service "presence" in the network can range from simple parametres, through specifications using more complex languages, to actual code. The full spectrum of mechanisms will be needed in a fully application-oriented network. What mechanism will be used for a specific action will not only depend on what degree of flexibility is needed, but also on practical considerations. For example, including service code for cell-level switching is impractical.

RESOURCE MANAGEMENT FRAMEWORK

While traditional networks allocate resources on a per packet or per connection basis, resource allocation in application-aware networks is subject to constraints and goals of a variety of entities including link owners, service providers, and applications. We briefly describe a hierarchical resource management framework that allows the systematic integration of these goals and constraints.

The resource allocation policy of a communication link is represented by a directed acyclic graph with a single root representing the link and leaf nodes representing individual traffic streams. Intermediate nodes represent organizational entities. Each node gets resources from its parents and specifies how its resources are distributed to its children. Examples of policies include fair-sharing at different granularities, reservation, and strict priority.

This graph is a language that can be used by different entities to specify how traffic streams or collections of traffic streams should share bandwidth. By combining subgraphs, the resource management policies set by different entities (link, service providers, applications) can be represented simultaneously. Tools are used to translate a graph into a schedule that can be used by switch nodes, and incremental changes in the graph translate into incremental changes in the schedule.

ROBUSTNESS AND SECURITY

Our approach lends itself naturally to dealing with failure recovery in an integrated fashion throughout the resource allocation process. One of the "changes" that can be considered during the creation of the virtual mesh is the failure of nodes and links, and both the topology of the virtual application mesh and the instructions to switching points can implicitly and explicitly prepare for a quick response to failures. The degree of robustness can be application and service specific. The issue of security shows up in a number of areas. First, the network has to verify that application input (parametres, specification and programmes) can be acted upon safely since incorrect input can endanger the operation of the network. This requires a combination of language, compilation and runtime techniques, and we plan to use mostly existing technology for this security aspect. Second, the network has to guarantee that only authorized entities can modify the network state. We plan to address this using existing authentication methods. Note that the virtual application mesh can form the basis for providing security. As part of the creation of the mesh, relationships of trust can be established between the nodes in the mesh. This can speed up security checking during execution.

EXPERIMENTAL APPROACH

Carnegie Mellon University is developing a comprehensive suite of resource management mechanisms in support of such "application-aware" networks. We will support resource allocation along three dimensions: resource allocation in the "space" consisting of the physical network infrastructure and attached processing and storage resources; decision making on different time scales, ranging from application startup to packet and cell scheduling; and resource allocation by different organizational entities sharing the infrastructure.

In all three dimensions, the mechanisms we develop will provide for extensive tailoring to application requirements. The resource management techniques will be evaluated in a testbed driven by increasingly more aggressive applications and services. Tesbed development will take place in three steps. Initially, we will use the existing Credit Net ATM network for quick experiments that will guide the design of interfaces and protocols. A second step will be a local area version of our network architecture and resource management software. Finally, we plan to perform a wide area evaluation, hopefully in cooperation with groups working on related research topics.

NETWORK STRUCTURE

ARCHITECTURE AND STRUCTURE

The importance of having standardised networking protocols have led to the evolution of several networking reference models. The Open System Interconnection (OSI) and the TCP/IP models will be looked at. These models allow us to more easily study the structure of networks.

OSI Reference Model

The OSI model is based on a proposal by the International Standards Organisation. The OSI reference model has a layered architecture, whereby each layer encapsulates a function of the overall complex task. The proposed model has 7 layers. The key idea is that although data is transmitted vertically, each layer is programmed horizontally. Each layer ignores the complications of the lower layers and assumes that the information it passes out is immediately seen by destination host. At each layer, appropriate headers are appended onto the data when sending, and are removed as the data is decoded. Since the headers from the lower levels are removed before the next higher level looks at the data, the concept of horizontal coding is preserved.

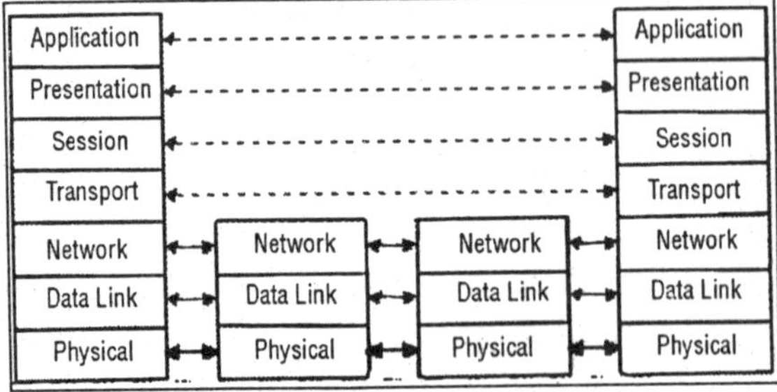

Layer 1: The physical layer, and is concerned with transmitting raw bits over a communication channel.

Layer 2: The data link layer, handles error correction and flow regulation.

Layer 3: The network layer. It is concerned with the operation of the subnet, that is, it determines how packets are routed from source to destination. Routes can be based on hardwired static tables, or can be highly dynamic, where each packet is assigned a different route through the network, depending on the network load. In broadcast networks, routing is simple, and hence the network layer is often thin or non-existent.

Layer 4: The transport layer. Data accepted from the session layer is split into smaller units if need be and passed to the network layer. It is also in charge of ensuring that the information arrives correctly on the other end. Connections across the network, are established and deleted from this layer. There are mechanisms to regulate flow of information between fast and slow host machines. This flow control is distinct from the flow control talked about in layer 2.

Layer 5: The session layer implements a set of rules for establishing and terminating data streams between hosts. Services provided include dialogue control(full of half duplex), token management and other end to end data control.

Layer 6: The presentation layer, and it performs certain functions requested sufficiently often enough to warrant finding a general solution for them, rather than letting each user solve them. It manages between different abstract data types like ASCII, Unicode, integer representation, one's and two's complements etc. This allows computers with different data representations to communicate.

Layer 7: The application layer and is charged with translating between different applications. For example, for a screen editor to work over a network, it has to know the different escape codes of different terminals. Similarly with FTP. Different systems have different file naming conventions, different ways of representing text. The applications layer takes care of these complications.

TCP/IP Reference

The underpinnings of the Internet are formed by the global

interconnection of hundreds of thousands of otherwise independent computers, communications entities and information systems. What makes this interconnection possible is the use of a set of communication standards, procedures and formats in common among the networks and the various devices and computational facilities connected to them. The procedures by which computers communicate with each other are called "protocols." While this infrastructure is steadily evolving to include new capabilities, the protocols initially used by the Internet are called the "TCP/IP" protocols, named after the two protocols that formed the principal basis for Internet operation.

On top of this infrastructure is an emerging set of architectural concepts and data structures for heterogeneous information systems that renders the Internet a truly global information system. In essence, the Internet is an architecture, although many people confuse it with its implementation. When the Internet is looked at as an architecture, it manifests two different abstractions. One abstraction deals with communications connectivity, packet delivery and a variety of end-end communication services. The other abstraction deals with the Internet as an information system, independent of its underlying communications infrastructure, which allows creation, storage and access to a wide range of information resources, including digital objects and related services at various levels of abstraction.

Interconnecting computers is an inherently digital problem. Computers process and exchange digital information, meaning that they use a discrete mathematical "binary" or "two-valued" language of 1s and 0s. For communication purposes, such information is mapped into continuous electrical or optical waveforms. The use of digital signaling allows accurate regeneration and reliable recovery of the underlying bits. We use the terms "computer," "computer resources" and "computation" to mean not only traditional computers, but also devices that can be controlled digitally over a network, information resources such as mobile programmes and other computational capabilities.

The telephone network started out with operators who manually connected telephones to each other through "patch panels" that accepted patch cords from each telephone line and electrically connected them to one another through the panel, which operated, in effect, like a switch. The result was called circuit switching, since at its conclusion, an electrical circuit was made between the calling telephone and the called telephone.

Conventional circuit switching, which was developed to handle telephone calls, is inappropriate for connecting computers because it makes limited use of the telecommunication facilities and takes too long to set up connections. Although reliable enough for voice communication, the circuit-switched voice network had difficulty delivering digital information without errors.

For digital communications, packet switching is a better choice, because it is far better suited to the typically "burst" communication style of computers. Computers that communicate typically send out brief but intense bursts of data, then remain silent for a while before sending out the next burst. These bursts are communicated as packets, which are very much like electronic postcards. The postcards, in reality packets, are relayed from computer to computer until they reach their destination. The special computers that perform this forwarding function are called variously "packet switches" or "routers" and form the equivalent of many bucket brigades spanning continents and oceans, moving buckets of electronic postcards from one computer to another. Together these routers and the communication links between them form the underpinnings of the Internet.

Without packet switching, the Internet would not exist, as we now know it. Going back to the postcard analogy, postcards can get lost. They can be delivered out of order, and they can be delayed by varying amounts. The same is true of Internet packets, which, on the Internet, can even be duplicated. The Internet Protocol is the postcard layer of the Internet. The next higher layer of protocol, TCP, takes care of re-sending the "postcards" to recover packets that might have been lost, and putting packets back in order if they have become disordered in transit. Thus, the evolution of the Internet was based on two technologies and a research dream. The technologies were packet switching and computer technology, which, in turn, drew upon the underlying technologies of digital communications and semiconductors. The research dream was to share information and computational resources. But that is simply the technical side of the story. Equally important in many ways were the other dimensions that enabled the Internet to come into existence and flourish. This aspect of the story starts with cooperation and far-sightedness in the U.S. Government, which is often derided for lack of foresight but is a real hero in this story.

It leads on to the enthusiasm of private sector interests to build upon the government funded developments to expand the Internet and make it available to the general public. Perhaps most important, it is fueled by the development of the personal computer industry and significant changes in the telecommunications industry in the 1980s, not the least of which was the decision to open the long distance market to competition. The role of workstations, the Unix operating system and local area networking (especially the Ethernet) are themes contributing to the spread of Internet technology in the 1980s into the research and academic community from which the Internet industry eventually emerged.

Many individuals have been involved in the development and evolution of the Internet covering a span of almost four decades if one goes back to the early writings on the subject of computer networking by Kleinrock, Licklider, Baran, Roberts, and Davies. The ARPANET, described below, was the first wide-area computer network. The NSFNET, which followed more than a decade later under the leadership of Erich Bloch, Gordon Bell, Bill Wulf and Steve Wolff, brought computer networking into the mainstream of the research and education communities. It is not our intent here to attempt to attribute credit to all those whose contributions were central to this story, although we mention a few of the key players.

The TCP/IP model was born out of the U.S. Department of Defence ARPANET. It consist of 4 layers and is named after the two protocols used.

- *Layer 4 is the application layer*: The TCP/IP model does not have a session or presentation layer. No need for them were perceived. Hence the application layer here corresponds to layers 5-7 in the OSI model. It contains higher protocols such as FTP, TELNET, HTTP etc.
- *Layer 3, the transport layer corresponds to the layer 4 in the OSI model*: The transport layer was designed to allow peer entities on the source and destination hosts to establish a conversation. Two end to end protocols are defined here. Transmission Control Protocol (TCP) is a reliable connection oriented protocol that allows a byte stream originating from one machine to de delivered without error to any other machine in the Internet. Incoming messages are fragmented into discrete messages before being transmitted. At the destination, TCP reassembles the received messages into the output stream. The second protocol, User Datagram Protocol (UDP) is an unreliable connectionless protocol. It is used for applications that do not want TCP's sequencing or flow control and wish to implement their own. It is widely used for one shot, client server type request-reply queries and applications in which prompt delivery is more important than accurate delivery. *E.g.* speech or video streams.
- *Layer 2 is the Internet layer*: The requirement that the network should survive a loss of subnet hardware, led to the choice of a packet switching network based on a connectionless layer. The job of the Internet layer is to permit hosts to inject packets into the network and have them travel independently to the destination. The Internet layer defines an official format and protocol called Internet Protocol (IP). The primary job here is one of packet routing and

avoidance of congestion. It is very similar to the OSI network layer.

- *The final layer is the host to network layer*: The TCP/IP model does not say much about what occurs here, except to point out that the host has to connect to the network using some protocol so it can send IP packets to the network.

Hardware Components

Here we will examine the different hardware that makes up a network. The most basic hardware that makes up a network is the transmission medium. The oldest and most common transmission medium is twisted pair wires. It consists of two insulated copper wires, typically about 1mm thick. The purpose of twisting is to reduce electrical interference.

The bandwidth depends on the thickness of the wires and distance travelled, but several megabytes/sec can be achieved for a few kilometres. Twisted pair cabling comes in several varieties, one of which is the Unshielded Twisted Pair (UTP) category 5 cabling. Category 5 UTP wires have more twists per centimetre than other twisted pair cabling, and has Teflon insulation. This results in less cross talk and a better quality signal over longer distances.

Coaxial cables are another popular form of transmission medium. It has better shielding than UTP so it can span for longer distances and at higher speeds. A coax cable is made up of a copper core, covered by a layer of insulating material, a braided outer conductor and finally a protective plastic covering. For 1 kilometre cables, bandwidths of 1 to 2 Gbps are feasible.

Fibre optic cables have a glass core centre, from which light propagates. It is next enclosed by a cladding of glass with a lower index of refraction than the core. This keeps the light within the core. A plastic jacket is the last layer and is to protect the cladding. Fibres are typically grouped into bundles, protected by another outer sheath.

The achievable bandwidth (about 1 Gbps) of fibre is current restricted by the ability to convert between electrical to optical signals. Speeds of 100Gbps are feasible and terabit performance is just a few years down the road. Fibre has many advantages over copper. It can handle higher bandwidths, due to lower attenuation, it only requires repeaters every 30 km as opposed to 5 km for copper. Fibre is also not affected by power surges, electromagnetic interference or power failures. Fibre does not leak light and thus is difficult to tap into. Fibre is light weight and its lower installation cost makes it a good choice over copper.

A repeater operates at the physical layer. It regenerates a signal received on one cable segment and retransmits it on another cable segment. A repeater can be used to extend the coverage of a network, and also to connect networks. Although a network can be extended with a repeater, a network is still constrained by the maximum permissible length of that LAN. Since a repeater functions at the physical layer, it is transparent to data flow and hence is limited to connecting two similar networks. Repeaters also cause problems with traffic.

If two networks are connected via a repeater, all messages from one network is passed to the other network, regardless of the intended recipient. If implemented without knowledge concerning the traffic flow on each LAN, performance problems will arise.

Application			Application
Presentation			Presentation
Session			Session
Transport			Transport
Network			Network
Data Link	Data Link	Data Link	Data Link
Physical	Physical	Physical	Physical

Bridge
Repeater

Bridges are more intelligent than repeaters. A bridge connects at the data link layer, where it can examine each frame that passes through it.

The bridge looks at the destination address of the incoming frame; if the destination is for the network across the bridge, it translates the frame, and retransmits it on the other network. If the frame is for a destination from the source network, the bridge repeats back the frame. There are typically two types of bridges. Transparent bridge and translating bridge. A transparent bridge connects two networks that employ the same protocol at the data link layer, whereas a translating bridge provides a connection capability between two networks that have differing protocols at the data link layer.

Routers operate one level higher, at the network layer. By operating at the network layer, routers are able to make decisions about how packets are routed between networks. Although multiported bridges can be said to have routing capabilities, this is usually for one point to point link within a network. A router has the ability to fragment and dynamically re-route the message across networks, making use of the most efficient paths. Routers are known to workstations that use their service, hence packets can be sent directly to routers. This means that routers do not have to examine in detail every packet it receives, and this makes them more efficient. However, the higher functionality of routers over bridges means that on average, routers perform a half to two thirds more processing over bridges.

Gateways function through all layers. Essentially, gateways perform protocol translation between networks. Gateways are generally designed and used for LAN-WAN connections and not for inter LAN communications.

The idea of intelligent hubs came about because running cables all over the building made it hard to configure and repair networks. Instead, collapse the LAN topology and put it in a box; terminate all devices in the network at the box using separate wires for each device. This centralised location makes it more convenient for network configuration, management and monitoring. Intelligent hubs are a level above normal hubs and wiring cabinets. Intelligent hubs are becoming key network management points as functionality such as bridges, routers and servers are built into them. Some intelligent hubs provide remote management capabilities that makes it easier to diagnose problems at distant locations and isolate faults from the rest of the network.

REFERENCE MODEL

HISTORY

The idea behind the creation of networking standards is to define widely-accepted ways of setting up networks and connecting them together. The OSI Reference Model represented an early attempt to get all of the various hardware and software manufacturers to agree on a framework for developing various networking technologies.

In the late 1970s, two projects began independently, with the same goal: to define a unifying standard for the architecture of networking systems. One was administered by the *International Organization for Standardization (ISO),* while the other was undertaken by the *International Telegraph and Telephone Consultative Committee,* or *CCITT* (the abbreviation is from the French version of the name). These two international standards bodies each developed a document that defined similar networking models.

In 1983, these two documents were merged together to form a standard called *The Basic Reference Model for Open Systems Interconnection.* That's a mouthful, so the standard is usually referred to as the *Open Systems Interconnection Reference Model,* the *OSI Reference Model,* or even just the *OSI Model.* It was published in 1984 by both the ISO, as standard ISO 7498, and the renamed CCITT (now called the *Telecommunications Standardization Sector of the International Telecommunication Union* or *ITU-T*) as standard X.200.

Incidentally, isn't the new name for the CCITT *much* catchier than the old one? Just rolls off the old tongue, doesn't it. J. One interesting aspect of the history of the OSI Reference Model is that the original objective was *not* to create a model primarily for educational purposes—even though many people today think that this was the case.

The OSI Reference Model was intended to serve as the foundation for the establishment of a widely-adopted suite of protocols that would be used by international internetworks—basically, what the Internet became. This was called, unsurprisingly, the OSI Protocol Suite.

The OSI model itself, however, found a home as a device for explaining the operation of not just the OSI protocols, but networking in general terms. It was used widely as an educational tool—much as I use it myself in this Guide—and also to help describe interactions between the components of other protocol suites and even hardware devices. While most technologies were not designed specifically to meet the dictates of the OSI model, many are described in terms of how they fit into its layers.

OSI

The OSI reference model specifies standards for describing "Open Systems Interconnection" with the term 'open' chosen to emphasise the fact that by using these international standards, a system may be defined which is open to all other systems obeying the same standards throughout the world. The definition of a common technical language has been a major catalyst to the standardization of communications protocols and the functions of a protocol layer.

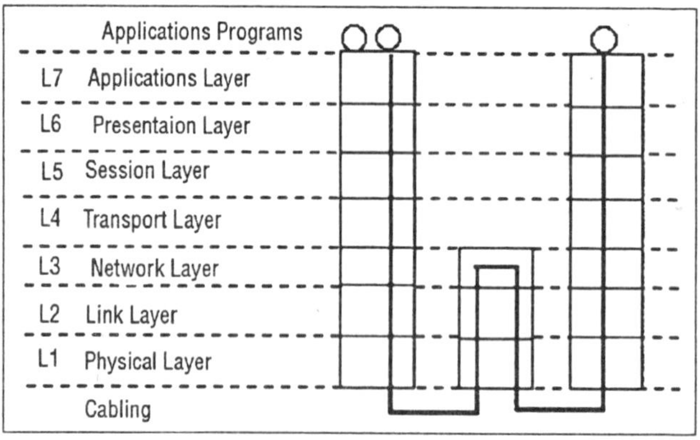

Applications Programs
L7 Applications Layer
L6 Presentaion Layer
L5 Session Layer
L4 Transport Layer
L3 Network Layer
L2 Link Layer
L1 Physical Layer
Cabling

Fig. The Seven Layers of the OSI Reference Model

The structure of the OSI architecture is given in the figure above, which indicates the protocols used to exchange data between two users A and B. The figure shows bidirectional (duplex) information flow; information in either direction passes through all seven layers at the end points. When the communication is via anetwork of intermediate systems, only the lower three layers of the OSI protocols are used in the intermediate systems.

OSI (Open Systems Interconnection) is a standard description or "reference model" for how messages should be transmitted between any two points in a telecommunication network. Its purpose is to guide product implementors so that their products will consistently work with other products.

The reference model defines seven layers of functions that take place at each end of a communication. Although OSI is not always strictly adhered to in terms of keeping related functions together in a well-defined layer, many if not most products involved in telecommunication make an attempt to describe themselves in relation to the OSI model. It is also valuable as a single reference view of communication that furnishes everyone a common ground for education and discussion.

The main idea in OSI is that the process of communication between two end points in a telecommunication network can be divided into layers, with each layer adding its own set of special, related functions.

Each communicating user or programme is at a computer equipped with these seven layers of function. So, in a given message between users, there will be a flow of data through each layer at one end down through the layers in that computer and, at the other end, when the message arrives, another flow of data up through the layers in the receiving computer and ultimately to the end user or programme. The actual programming and hardware that furnishes these seven layers of function is usually a combination of the computeroperating system, applications (such as your Web browser), TCP/IP or alternative transport and network protocols, and the software and hardware that enable you to put a signal on one of the lines attached to your computer.

OSI divides telecommunication into seven layers. The layers are in two groups. The upper four layers are used whenever a message passes from or to a user. The lower three layers (up to the network layer) are used when any message passes through the host computer.

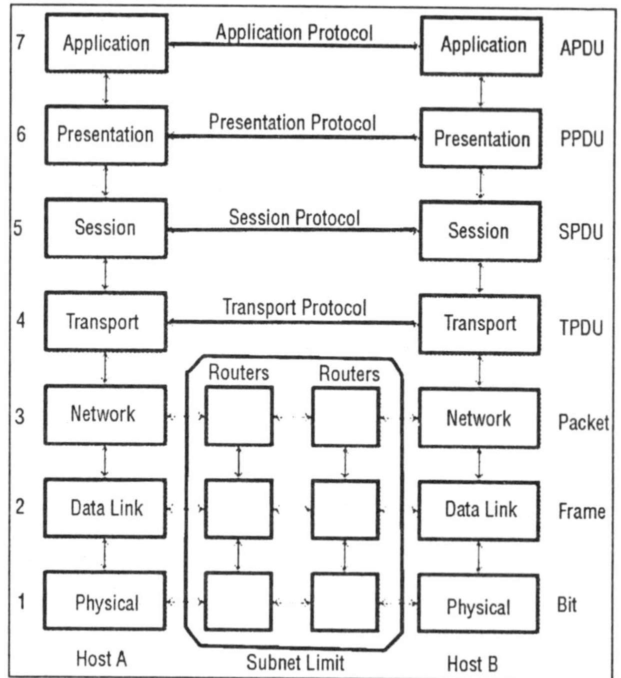

Messages intended for this computer pass to the upper layers. Messages destined for some other host are not passed up to the upper layers but are forwarded to another host.

The seven layers are:

Physical Layer

Provides electrical, functional, and procedural characteristics to activate, maintain, and deactivate physical links that transparently send the bit stream; only recognizes individual bits, not characters or multicharacter frames.

The physical layer (layer 1) of the OSI reference model serializes the frame (*i.e.* converts it to a series of bits) and sends it across a communications circuit (i.e cable) to the destination (or an intermediate) system.

There are a number of types of circuit/cable (sometimes also called "media") that may be used. these include:

- Open wire circuits
- Twisted pair cables

- Coaxial cables
- Fibre optic cables

Signaling of Bits

The physical layer defines the representation of ecah bit as a voltage, current, phase, or frequency.

Basic schemes are used:

- RZ, Return to Zero (Pulse signalling)
- NRZ, Non Return to Zero transmission (Level signalling)
- Manchester encoding (Edge/phase signalling)

In NRZ transmission, each data bit is represented by a level. A high level may represent a logic 1, where as a low level may represent a logic 0. The term is derived from the earlier transmission technique of sending pulses to represent bits (called Return to Zero, RZ) in which a logic 1 is represented by a pulse and a logic 0 by the absence of a pulse. (AMI and HDB3 are techniques derived from RZ). Manchester encoding uses a still different scheme where a logic 1 is represnted by a transition in a particular direction (usually a rising edge) in the centre of each bit. A transudation in the opposite direction (downward in this case) is used to represent a logic 0.

Timing of Bits

At the receiver, the remote system reassembles the series of bits to form a frame and forwards the frame for processing by the link layer. A clock (timing signal) is needed to identify the boundaries between the bits (in practice it is preferable to identify the centre of the bit - since this usually indicates the point of maximum signal power). There are two systems used to providing timing:

- Asynchronous Communication (independent transmit and receive clocks),
  - Simple interface (limited data rate < 19.2 kbps)
  - Used for connecting: Printer, Terminal, Modem
  - No clock sent (Tx and Rx have own clocks)
  - Requires start/stop which provides byte timing and increases overhead

  - Parity often used to validate correct reception
- Synchronous Communication (synchronised transmit and receive clocks),
  - More complex interface (high data rates supported upto ~ 1 Gbps)
  - Used for: LANs, MANs, WANs, Telephony
  - Clock sent with data (more configuration options)
  - Bit timing from transmission or by link protocol
  - Cyclic Redundancy Check (CRC) used to validate correct reception

Data Link Layer

Provides functional and procedural means to transfer data between network entities and (possibly) correct transmission errors; provides for activation, maintenance, and deactivation of data link connections, grouping of bits into characters and message frames, character and frame synchronisation, error control, media access control, and flow control (examples include HDLC and Ethernet)

The MAC Sublayer

The *medium access control (MAC) sublayer* is closely associated with the physical layer and defines the means by which the physical channel (medium) may be accessed. It coordinates the attempts to seize a shared channel by multiple MAC entities, much as a school teacher must arbitrate between pupils' conflicting desires to speak. The MAC layer commonly provides a limited form of error control, especially for any header information which defines the MAC-level destination and higher-layer access mechanism. *Ethernet (IEEE 802.3)* is a prime example of a shared medium with a defined MAC sublayer functionality. The shared medium in Ethernet has traditionally consisted of a coaxial cable into which multiple entities were "tapped," as depicted in Figure. Although this topology still applies conceptually, a hub and spoke medium is now typically used, in which the earlier coaxial cable has been physically collapsed into a *hub* device.

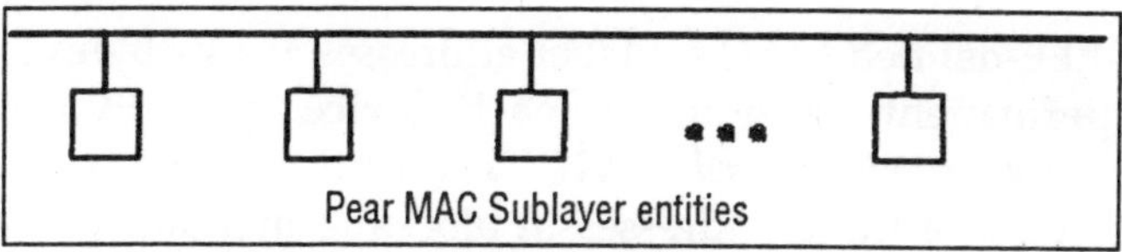

Fig: Ethernet MAC System

As a *contention* medium, Ethernet defines how devices *sense* a channel for its availability, wait when it is busy, *seize* the channel when it becomes available and*back-off* for a random length of time following a *collision* with another simultaneously transmitting device. On a shared channel, such as Ethernet, only a single entity can transmit at a time or messages will be garbled.

Not all shared channels involve contention. A prime example of a *contentionless* shared medium is *token ring (IEEE 802.5)*, in which control of the channel is rotated between the devices sharing the channel in a deterministic round-robin manner. Conceptually, control of the channel is given to the entity currently possessing a "token." If the device has nothing to transmit, it passes the token to the next device attached to the topological "ring,"

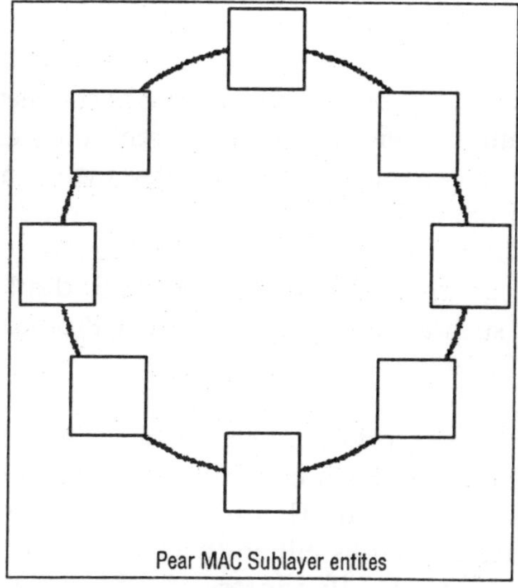

Fig. Token Ring MAC System

IEEE-defined MAC sublayer addresses are six bytes long and permanently assigned to each device, typically called a *network interface card* or*NIC. The*IEEE administers the assignment of these addresses in blocks to manufacturers to assure the global uniqueness that the MAC sublayer protocols rely on for "plug Ôn play" network setup. Each manufacturer must assure individual device identifier uniqueness within their assigned block.

Network layer

Provides independence from data transfer technology and relaying and routing considerations; masks peculiarities of data transfer medium from higher layers and provides switching and routing functions to establish, maintain, and terminate network layer connections and transfer data between users.

The Internetwork Protocol (IP)

The IP (Internet Protocol) is a protocol that uses data grams to communicate over a packet-switched network. The IP protocol operates at the network layer protocol of the OSI reference model and is a part of a suite of protocols known as TCP/IP. Today, with over 1.5 billion users worldwide, the current Internet is a great success in terms of connecting people and communities. Even though the current Internet continues to work and is capable of fulfilling its current missions, it also suffers from a relative œossification, a condition where technological innovation meets natural resistance, as exemplified by the current lack of wide deployment of technologies such as multicast or Internet Protocol version 6 (IPv6).

The Internetwork Protocol (IP) [RFC791] provides a best effort network layer service for connecting computers to form a computer network. Each computer is identified by one or more gloablly unique IP addresses. The network layer PDUs are known as either "packets" or "data grams". Each packet carries the IP address of the sending computer and also the address of the intended recipient or recipients of the packet. Other management information is also carried. The IP network service transmits datagrams between intermediate nodes using IP routers. The routers themselves are simple, since no information is stored concerning the datagrams which are forwarded on a link. The most complex part of an IP router is concerned with determining the optimum link to use to reach each destination in a network. This process is known as "routing". Although this process is computationally intensive, it is only performed at periodic intervals.

An IP network normally uses a dynamic routing protocol to find alternate routes whenever a link becomes unavailable. This provides considerable robustness from the failure of either links or routers, but does not guarentee reliable delivery. Some applications are happy with this basic service and use a simple transport protocol known as the User Datagram Protocol (UDP) to access this best effort service. Most Internet users need additional functions such as end-to-end error and sequence control to give a reliable service (equivalent to that provided by virtual circuits). This reliability is provided by the Transmission Control Protocol (TCP) which is used end-to-end across the Internet. In a LAN environment, the protocol is normally carried by Ethernet, but for long distance links, other link protocols using fibre optic links are usually used. Other protocols associated with the IP network layer are the Internet Control Message Protocol (ICMP) and the Address Resolution Protocol (arp).

Transport Layer

Provides transparent transfer of data between systems, relieving upper layers from concern with providing reliable and cost effective data transfer; provides end-to-end control and information interchange with quality of service needed by the application programme; first true end-to-end layer.

Session Layer

Provides mechanisms for organising and structuring dialogues between application processes; mechanisms allow for two-way simultaneous or two-way alternate operation, establishment of major and minor synchronisation points, and techniques for structuring data exchanges.

Presentation Layer

Provides independence to application processes from differences in data representation, that is, in syntax; syntax selection and conversion provided by allowing the user to select a "presentation context" with conversion between alternative contexts.

Application Layer

Concerned with the requirements of application. All application processes use the service elements provided by the application layer. The elements include library routines which perform interprocess communication, provide common procedures for constructing application protocols and for accessing the services provided by servers which reside on the network. The communications engineer is concerned mainly with the protocols operating at the bottom four layers (physical, data link, network, and transport) in the OSI reference model. These layers provide the basic communications service. The layers above are primarily the concern of computer scientists who wish to build distributed applications programmes using the services provided by the network.

SERVICES

WEB SERVICES PROTOCOL STACK

Web Services are a set of protocols based on XML (Extensible Markup Language). Many readers will be familiar with the following base protocols that formed the initial specification for Web Services.

- *Simple Object Access Protocol (SOAP)*: defines the runtime message that contains the service request and response. SOAP is independent of any particular transport and implementation technology.
- *Web Services Description Language (WSDL)*: describes a

Web Service and the SOAP Message. It provides a programmatic way to describe what a service does, paving the way for automation.

- *Universal Discovery, Description, Integration (UDDI)*: UDDI is a cross industry initiative to create a standard for service discovery together with a registry facility that facilitates the publishing and discovery processes.

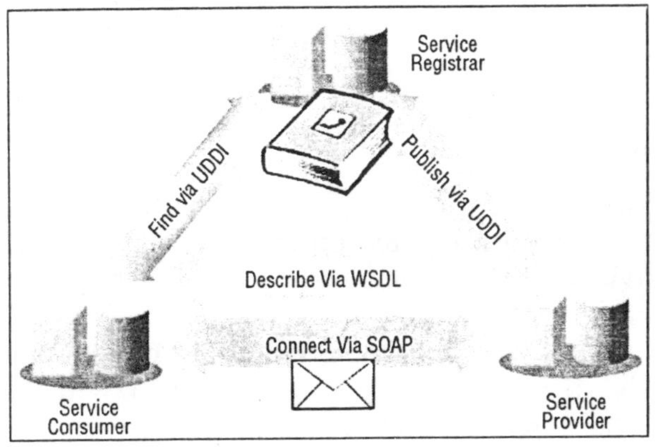

Fig. Base Web Service Protocols

These have effectively become de facto standards, with effectively universal acceptance and widespread implementation by vendors. Figure the way their application is typically illustrated. These base protocols have enabled many companies to put straightforward Web Services into production. However, to improve the security and reliability of Web Services and to address more complex business scenarios, a wide range of additional protocols have since been proposed. Some of these have since been merged with others or morphed into new proposals. The current proposals are illustrated in figure with further detail and links to the various specification is provided on Web service protocols summary table.

WEB SERVICES ARCHITECTURE

The additional protocols have been proposed within the context of a modular framework that would allow,

- Developers to only use the modules needed for their

Web Services. Each module can be lightweight and not overburdened with irrelevant syntax.

- Each module to evolve in isolation

There is no standard definition of the Web Services Protocol stack though the W3C Web Services Architecture Working Group did publish a Web Services Architecture document which provides an excellent context for the various protocols. Vendors often draw their own, but similar architecture.

CBDI ASSESSMENT

Additional Protocols Required

Taking all the proposals in Figure into consideration, the set of protocols required for secure, reliable 'Enterprise' Web Services is largely complete.

Areas not fully addressed are,

- *Management*: The OASIS WSDM Technical Committee is still in its early stages. WSDM will provide standard protocols for the Management Of Web Services (MOWS), and for Management Using Web Services (MUWS).
- *Service and Business Level Agreements*: These are identified by the W3C Web Service Architecture working group as part of the description layer, but as yet no proposals have been made in this area.
- *WS-Security*: The specifications for some elements of the WS-Security architecture have yet to be published. These are WS-Authorization and WS-Privacy.

Alternative Proposals

The degree of industry consensus on Web Service protocols has been significant. Though alternative proposals have been made in some areas, the formation of an appropriate working group in either W3C or OASIS has usually seen the subsequent convergence of all interested parties.

There are currently some areas where alternative proposals remain, namely in the areas of Reliable Messaging,

Orchestration, and Transaction Coordination. These alternatives have generally reflected an IBM/Microsoft led initiative on one side, and one led by Sun/Oracle on the other.

However, Microsoft and Sun earlier this year agreed to settle various antitrust and other issues, and announced greater cooperation in Web Services. Since then Sun has joined with BEA, IBM, Microsoft and SAP AG to submit the latest version of the WS-Addressing specification to the W3C. This will merge with the WS-MessageDelivery specification which Sun supported earlier along with Iona Nokia and Oracle.

This was followed by BEA, CA, IBM, Microsoft, Sun and TIBCO jointly publishing an update to the WS-Eventing specification, which proposes a way of communicating about events within and between Web services. This update sees CA, IBM and Sun joining BEA, Microsoft and TIBCO, who proposed the spec originally, and likely signals the prospect of greater interoperability with related specifications such as WS-Notification. Ca, Sun and WebMethods also joined with BEA, IBM, Microsoft, and SAP, in publishing the 2nd version of WS Metadata Exchange. These are welcome moves, and it augurs well for further cooperation in other pockets of overlapping proposals such as transaction co-ordination and choreography. Consequentl, it looks like any concerns over competing Web Service protocols delaying standardization, and hence adoption, should now disappear.

There has also been some overlap between Web Services and the ebXML initiative. ebXML uses SOAP at the transport level, but has its own registry and orchestration. Though ebXML is an approved, robust standard, its applicability is far narrower than Web Services. As an evolution of EDI, it primarily addresses the B2B domain only. As such we believe the Web Service protocols that are designed to address multiple requirements and usage scenarios will prove more valuable in time and that ebXML will probably evolve to adopt additional Web Service protocols as they mature and are approved. Part of the work of the OASIS ebSOA TC is to evolve the ebXML architecture and address the transition to the adoption of more Web Service protocols.

Standardization Process

Though the proposal of various Web Services protocols has been a fast moving area, their transition into actual open standards is inevitably much slower. There are only a few protocols that have, or a close to completing the standards process proper. Some key proposals have yet to be submitted to any standards body. We advise continuous monitoring of what are currently the two main standards groups involved in Web Services,

- *World Wide Web Consortium (W3C)*:
- Organization for the Advancement of Structured *Information Standards (OASIS)*: Web service protocols summary table indicates the current status of the various protocols in the standards process.

WS-Interoperability (WS-I)

WS-I is an open, industry group that was formed in 2002 to promote Web services interoperability across platforms, operating systems, and programming languages. Though this would appear to be the basic premise of Web Services and the role of standards bodies, WS-I still has a useful role to play, for example,

- Standards specifications are always open to interpretation to some extent. WS-I will provide guidelines and tools to help measure the conformance of various implementations, and to enable their interoperability
- As standards evolve, there is a need to understand what different versions might interoperate
- Publishing interoperability profiles to reflect the above, one of the key deliverables of WS-I.

ROADMAP ACTIONS

Apart from infrastructure and tools vendors, and early experimentation, organizations should avoid handcrafting the use of Web Service protocols wherever possible. It should not be necessary for developers to learn the low-level XML syntax of Web Services, delegating the generation of it instead to the infrastructure products and development tools.

NETWORK TOPOLOGY DESIGN

COMPUTER NETWORK TOPOLOGY

Network topology is one of the very important topics to learn when it comes to build up computer network. There are many Network Topologies on which network administrator decide to build the network on. Topology is basically defined as layout or design of network, and computers are connected using the design of the topology. These topologies can be either physical or logical design. Physical topology refers to physical design of network which includes devices, cables, location and installation of network where as in logical topology it is the amount of data to be transferred with in the network as apposed in its design.

There are five different Networking Topologies:

- Bus
- Star
- Ring
- Mesh
- Tree.

When networks are design using multiple topologies it is called Hybrid Networks, this concept is usually utilized in complex networks were larger number of computer clients are required.

Bus Topology

Bus topology is one the easiest topologies to install, it does not require lots of cabling. There are two most popular Ethernet cable types which are used in this topology they are 10Base-2 and 10BaseT. Bus topology based networks works with very limited devices. It performs fine as long as computer count remain with in 12 – 15, problems occurs when number of computer increases.

Bus topology uses one common cable (backbone) to connect all devices in the network in linear shape. Network interface cards of all network devices are attached to single communication medium backbone cable. When any computer sends out message in the network it is broadcasted in the entire network but only intended computer accepts the message and process it. Bus topology provide simplicity to the network, however there is big disadvantage of this topology, if main single network cable some how gets damaged, it will shut down the entire network no computer will run on network and no communication can be made among computers until backbone cable is replaced.

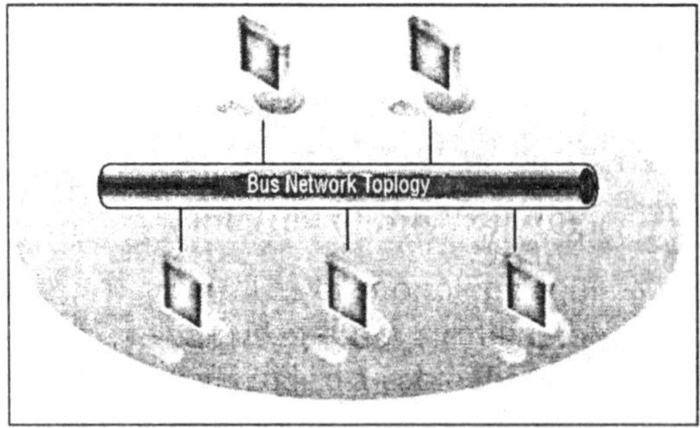

A bus topology is a method of transmission on networks that uses a common vehicle for transmissions and thus it is categorized as shared communication. Imagine a bus picking up various people from one stop and dropping of people as it travels and then picking a few more. That is what happens in a bus network exactly. A bus network uses a multi-drop transmission medium, all node on the network share a common bus and thus share communication. This allows only one device to transmit at a time. A distributed access protocol determines which station is to transmit. Data frames contain source and destination addresses, where each station monitors the bus and copies frames addressed to itself.

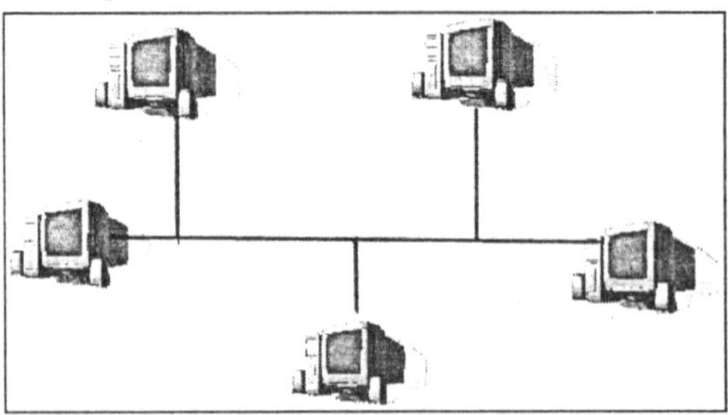

A bus topology connects each computer (nodes) to a single segment trunk (a communication line, typically coax cable, that is referred to as the 'bus'. The signal travels from one end of the bus to the other.

A terminator is required at each to absorb the signal so as it does not reflect back across the bus. A media access method called CSMA/MA is used to handle the collision that occur when two signals placed on the wire at the same time. The bus topology is passive. In other words, the computers on the bus simply 'listen' for a signal; they are not responsible for moving the signal along.

Function of Bus Topology

The bus topology connects each computer on the network into something called the segment trunk. A bus is usually referred to a cable that connects end to end and this is used to transmit the signals from one end to the other end. At every end a terminator is placed so that it understands in which direction the data is traveling and also the terminator is used to absorb the signals.

If the terminator does not absorb the signal then the same signal is reflected back to the bus confusing the whole data flow. The bus is considered to be a passive network because the computers are largely dependant on the signal that is being transmitted.

Advantages

The advantage of the Bus network is that if one computer fails in the network the others are still not affected and they continue to work. Bus network is very simple and easy to set up. If there is an urgent need to set up a network and perhaps be used on a short term basis then the Bus network is the best possibility. Bus networks use the least amount of cable to set up making it cost effective. Failure of one of the station does not affect others. Good compromise over the other two topologies as it allows relatively high rate of data tansmittion. Well suited for temporary networks that must be set up in a hurry. Easy to implement and extend.

Disadvantage

Require a network to detect when two nodes are transmitting at the same time. Does not cope well with heavy traffic rates Difficult to administer/troubleshoot. Limited cable length and number of stations. A cable brake can disable the entire network; no redundancy. Maintenance cost may be higher in the long run. Performance degrade as additional computers are added.

Limitations

In the bus network you will need a network connection in order to determine if the data is being transferred between two nodes. If the data transfer rate is high then the Bus network does not perform very well because the data travels in a stream and cannot be overloaded. The bus network is a bit challenging when you have to troubleshoot the problems. Bus networks are not suitable as large networks as there are limitations to the number of nodes you can set up for one single cable. As the number of computers increase in the network the data transfer rate goes down accordingly and noticeably.

Conclusion

The bus networks in spite of its limitations is considered to be the easiest and the fastest network that can be set up compared to the other kinds of network. In bus networks there is a collision handling system which ensures that data travels without errors and data is delivered correctly.

Ring Topology

Ring topology is one of the old ways of building computer network design and it is pretty much obsolete. FDDI, SONET or Token Ring technologies are used to build ring technology. It is not widely popular in terms of usability but incase if you find it any where it will mostly be in schools or office buildings.

In ring network topology computers and other networking devices are attached to each other in such a way that they have devices adjacent to each other (Left and right side). All messages are travelled in the same directory either clockwise or anticlockwise.

A ring topology is a network topology or circuit arrangement in which each network device is attached along the same signal path to two other devices, forming a path in the shape of a ring.

Each device in the network that is also referred to as node handles every message that flows through the ring. Each node in the ring has a unique address.

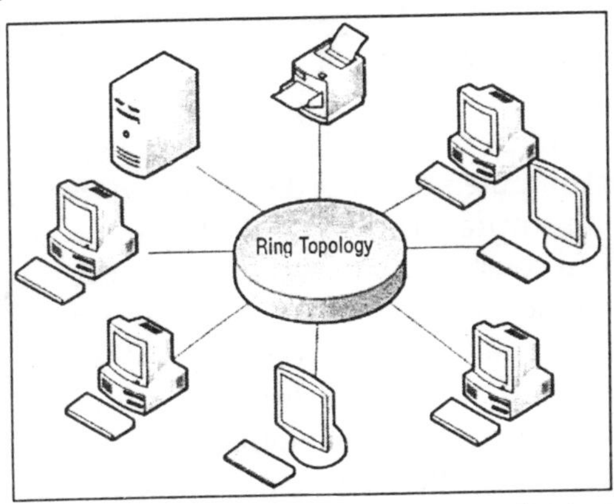

The redundant topologies are used to eliminate network downtime caused by a single point of failure. All networks need redundancy for enhanced reliability. Network reliability is achieved through reliable equipment and network designs that are tolerant to failures and faults.

The FDDI networks overcome the disruption in the network by sending data on a clockwise and a counter clockwise ring. In case there is a break in data flow,the data is wrapped back onto the complementary ring before it reaches the end of the cable thereby maintaining a path to every node within the complementary ring.

Each station on the ring has equal access but only one station can talk at a time. To allow an orderly access to the ring, a single electronic token passes from one computer to the next around the ring as seen in (token ring). A computer can only transmit data when it capture the token.

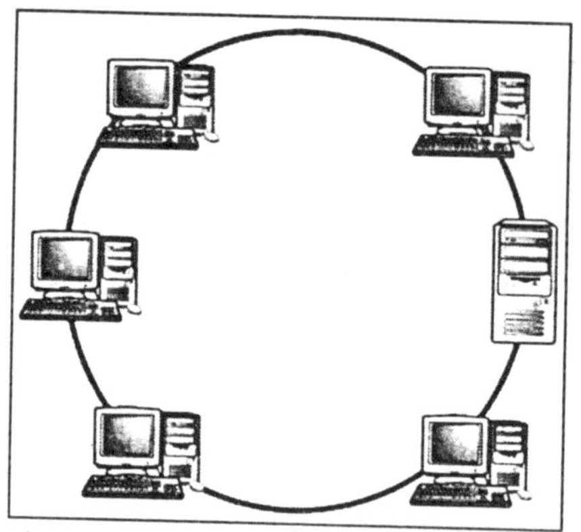

In a true ring topology, if a single computer or section of cable fails, there is an interruption in the signal. The entire network becomes inaccessible. Network disruption can also occur when computers are added or removed from the network, making it an impractical network design in environments where there is constant change to the network. Ring networks are most commonly wired in a star configuration. In a Token Ring network, a multistation access unit (MSAU) is equivalent to a hub or switch on an Ethernet network. The MSAU performs the token circulation internally. To create the complete ring, the ring in (RI) port on each MSAU is connected to the ring out (RO) port on another MSAU.

Advantages

An orderly network where every device has access to the token and the opportunity to transmit Under heavy network load performs better than a start topology. To manage the connectivity between the computers it doesnt need network server.

DisadvAntages

One malfunctioning workstation can throw away the entire network. Moves, adds and changes of devices can affect the entire network. It is slower than an Ethernet network.

Star Topology

This is the most commonly used network topology design

you will come across in LAN computer networks. In Star, all computers are connected to central device called hub, router or switches using Unshielded Twisted Pair (UTP) or Shielded Twisted Pair cables.

In star topology, we require more connecting devices like routers, cables unlike in bus topology where entire network is supported by single backbone. The most practical point of Star topology success is that the entire network does not go down incase of failure of a computer or cable or device, it will only affect the computer whose wire failed rest of the network will be working fine. However, incase of failure of central communication device such as Hub, Router or Switch the entire network will collapse. Star topology is widely used in homes, offices and in buildings because of its commercial success.

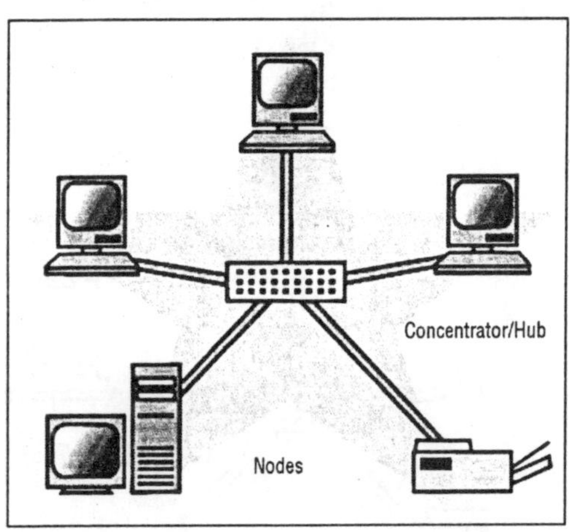

Star topology is the most commonly used physical technology in Ethernets LANS, when installed, the star topology resembles spokes I n a bicycle wheel. The star topology is made up of a central connection point that is a device such as a hub, switch, or router, where all the cabling segments meet. Each host in the network is connected to the central devices with its own cables although a physical star topology costs more to implement than the physical bus topology , the advantage of star topology make it worth the additional cost.

Because each host it connected to the central device with its own cable, when that cable has a problem, only that host is affected, the rest of the network remains operational this benefit is extremely important and is why virtually every newly designed Ethernet a central connection point might be desirable for security or restricted access, but this is also a main disadvantage of a star topology.if the central device fails, the whole network become disconnected.when a star network is expanded to include an additional networking device that is connected for the main networking device, it is called an extended star topology.

Description

A star topology is designed with each node (file server, workstations, and peripherals) connected directly to a central network hub or concentrator as shown in figure below:

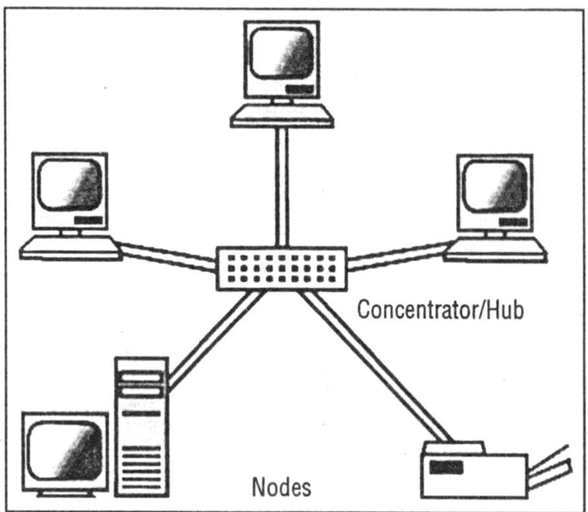

Data on a star network passes through the hub or concentrator before continuing to its destination. The hub or concentrator manages and controls all functions of the network. It also acts as a repeater for the data flow. This configuration is common with twisted pair cable; however, it can also be used with coaxial cable or fibre optic cable.

Many businesses and home networks use the star topology. A star network features a central connection point called a "hub" that may be an actual hub or a switch as shown below:

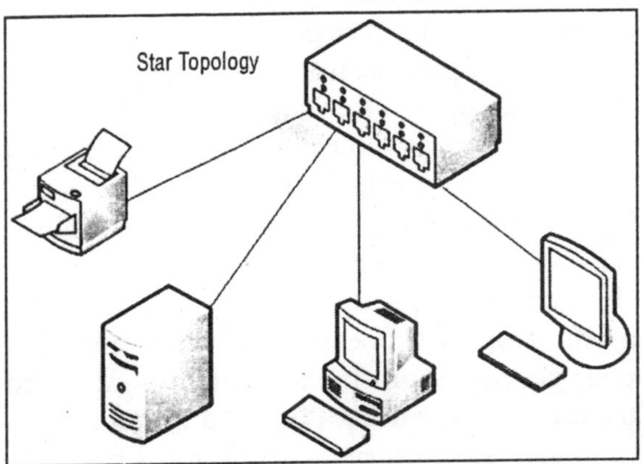

Devices typically connect to the hub with Unshielded Twisted Pair (UTP) Ethernet cables also known as RJ45 cables. Compared to the bus topology, a star network generally requires more cable, but a failure in any star network cable will only take down one computer's network access and not the entire LAN. (If the hub fails, however, the entire network also fails.)

Star Topology has the Following Advantages

- Easy to manage.
- Easy to locate problems (cable/workstations).
- Easier to expand than a bus or ring topology.
- Easy to Install and Wire.
- No disruptions to the network then connecting or removing devices.
- Easy to detect faults and to remove parts.

Star Topology has Following Disadvantages

- It is susceptible to a single point of failure be it the server or hub/switch.
- With Increased devices and traffic can make the network slow.

- Requires more Cable Length.
- If the hub or concentrator fails, nodes attached are disabled.
- More expensive than linear bus topologies because of the cost of the concentrators.

Since all the computers on the network have independent control of their networks and only dependant on the central hub computer, the failures in transmission and other possible problems in this area are less likely. Also if the hub is safe then every computer in the network is safe. This type of network also offers more privacy than any other network.

All the computers in the network are communicating with one main centrally located computer and there is no peer to peer coordination. If the peer to peer coordination takes place it is routed through the central hub. This way the privacy of each and every computer on the network is maintained.

If one computer fails in the network it does not affect any other computer in the network and the tasks of this computer can be easily switched very to the next computer easily using the hub controls. In a Star Network Topology it is possible to have all the important data back ups on the hub in a private folder and this way if the computer fails you can still use your data using the next computer in the network and accessing the backup files on the hub.

New devices or nodes can easily be added to the Star Network by just extending a cable from the hub. Since the hub controls everything the addition or removal of devices are done using g the hub.

Tree Topology

Just as name suggest, the network design is little confusing and complex to understand at first but if we have better understanding of Star and Bus topologies then Tree is very simple. Tree topology is basically the mixture of many Star topology designs connected together using bus topology. Devices like Hub can be directly connected to Tree bus and each hub performs as root of a tree of the network devices.

Tree topology is very dynamic in nature and it holds potential of expandability of networks far better than other topologies like Bus and Star.

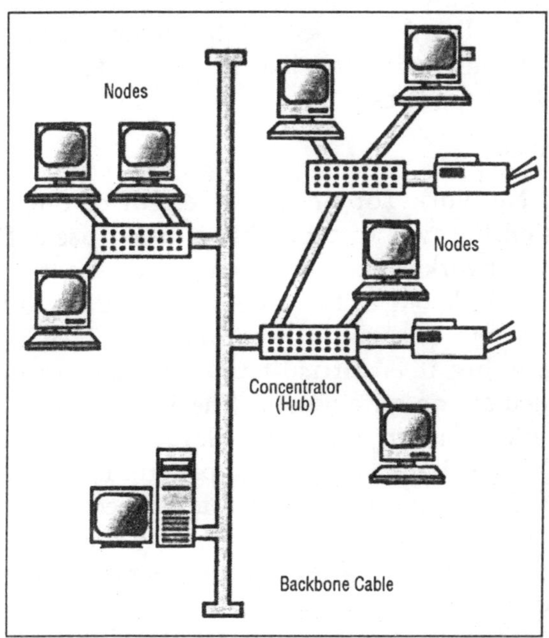

Among all the Network Topologies we can derive that the Tree Topology is a combination of the bus and the Star Topology. The tree like structure allows you to have many servers on the network and you can branch out the network in many ways.

This is particularly helpful for colleges, universities and schools so that each of the branches can identify the relevant systems in their own network and yet connect to the big network in some way.

A Tree Structure suits best when the network is widely spread and vastly divided into many branches. Like any other topologies, the Tree Topology has its advantages and disadvantages. A Tree Network may not suit small networks and it may be a waste of cable to use it for small networks. Tree Topology has some limitations and the configuration should suit those limitations.

Benefits

A Tree Topology is supported by many network vendors ad even hardware vendors. A point to point connection is possible with Tree Networks. All the computers have access to the larger and their immediate networks. Best topology for branched out networks.

Limitations

In a Network Topology the length of the network depends on the type of cable that is being used. The Tree Topology network is entirely dependant on the trunk which is the main backbone of the network. If that has to fail then the entire network would fail. Since the Tree Topology network is big it is difficult to configure and can get complicated after a certain point. The Tree Topology follows a hierarchical pattern where each level is connected to the next higher level in a symmetrical pattern. Each level in the hierarchy follows a certain pattern in connecting the nodes. Like the top most level might have only one node or two nodes and the following level in the hierarchy might have few more nodes which work on the point to point connectivity and the third level also has asymmetrical node to node pattern and each of these levels are connected to the root level in the hierarchy. Think of a tree that branches out in various directions and all these branches need the roots and the tree trunk to survive. A Tree Structured network is very similar to this and that is why it is called the Tree Topology.

Features

There will be at least three levels of hierarchy in the Tree Network Topology and they all work based on the root node. The Tree Topology has two kinds of topology integral in it, the star and the linear way of connecting to nodes. The Tree Topology functions by taking into account the total number of nodes present in the network. It does not matter how many nodes are there on each level. Nodes can be added to any level of the hierarchy and there are no limitations a far as the total number of nodes do not exceed.

Advantages of a Tree Topology

- Point-to-point wiring for individual segments.
- Supported by several hardware and software venders.

Disadvantages of a Tree Topology

- Overall length of each segment is limited by the type of cabling used.
- If the backbone line breaks, the entire segment goes down.
- More difficult to configure and wire than other topologies.

Tree Network Topology Benefits

- A Tree Topology is supported by many network vendors ad even hardware vendors.
- A point to point connection is possible with Tree Networks.
- All the computers have access to the larger and their immediate networks.
- Best topology for branched out networks.

The Tree Topology follows a hierarchical pattern where each level is connected to the next higher level in a symmetrical pattern. Each level in the hierarchy follows a certain pattern in connecting the nodes. Like the top most level might have only one node or two nodes and the following level in the hierarchy might have few more nodes which work on the point to point connectivity and the third level also has asymmetrical node to node pattern and each of these levels are connected to the root level in the hierarchy.

Tree Topology Qualities

- There will be at least three levels of hierarchy in the Tree Network Topology and they all work based on the root node.
- The Tree Topology has two kinds of topologyintegral in it, the star and the linear way of connecting to nodes.

- The Tree Topology functions by taking into account the total number of nodes present in the network. It does not matter how many nodes are there on each level. Nodes can be added to any level of the hierarchy and there are no limitations a far as the total number of nodes do not exceed.
- The higher levels in the hierarchy are expected to perform more functions than the lower levels in the network.

Mesh Topology

Mesh topology is designed over the concept of routing. Basically it uses router to choose the shortest distance for the destination. In topologies like star, bus etc, message is broadcasted to entire network and only intended computer accepts the message, but in mesh the message is only sent to the destination computer which finds its route it self with the help of router. Internet is based on mesh topology. Routers plays important role in mesh topology, routers are responsible to route the message to its destination address or computer. When every device is connected to every other device it is known as full mesh topology and if every device is connected indirectly to each other then it is called partial mesh topology.

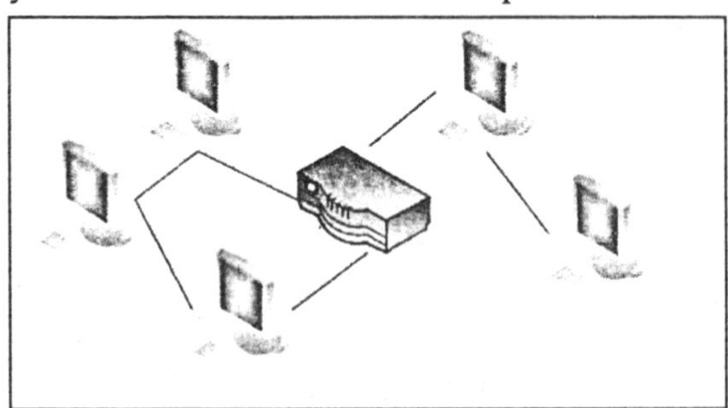

A type of network setup where each of the computers and network devices are interconnected with one another, allowing for most transmissions to be distributed, even if one of the connections go down.

The *mesh* topology incorporates a unique network design in which each computer on the network connects to every other, creating a point-to-point connection between every device on the network. The purpose of the mesh design is to provide a high level of redundancy.

Wireless Mesh Networks

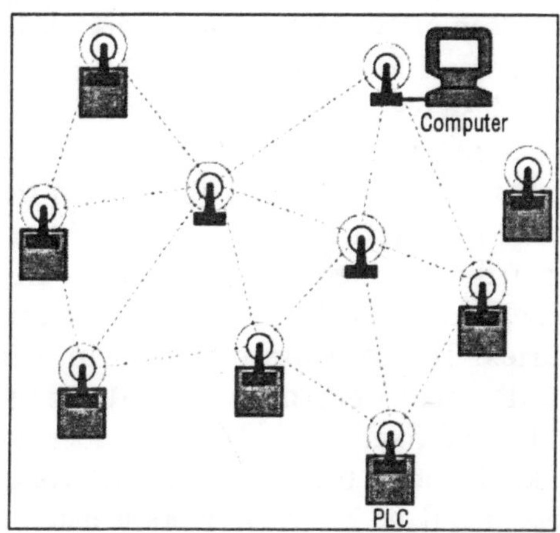

Wireless Mesh Networks work based on the radio frequencies and was originally developed by the army to be able to communicate. The reliability factor is high in any kind of Mesh Network. There are three types of wireless Mesh Topologies.

- Fixed Wireless Connections
- Peer to Peer or Adhoc Networks
- Node to Node

Fixed Mesh Networks

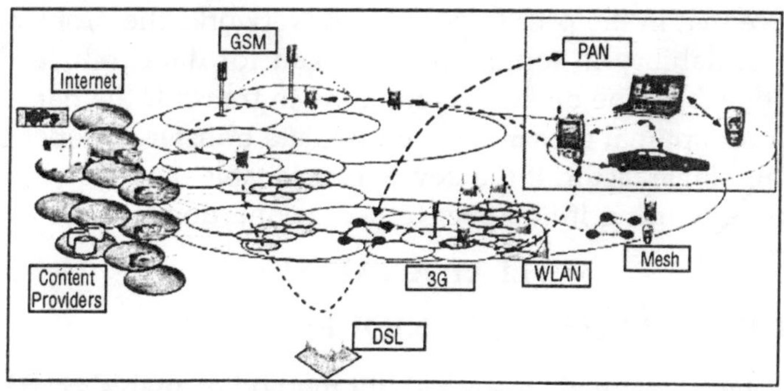

The fixed Mesh Networks will work only in the specified location and they are not mobile networks. They are meant to be used in a limited surrounding with boundaries. The location of nodes in affixed Mesh Network is all pre determined and they are not interchangeable.

The fixed Mesh Network does not work on line of sight like the other types of Mesh Networks. The total number of hops in a fixed Mesh Network is usually fixed and also short. There may not be many nodes as this kind of Mesh Networks exist within an office or building. More often than not the data travels ion a specific direction. The fixed Mesh Networks will work only in the specified location and they are not mobile networks. They are meant to be used in a limited surrounding with boundaries. The location of nodes in affixed Mesh Network is all pre determined and they are not interchangeable. The fixed Mesh Network does not work on line of sight like the other types of Mesh Networks. The total number of hops in a fixed Mesh Network is usually fixed and also short. There may not be many nodes as this kind of Mesh Networks exist within an office or building. More often than not the data travels ion a specific direction.

Peer to Peer Mobile Networks

In a peer to peer mobile network the individual devices connect to each other using the Mesh Network. The peer does not require connecting to the main node and they can still communicate from one device to another device by taking the shortest possible data transfer route. However many experts believe that in the peer to peer Mesh Networks the problems with scalability in terms of time taken for data transfer is questionable. The device has to know to transmit the data in the most optimal path and the entire data transfer or depends on this single factor. If the device is incapable then the whole purpose of using it in a peer to peer connection is lost.

DELAY ANALYSIS

DELAY ANALYSIS TECHNIQUES

The as-planned versus as-built method of analysis can be

carried out without the need for complex computer project management software, although such software is usually used for its presentation. This method is described by a number of English and American commentators as well as being referred to in SCL Delay and Disruption Protocol.

The method merely compares the durations of the planned activities with the as-built durations, and attributes the variance between the planned construction period and the as-built construction period as an entitlement to an extension of time. The approach is illustrated in the programme chart above right. It therefore assumes that the as-built situation arises by reason of variations or other reasons for which the contractor is entitled to an extension of time and not due to its own culpability.

Selection Criteria

This method is well suited for relatively simple projects where it is easy to identify where the main delays arose. Clearly it requires the planned programme and as-built information in sufficient detail to compare as-built activities with the same planned activities. This method is useful to identify the difference between the planned and actual durations and sequence of events in order to focus the further investigation on areas which appear to have gone particularly wrong and which appear to have been critical.

Issues

This is obviously a very simplistic method of analysis. Indeed it is questionable whether this can really be called a method of analysis in the way that it is described by commentators. It is unlikely that it can credibly be concluded that the difference between the planned and as-built programmes gives rise to an extension of time.

To do so assumes that the planned programme was realistic and achievable, the work was appropriately resourced to enable that plan to be achieved and that the only reason for the delay was because of an event for which the contractor is entitled to an extension of time. What is needed is a careful consideration of the facts from which one should seek to determine an actual period of delay, which either will or will not sufficiently explain the difference between the planned and as-built programmes.

For example, if one looks at the programme above, it may be that the planned duration for Activity 1 was an underestimate and there was no event affecting it, that the same applies to Activity 2, and Activity 3 was an overestimate, but was subject to a delay of four days, thus explaining four of the seven days of delay to completion.

None of this would be apparent from the simple comparison shown in the chart, but would become apparent from an investigation of the facts.

Further, the planned programme may well not be in sufficient detail to enable a credible conclusion that the difference between the planned and actual activity durations is explainable by the events relied upon.

Advantages

This method of analysis is generally the cheapest and simplest to perform, although assuming a planned programme exists, it still requires the production of an as-built programme. This approach can be useful in relation to events that are clearly on the critical path.

Disadvantages

It has been observed that the fact that this is not a CPM-based method means that it is impossible to demonstrate with any precision the effects of concurrency or parallel delays; unproductive working; the effects of secondary or consequential delay; acceleration; resequencing or mitigation. This is not necessarily so, since many of these issues are a question of fact and how they are presented. If this method is modified to reflect and present the actual delays determined from a proper investigation of the facts, then this approach has its place. However, the use of this method of analysis in its simplest form is easily criticised and is unlikely to be reliable in dispute resolution.

BACK BONE DESIGN

In early data networking, the topology for the network backbone was relatively simple: Operations were centralized, so a star topology made the most sense—and, in some cases, this was the only topology the technology would support. This did cause the centre of the star to become a single point of failure, but because no real traffic flows existed between spokes on the star, this was not a major cause for concern. With the move toward multiple client-server and peer-to-peer relationships, the choice of core network topology is not as clear. The purpose of the backbone is to connect regional distribution networks and, in some instances, to provide connectivity to other peer networks. A national infrastructure usually forms a significant part of the operational cost of the network. Given its position at the top of the network hierarchy, two requirements of the backbone topology are clear: it must be reliable and it must scale.

BACKBONE RELIABLE

Reliability can be acquired by employing two methods. First, you can create more reliable routers through the use of "carrier-class" characteristics, such as multiple CPUs, power supplies, and generators; and even redundant routers. Ultimately, however, any backbone will include WAN links that rely on a great deal of equipment and environmental stability for their operation, which represents a real risk of ultimate failure. If the carrier's up-time guarantees are not sufficient, you have no choice but to design a backbone that is resilient to link failure.

The second option is to simply connect all distribution networks with a full mesh. However, in terms of minimizing hop count within the network, the full mesh approach has several drawbacks:

- First, given N regional distribution networks, you must have N(N-1)/2 backbone links in the core. This creates expense in WAN circuitry, as well as in router and WAN switch hardware (channelized or ATM technology can reduce these issues).

- Moreover, PVC sizing requires that the traffic levels between any two distribution networks should be well understood, or that the network has the capability to circumvent congestion. Although traffic engineering calculations and circumventing congestion are common in the telephone network, common IP networks and their associated routing protocols do not provide this capability as readily. One good reason is that the resources required by any TCP/IP session are not known *a priori,* and IP networks are traditionally engineered as best-effort.
- A full PVC mesh can also obviate one of the benefits of multiplexing, or *trunking,* in a best-effort network. Round-trip time and TCP window size permitting, any user can burst traffic up to the full line rate of the trunk. Furthermore, the routing complexity in a full mesh can consume bandwidth, computational, and operational management resources.

BACKBONE TOPOLOGY

Because you have a basic need for resilience in the backbone, a good starting point for the backbone topology is a ring connecting all distribution networks. This ring could represent the minimum cost of WAN circuits, compromised by an initial estimate of major traffic flows, and possibly some very particular delay requirements (although this is rare, with notable exceptions being high-performance networks).

Next, existing links can be fattened, or direct connections between backbone routers can be added as required or as is cost-effective. This incremental approach should be considered when selecting WAN technologies, routing nodes, and interface types.

Backbone routing protocols, such as IBGP, properly coupled with OSPF, IS-IS, and Enhanced IGRP, can rapidly circumvent failures by simple link-costing mechanisms. However, the bandwidth allocations with the core topology should consider failure modes. What happens when the ring is broken due to WAN or node failure? Is the re-routed path sufficient to carry the additional traffic load? Although TCP performs extremely well in congested environments compared with other protocols, it is still possible to render the network useless for most practical applications.

Analysis of historical traffic levels, captured by SNMP, for example, provides for a relatively accurate estimation of the consolidated load on the remaining links during various failure modes. Traditionally, the use of a ring topology made it difficult to estimate the traffic levels between individual distribution networks. SNMP statistics, for example, provided only input and output byte counts for WAN interfaces, making it difficult to determine the appropriate sizing for new direct links between distribution networks.

Typically, this had to be accomplished using a cumbersome approach, such as "sniffers" on WAN links, or through accounting capabilities within routers that scaled rather poorly. However, IP accounting facilities, such as Netflow, now provide a scalable way for network managers to collect and analyse traffic flows, based on source and destination addresses, as well as many other flow parametres. This significantly eases traffic engineering and accounting activities.

LOCAL ACCESS NETWORK DESIGN

LOCAL AREA NETWORK (LAN)

Is a data communications network connecting terminals, computers and printers within a building or other geographically limited areas. These devices could be connected through wired cables or wireless links. Ethernet, Token Ring and Wireless LAN using IEEE 802.11 are examples of standard LAN technologies.

Ethernet is by far the most commonly used LAN technology. Token Ring technology is still used by some companies. FDDI is sometimes used as a backbone LAN interconnecting Ethernet or Token Ring LANs. WLAN using IEEE 802.11 technologies is rapidly becoming the new leading LAN technology for its mobility and easy to use features. Local Area Network could be interconnected using Wide Area

Network (WAN) or Metropolitan Area Network (MAN) technologies. The common WAN technologies include TCP/IP, ATM, Frame Relay etc. The common MAN technologies include SMDS and 10 Gigabit Ethernet.

LANs are traditionally used to connect a group of people who are in the same local area. However, the working group are becoming more geographically distributed in today's working environment. There, virtual LAN (VLAN) technologies are defined for people in different places to share the same networking resource.

LOCAL AREA NETWORK DIAGRAM SOFTWARE

Edraw Network Diagram is ideal for network engineers and network designers who need to draw wan diagrams. It had defined some common used WAN symbols in drawing WAN diagrams. Just drag and drop pre-drawn shapes representing computers and network devices. Double click and set equipment data.

EXAMPLES

Examples of Wide Area Network Technologies Created by Edraw!

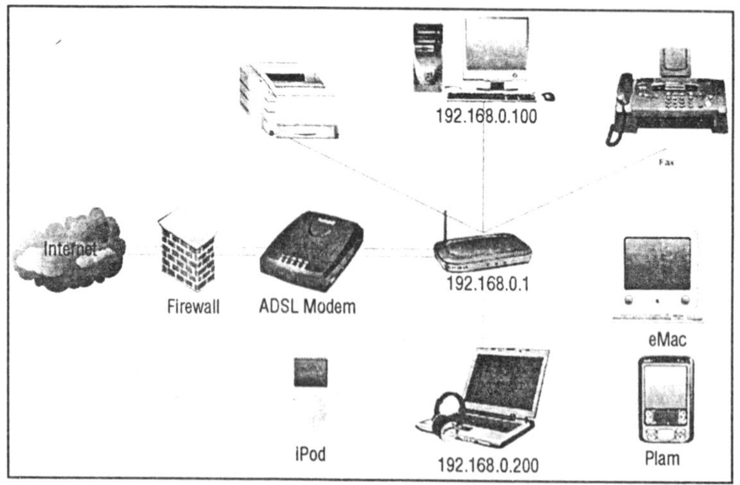

Fig. Wireless LAN Diagram

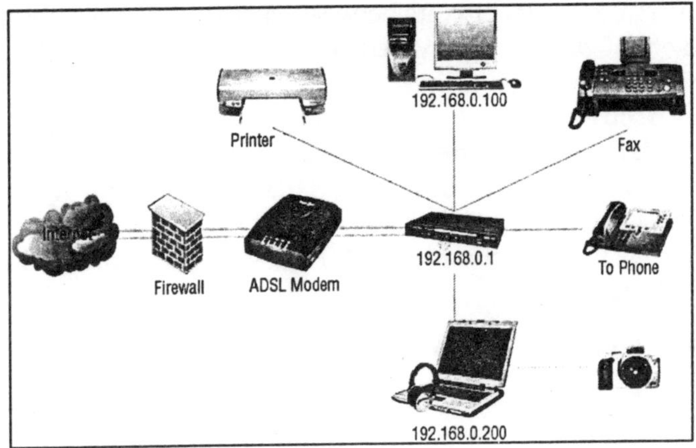

Fig. Home LAN Diagram

WIDE AREA NETWORK TECHNOLOGIES

A Wide Area Network (WAN) is a computer network covering multiple distance areas, which may spread across the entire world.

WANs often connect multiple smaller networks, such as local area networks (LANs) or metro area networks (MANs). The world's most popular WAN is the Internet. Some segments of the Internet are also WANs in themselves. The key difference between WAN and LAN technologies is scalability C WAN must be able to grow as needed to cover multiple cities, even countries and continents.

A set of switches and routers are interconnected to form a Wide Area Network. The switches can be connected in different topologies such as full mesh and half mesh. A wide area network may be privately owned or rented from a service provider, but the term usually connotes the inclusion of public (shared user) networks.

Both packet switching and circuit switching technologies are used in the WAN. Packet switching allows users to share common carrier resources so that the carrier can make more efficient use of its infrastructure. In a packet switching setup, networks have connections into the carrier's network, and many customers share the carrier's network. The carrier can then create virtual circuits between customers' sites by which packets of data are delivered from one to the other through the network.

Circuit Switching allows data connections to be established when needed and then terminated when communication is complete. This works like a normal telephone line works for voice communication. Integrated Services Digital Network (ISDN) is a good example of circuit switching.

WAN Diagram Software

Edraw Network Diagram is ideal for network engineers and network designers who need to draw wan diagrams. It had defined some common used WAN symbols in drawing WAN diagrams. Just drag and drop pre-drawn shapes representing computers and network devices. Double click and set equipment data.

Examples of Wide Area Network Technologies

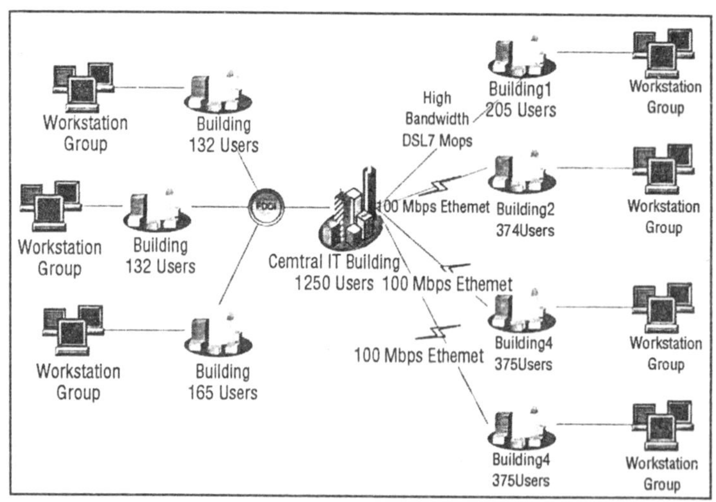

Fig. Wide Area Network

Virtual private network (VPN) is a tecnology widely used in a public switched network (PSTN) to provide private and secured WAN for an organization. VPN uses encryption and other techniques to make it appear that the organisation has a dedicated network, while making use of the shared infrastructure of the WAN.

WAN technologies generally function at the lower three layers of the OSI reference model: the physical layer, the data link layer, and the network layer. Key technologies often found in WANs include SONET, Frame Relay, X.25, ATM and PPP.

- *ATM*: A dedicated-connection switching technology that organizes digital data into 53-byte cell units. Individually, a cell is processed asynchronously relative to other related cells and is queued before being multiplexed over the transmission path. Speeds on ATM networks can reach 10 Gbps.
- *Frame Relay*: (FR). A high-speed packet-switched data communications service, similar to X.25. Frame relay is widely used for LAN-to-LAN interconnect services, and is well suited to the bursty demands of LAN environments.
- *SONET/SDH*: Synchronous Optical Network is an international standard for high speed communication over fibre-optic networks. The SONET establishes Optical Carrier (OC) levels from 51.8 Mbps to 10 Gbps (OC-192) or even higher. Synchronous Digital Hierarchy (SDH) is a European equivalent of SONET.
- *X.25*: The X.25 protocol allows computers on different public networks to communicate through an intermediary computer at the network layer level.
- *PPP*: A *point-to-point link* provides a single, pre-established WAN communications path from the customer premises through a carrier network, such as a telephone company, to a remote network. Point-to-point lines are usually leased from a carrier and thus are often called leased lines. For a point-to-point line, the carrier allocates pairs of wire and facility hardware to your line only.

IP can also be considered as a WAN technology in the packet switching environment.

PHYSICAL LAYER TRANSMISSION MEDIA

DEFINITION

The Physical Layer resides immediately below the Data Link Layer. The Physical Layer is responsible for bit-level transmission between network nodes. In copper networks, the Physical Layer is responsible for defining specifications for electrical signals. In fibre optic networks, the Physical Layer is responsible for defining the characteristics of light signals. The Physical Layer defines items such as: connector types, cable types, voltages, and pin-outs.

The lowest layer of the OSI Reference Model is layer 1, the *physical layer*; it is commonly abbreviated "PHY". The physical layer is special compared to the other layers of the model, because it is the only one where data is physically moved across the network interface. All of the other layers perform useful functions to create messages to be sent, but they must all be transmitted down the protocol stack to the physical layer, where they are actually sent out over the network.

Note: The physical layer is also "special" in that it is the only layer that really does not apply specifically to TCP/IP. Even in studying TCP/IP, however, it is still important to understand its significance and role in relation to the other layers where TCP/IP protocols reside.

ROLE OF PHYSICAL LAYER

The name "physical layer" can be a bit problematic. Because of that name, and because of what I just said about the physical layer actually transmitting data, many people who study networking get the impression that the physical layer is only about actual network hardware. Some people may say the physical layer is "the network interface cards and cables". This is not actually the case, however. The physical layer defines a number of network functions, not just hardware cables and cards.

A related notion is that "all network hardware belongs to the physical layer". Again, this isn't strictly accurate. All hardware must have *some* relation to the physical layer in order to send data over the network, but hardware devices generally implement multiple layers of the OSI model, including the physical layer but also others. For example, an Ethernet network interface card performs functions at both the physical layer and the data link layer.

PHYSICAL LAYER FUNCTIONS

The following are the main responsibilities of the physical layer in the OSI Reference Model:

- *Definition of Hardware Specifications*: The details of operation of cables, connectors, wireless radio transceivers, network interface cards and other hardware devices are generally a function of the physical layer (although also partially the data link layer; see below).
- *Encoding and Signaling*: The physical layer is responsible for various encoding and signaling functions that transform the data from bits that reside within a computer or other device into signals that can be sent over the network.
- *Data Transmission and Reception*: After encoding the data appropriately, the physical layer actually transmits the data, and of course, receives it. Note that this applies equally to wired and wireless networks, even if there is no tangible cable in a wireless network!
- *Topology and Physical Network Design*: The physical layer is also considered the domain of many hardware-related network design issues, such as LAN and WAN topology.

In general, then, physical layer technologies are ones that are at the very lowest level and deal with the actual ones and zeroes that are sent over the network. For example, when considering network interconnection devices, the simplest ones operate at the physical layer: repeaters, conventional hubs and transceivers. These devices have absolutely no knowledge of the contents of a message. They just take input bits and send them as output. Devices like switches and routers operate at higher layers and look at the data they receive as being more than voltage or light pulses that represent one or zero.

CAN PHYSICAL LAYER

The Controller Area Network (CAN) protocol defines the data link layer and part of the physical layer in the OSI model, which consists of seven layers. The International Standards Organization (ISO) defined a standard, which incorporates the CAN specifications as well as a part of physical layer: the physical signaling, which comprises bit encoding and decoding (Non Return to Zero, NRZ) as well as bit-timing and synchronization.

Bit Encoding

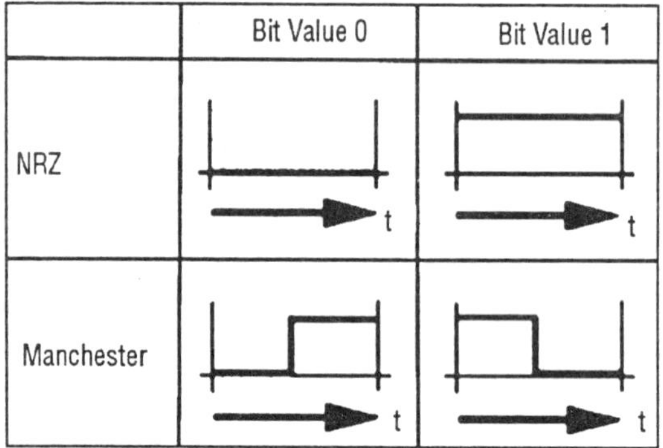

Fig. NRZ Compared with Manchester Bit Representation

In the chosen Non Return to Zero (NRZ) bit coding the signal level remains constant over the bit time and thus just one time slot is required for the representation of a bit (other methods of bit encoding are e. g. Manchester or Pulse-width-modulation). The signal level can remain constant over a longer period of time; therefore measures must be taken to ensure that the maximum permissible interval between two signal edges is not exceeded. This is important for synchronization purposes. Bit stuffing is applied by inserting a complementary bit after five bits of equal value. Of course the receiver has to un-stuff the stuff-bits so that the original data content is processed.

Interdependency of Data Rate and Bus Length

Depending on the size of the propagation delay segment the maximum possible bus length at a specific data rate (or the maximum possible data rate at a specific bus length) can be determined. The signal propagation is determined by the two nodes within the system that are farthest apart from each other. It is the time that it takes a signal to travel from one node to the one farthest apart (taking into account the delay caused by the transmitting and receiving node), synchronization and the signal from the second node to travel back to the first one. Only then can the first node decide whether its own signal level (recessive in this case) is the actual level on the bus or whether it has been replaced by the dominant level by another node. This fact is important for bus arbitration. Some modern transceivers support no low data rates. Therefore on acquisition of transceivers the maximal required network length must be considered.

PHYSICAL MEDIA

This clause is most interesting for system designers: The basis for transmitting CAN messages and for competing for bus access is the ability to represent a dominant and a recessive bit value. This is possible for electrical and optical media so far. Also powerline and wireless transmission is possible. For electrical media the differential output bus voltages are defined in ISO 11898-2 and ISO 11898-3, in SAE J2411, and ISO 11992.

With optical media the recessive level is represented by "dark" and the dominant level by "light". The physical media most commonly used to implement CAN networks is a differentially driven pair of wired with common return. For vehicle body electronics single wire bus lines are also used. Some efforts have been made to develop a solution for the transmission of CAN signals on the same line as the power supply.

The parametres of the electrical medium become important when the bus length is increased. Signal propagation, the line resistance and wire cross sections are factors when dimensioning a network. In order to achieve the highest possible bit rate at a given length, a high signal speed is required. For long bus lines the voltage drops over the length of the bus line. The wire cross section necessary is calculated by the permissible voltage drop of the signal level between the two nodes farthest apart in the system and the overall input resistance of all connected receivers. The permissible voltage drop must be such that the signal level can be reliably interpreted at any receiving node.

Network Topology

This clause is most interesting for system designers.

Electrical signals on the bus are reflected at the ends of the electrical line unless measures against that have been taken. For the node to read the bus level correctly it is important that signal reflections are avoided. This is done by terminating the bus line with a termination resistor at both ends of the bus and by avoiding unnecessarily long stubs lines of the bus. The highest possible product of transmission rate and bus length line is achieved by keeping as close as possible to a single line structure and by terminating both ends of the line. Specific recommendations for this can be found in the according standards (*i.e.* ISO 11898-2 and -3).

It is possible to overcome the limitations of the basic line topology by using repeaters, bridges or gateways. A repeater transfers an electrical signal from one physical bus segment to another segment. The signal is only refreshed and the repeater can be regarded as a passive component comparable to a cable. The repeater divides a bus into two physically independent segments. This causes an additional signal propagation time. However, it is logically just one bus system.

A bridge connects two logically separated networks on the data link layer (OSI layer 2). This is so that the CAN identifiers are unique in each of the two bus systems. Bridges implement a storage function and can forward messages or parts thereof in an independent time-delayed transmission. Bridges differ from repeaters since they forward messages, which are not local, while repeaters forward all electrical signals including the CAN identifier. A gateway provides the connection of networks with different higher-layer protocols. It therefore performs the translation of protocol data between two communication systems. This translation takes place on the application layer (OSI layer 7).

Bus Access

The connection between a CAN controller chip and a two-wire differential bus a variety of CAN transceiver chips according to different physical layer standards are available. This interface basically consists of a transmitting amplifier and a receiving amplifier (transceiver = transmit and receive). Aside from the adaptation of the signal representation between chip and bus medium the transceiver has to meet a series of additional requirements. As a transmitter it provides sufficient driver output capacity and protects the on-controller-chip driver against overloading. It also reduces electromagnetic radiation. As a receiver the CAN transceiver provides a defined recessive signal level and protects the on-controller-chip input comparator against over-voltages on the bus lines. It also extends the common mode range of the input comparator in the CAN controller and provides sufficient input sensitivity. Furthermore it detects bus errors such as line breakage, short circuits, shorts to ground, etc. A further function of the transceiver can also be the galvanic isolation of a CAN node and the bus line.

SWITCHING METHODS

CHANNEL BASED SWITCHING

You have known the telephone network for a long time: When you call a participant, a continuous connection (a channel) to your communication partner is created and you can use this channel exclusively for yourself. Because only complete channels are provided, this is called channel based switching. In our example, Hänsel and Gretel as well as Max and Moritz occupy a channel. A request for a connection from Findus to Pettersson has to be refused, because there are no channels available. When using channel based switching, you have a channel exclusively for yourself - if you get one. But it costs you, even when you actually don't use it, because you are *e.g.* thinking. When computers communicate with each other, the volume of data is very irregular: For example, when you want to look at a web site, a lot of data has to be transmitted to load it. But as soon as the web site has been completely loaded and you are reading it, no data is transmitted. In this case, a channel would be either completely busy or not busy at all.

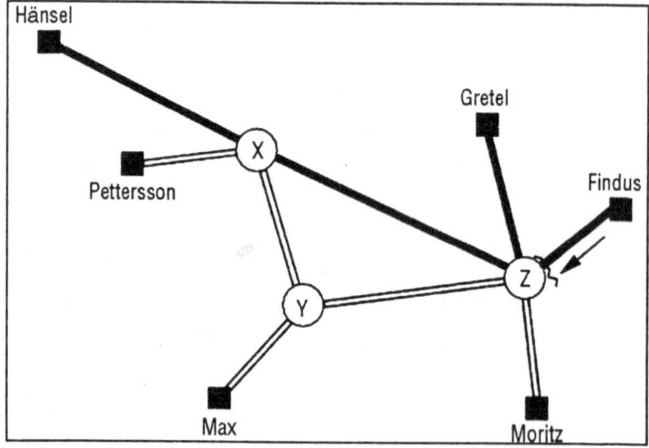

Fig. Example of Channel Based Switching

MESSAGE BASED SWITCHING

If data has to be transmitted only occasionally, the computers don't need switched-through connections for communication. It is absolutely sufficient to transport separate messages. This solves the problems of channel based switching, but immediately creates a new one: If a very large message has to be transported, it could easily happen that many shorter messages have to wait. Because of that, it is better to split the messages into smaller packets and transfer them separately.

PACKET BASED SWITCHING

Packet based switching splits each message into packets.

These receive sender and addressee information each and are sent separately. The packets can have different sizes but must not exceed a maximum size. We can see, that now also Findus is able to communicate. But we also see, that the line between X and Z cannot cope with many more packets. If other participants also want to transfer data over this line, they will sometimes have to wait for a packet. In contrast to channel based switching, a line cannot be busy, but the users actually have to share the lines. Thus, a user who transmits many packets can hinder other users.

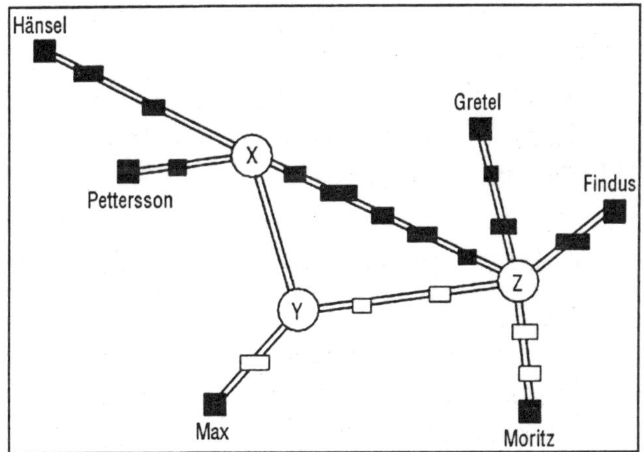

Fig. Example of Packet Based Switching

Let's imagine, the connection between X and Z breaks down, *e.g.* because a dredger has cut the cable. If the switching stations know, that there exists a redirection over Y, they can send the packets over this alternative route. As soon as the damage is repaired, the old route will be used again. It is clear, that by this means it is possible for packets to overtake each other. Packets can also get lost, because for example a switching station's capacity is overloaded.

What we see here is a model of the Internet. Within the Internet, data that computers want to exchange is split in exactly such packets and sent on the way. The computers only have to learn how to wrap and unwrap the packets.

The Internet Protocol (IP) is a rule describing the structure of data packets in the Internet. This protocol also determines the way how switching stations and terminals (*e.g.* your PC) have to handle the packets. But the Internet Protocol does not make sure that each packet always arrives or that the order of the packets is correct. The Transmission Control Protocol (TCP) takes care of this. It controls the transmission of data. Only both protocols together allow for a data exchange without losses, so this is often called TCP/IP transmission. Rules describing the communication between several participants are called protocol.

The protocol which describes the opening of a phone call could be outlined as follows:

- Max calls Moritz. The phone rings.
- Moritz responds with "Hello".
- Max introduces himself....

ROUTERS AND GATEWAYS

You can see in figure how packets pass through several switching stations (X, Y and Z). These stations are also called routers or gateways. They know their environment and decide which route a packet should take from there. Therefore a computer at the end of the network can be "stupid", it just has to know the address of the next router or routers to reach all computers in the network.

If you connect a computer to the network you usually have to specify a default router or default gateway where all those packets will be sent to that cannot be directly delivered.

INTEGRATED SERVICES DIGITAL NETWORK

DEFINITION

Integrated Services Digital Network(ISDN) is a state-of-the-art Public Switched Digital Network for provisioning of different services – voice, data and image transmission over the telephone line through the telephone network.

ISDN, which stands for Integrated Services Digital Network, is a system of digital phone connections which has been available for over a decade. This system allows voice and data to be transmitted simultaneously across the world using end-to-end digital connectivity. With ISDN, voice and data are carried by bearer channels (B channels) occupying a bandwidth of 64 kb/s (bits per second). Some switches limit B channels to a capacity of 56 kb/s. A data channel (D channel) handles signaling at 16 kb/s or 64 kb/s, depending on the service type.

Note that, in ISDN terminology, "k" means 1000 (10^3), not 1024 (2^{10}) as in many computer applications (the designator "K" is sometimes used to represent this value); therefore, a 64 kb/s channel carries data at a rate of 64000 b/s. A new set of standard prefixes has recently been created to handle this. Under this scheme, "k" (kilo-) means 1000 (10^3), "M" (mega-) means 1000000 (10^6), and so on, and "Ki" (kibi-) means 1024 (2^{10}), "Mi" (mebi-) means 1048576 (2^{20}), and so on. (An alert reader pointed out some inconsistencies in my use of unit terminology throughout this Tutorial. He also referred me to a definitive web site. As a result, I have made every effort to both conform to standard terminology, and to use it consistently. I appreciate helpful user input like this!)

There are two basic types of ISDN service: Basic Rate Interface (BRI) and Primary Rate Interface (PRI). BRI consists of two 64 kb/s B channels and one 16 kb/s D channel for a total of 144 kb/s. This basic service is intended to meet the needs of most individual users. PRI is intended for users with greater capacity requirements.

Typically the channel structure is 23 B channels plus one 64 kb/s D channel for a total of 1536 kb/s. In Europe, PRI consists of 30 B channels plus one 64 kb/s D channel for a total of 1984 kb/s. It is also possible to support multiple PRI lines with one 64 kb/s D channel using Non-Facility Associated Signaling (NFAS).

H channels provide a way to aggregate B channels. They are implemented as:

- H0=384 kb/s (6 B channels)
- H10=1472 kb/s (23 B channels)
- H11=1536 kb/s (24 B channels)
- H12=1920 kb/s (30 B channels) - International (E1) only

To access BRI service, it is necessary to subscribe to an ISDN phone line. Customer must be within 18000 feet (about 3.4 miles or 5.5 km) of the telephone company central office for BRI service; beyond that, expensive repeater devices are required, or ISDN service may not be available at all. Customers will also need special equipment to communicate with the phone company switch and with other ISDN devices. These devices include ISDN Terminal Adapters(sometimes called, incorrectly, "ISDN Modems") and ISDN Routers.

HISTORY

A standards movement was started by the International Telephone and Telegraph Consultative Committee (CCITT), now known as the International Telecommunications Union (ITU). The ITU is a United Nations organization that coordinates and standardizes international telecommunications. Original recommendations of ISDN were in CCITT Recommendation I.120 (1984) which described some initial guidelines for implementing ISDN.

Local phone networks, especially the regional Bell operating companies, have long hailed the system, but they had been criticized for being slow to implement ISDN. One good reason for the delay is the fact that the two major switch manufacturers, Northern Telecom (now known as Nortel Networks), and AT&T(whose switch business is now owned by Lucent Technologies), selected different ways to implement the CCITT standards. These standards didn't always interoperate. This situation has been likened to that of earlier 19th century railroading. "People had different gauges, different tracks... nothing worked well."

In the early 1990s, an industry-wide effort began to establish a specific implementation for ISDN in the U.S. Members of the industry agreed to create the National ISDN 1 (NI-1) standard so that end users would not have to know the brand of switch they are connected to in order to buy equipment and software compatible with it. However, there were problems agreeing on this standard. In fact, many western states would not implement NI-1. Both Southwestern

Belland U.S. West (now Qwest) said that they did not plan to deploy NI-1 software in their central office switches due to incompatibilities with their existing ISDN networks. Ultimately, all the Regional Bell Operating Companies (RBOCs) did support NI-1. A more comprehensive standardization initiative, National ISDN 2 (NI-2), was later adopted. Some manufacturers of ISDN communications equipment, such as Motorola and U S Robotics (now owned by 3Com), worked with the RBOCs to develop configuration standards for their equipment. These kinds of actions, along with more competitive pricing, inexpensive ISDN connection equipment, and the desire for people to have relatively low-cost high-bandwidth Internet access have made ISDN more popular in recent years. Most recently, ISDN service has largely been displaced by broadband internet service, such as xDSL and Cable Modem service. These services are faster, less expensive, and easier to set up and maintain than ISDN. Still, ISDN has its place, as backup to dedicated lines, and in locations where broadband service is not yet available.

ADVANTAGES OF ISDN

Speed

The modem was a big breakthrough in computer communications. It allowed computers to communicate by converting their digital information into an analog signal to travel through the public phone network. There is an upper limit to the amount of information that an analog telephone line can hold. Currently, it is about 56 kb/s bidirectionally. Commonly available modems have a maximum speed of 56 kb/s, but are limited by the quality of the analog connection and routinely go about 45-50 kb/s.

Some phone lines do not support 56 kb/s connections at all. There were currently 2 competing, incompatible 56 kb/s standards (X2 from U S Robotics (recently bought by 3Com), and K56flex from Rockwell/Lucent). This standards problem was resolved when the ITU released the V.90, and later V.92, standard for 56 kb/s modem communications.

ISDN allows multiple digital channels to be operated simultaneously through the same regular phone wiring used for analog lines. The change comes about when the telephone company's switches can support digital connections. Therefore, the same physical wiring can be used, but a digital signal, instead of an analog signal, is transmitted across the line.

This scheme permits a much higher data transfer rate than analog lines. BRI ISDN, using a channel aggregation protocol such as BONDING or Multilink-PPP, supports an uncompressed data transfer speed of 128 kb/s, plus bandwidth for overhead and signaling. In addition, the latency, or the amount of time it takes for a communication to begin, on an ISDN line is typically about half that of an analog line. This improves response for interactive applications, such as games.

Multiple Devices

Previously, it was necessary to have a separate phone line for each device you wished to use simultaneously. For example, one line each was required for a telephone, fax, computer, bridge/router, and live video conference system. Transferring a file to someone while talking on the phone or seeing their live picture on a video screen would require several potentially expensive phone lines.

ISDN allows multiple devices to share a single line. It is possible to combine many different digital data sources and have the information routed to the proper destination. Since the line is digital, it is easier to keep the noise and interference out while combining these signals. ISDN technically refers to a specific set of digital services provided through a single, standard interface. Without ISDN, distinct interfaces are required instead.

Signaling

Instead of the phone company sending a ring voltage signal to ring the bell in your phone ("In-Band signal"), it sends a digital packet on a separate channel ("Out-of-Band signal"). The Out-of-Band signal does not disturb established connections, no bandwidth is taken from the data channels, and call setup time is very fast. For example, a V.90 or V.92 modem typically takes 30-60 seconds to establish a connection; an ISDN call setup usually takes less than 2 seconds.

The signaling also indicates who is calling, what type of call it is (data/voice), and what number was dialed. Available ISDN phone equipment is then capable of making intelligent decisions on how to direct the call.

INTERFACES

In the U.S., the telephone company provides its BRI customers with a U interface. The U interface is a two-wire (single pair) interface from the phone switch, the same physical interface provided for POTS lines. It supports full-duplex data transfer over a single pair of wires, therefore only a single device can be connected to a U interface. This device is called an Network Termination 1 (NT-1). The situation is different elsewhere in the world, where the phone company is allowed to supply the NT-1, and thereby the customer is given an S/T interface.

The NT-1 is a relatively simple device that converts the 2-wire U interface into the 4-wire S/T interface. The S/T interface supports multiple devices (up to 7 devices can be placed on the S/T bus) because, while it is still a full-duplex interface, there is now a pair of wires for receive data, and another for transmit data. Today, many devices have NT-1s built into their design. This has the advantage of making the devices less expensive and easier to install, but often reduces flexibility by preventing additional devices from being connected.

Technically, ISDN devices must go through an Network Termination 2 (NT-2) device, which converts the T interface into the S interface (Note: the S and T interfaces are electrically equivalent). Virtually all ISDN devices include an NT-2 in their design. The NT-2 communicates with terminal equipment, and handles the Layer 2 and 3 ISDN protocols. Devices most commonly expect either a U interface connection (these have a built-in NT-1), or an S/T interface connection. Devices that connect to the S/T (or S) interface include ISDN capable telephones and FAX machines, video teleconferencing equipment, bridge/routers, and terminal adapters. All devices that are designed for ISDN are designated Terminal Equipment 1 (TE1).

All other communication devices that are *not* ISDN capable, but have a POTS telephone interface (also called the R interface), including ordinary analog telephones, FAX machines, and modems, are designatedTerminal Equipment 2 (TE2). A Terminal Adapters (TA) connects a TE2 to an ISDN S/T bus.

Going one step in the opposite direction takes us inside the telephone switch. Remember that the U interface connects the switch to the customer premises equipment. This local loop connection is called *Line Termination* (LT function). The connection to other switches within the phone network is called *Exchange Termination* (ET function).

LAYER 1 - PHYSICAL LAYER

The ISDN Physical Layer is specified by the ITU I-series and G-series documents. The U interface provided by the telco for BRI is a 2-wire, 160 kb/s digital connection. Echo cancellation is used to reduce noise, and data encoding schemes (2B1Q in North America, 4B3T in Europe) permit this relatively high data rate over ordinary single-pair local loops.

2B1Q

2B1Q (2 Binary 1 Quaternary) is the most common signaling method on U interfaces. This protocol is defined in detail in 1988 ANSI spec T1.601.

In summary, 2B1Q provides:

- Two bits per baud
- 80 kilobaud (baud = 1 modulation per second)
- Transfer rate of 160 kb/s

Bits	QuaternarySymbol	VoltageLevel
00	–3	–2.5
01	–1	–0.833
10	+3	+2.5
11	+1	+0.833

This means that the input voltage level can be one of 4 distinct levels.

These levels are called Quaternaries. Each quaternary represents 2 data bits, since there are 4 possible ways to represent 2 bits, as in the table above.

Frame Format

Each U interface frame is 240 bits long. At the prescribed data rate of 160 kb/s, each frame is therefore 1.5 ms long.

Each frame consists of:

- Frame overhead - 16 kb/s
- D channel - 16 kb/s
- 2 B channels at 64 kb/s - 128 kb/s

Sync	12 * (B_1 + B_2 + D)	Maintenance6
18 bits	216 bits	6 bits

- The Sync field consists of 9 Quaternaries (2 bits each) in the pattern +3 +3 –3 –3 –3 +3 –3 +3 –3.
- (B_1 + B_2 + D) is 18 bits of data consisting of 8 bits from the first B channel, 8 bits from the second B channel, and 2 bits of D channel data.
- The Maintenance field contains CRC information, block error detection flags, and "embedded operator commands" used for loopback testing without disrupting user data.

Data is transmitted in a superframe consisting of 8 240-bit frames for a total of 1920 bits (240 octets). The sync field of the first frame in the superframe is inverted (*i.e.* –3 –3 +3 +3 +3 –3 +3 –3 +3).

LAYER 2 - DATA LINK LAYER

The ISDN Data Link Layer is specified by the ITU Q-series documents Q.920 through Q.923. All of the signaling on the D channel is defined in the Q.921 spec.

LAP-D

Link Access Protocol - D channel (LAP-D) is the Layer 2 protocol used. This is almost identical to the X.25 LAP-B protocol.

Here is the structure of a LAP-D frame:

Flag	Address	Control	Information	CRC	Flag

Flag (1 octet) - This is always $7E_{16}$ ($0111\ 1110_2$)

Address (2 octets)							
1	2	3	4	5	6	7	8
		SAPI (6 bits)				C/R	EA0
		TEI(7bits)					EA1

SAPI (Service access point identifier), 6-bits. C/R (Command/Response) bit indicates if the frame is a command or a response. EA0 (Address Extension) bit indicates whether this is the final octet of the address or not. TEI (Terminal Endpoint Identifier) 7-bit device identifier. EA1 (Address Extension) bit, same as EA0:

- *Control (2 octets):* The frame level control field indicates the frame type (Information, Supervisory, or Unnumbered) and sequence numbers (N(r) and N(s)) as required.
- *Information*: Layer 3 protocol information and User data
- *CRC (2 octets):* Cyclic Redundancy Check is a low-level test for bit errors on the user data.
- *Flag (1 octet):* This is always $7E_{16}$ ($0111\ 1110_2$)

SAPIs

The Service Access Point Identifier (SAPI) is a 6-bit field that identifies the point where Layer 2 provides a service to Layer 3.

Table. See the Following Table.

SAPI	Description
0	Call control procedures
1	Packet Mode using Q.931 call procedures
16	Packet Mode communications procedures
32-47	Reserved for national use
63	Management Procedures
Others	Reserved for Future Use

TEIs

Terminal Endpoint Identifiers (TEIs) are unique IDs given to each device (TE) on an ISDN S/T bus. This identifier can be dynamic; the value may be assigned statically when the TE is installed, or dyn amically when activated.

TEI	Description
0-63	Fixed TEI assignments
64-126	Dynamic TEI assignment (assigned by the switch)
127	Broadcast to all devices

Establishing the Link Layer

The Layer 2 establishment process is very similar to the X.25 LAP-B setup, if you are familiar with it.

- The TE (Terminal Endpoint) and the Network initially exchange Receive Ready (RR) frames, listening for someone to initiate a connection
- The TE sends an Unnumbered Information (UI) frame with a SAPI of 63 (management procedure, query network) and TEI of 127 (broadcast)
- The Network assigns an available TEI (in the range 64-126)
- The TE sends a Set Asynchronous Balanced Mode (SABME) frame with a SAPI of 0 (call control, used to initiate a SETUP) and a TEI of the value assigned by the network
- The network responds with an Unnumbered Acknowledgement (UA), SAPI=0, TEI=assigned.

At this point, the connection is ready for a Layer 3 setup.

LAYER 3 - NETWORK LAYER

The ISDN Network Layer is also specified by the ITU Q-series documents Q.930 through Q.939. Layer 3 is used for the establishment, maintenance, and termination of logical network connections between two devices.

SPIDs

Service Profile IDs (SPIDs) are used to identify what

services and features the telco switch provides to the attached ISDN device. SPIDs are optional; when they are used, they are only accessed at device initialization time, before the call is set up. The format of the SPID is defined in a recommendation document, but it is only rarely followed. It is usually the 10-digit phone number of the ISDN line, plus a prefix and a suffix that are sometimes used to identify features on the line, but in reality it can be whatever the telco decides it should be. If an ISDN line requires a SPID, but it is not correctly supplied, then Layer 2 initialization will take place, but Layer 3 will not, and the device will not be able to place or accept calls. See ITU spec Q.932 for details.

Information Field Structure

The Information Field is a variable length field that contains the Q.931 protocol data.

Information Field							
1	2	3	4	5	6	7	8
Protocol Discriminator							
0	0	0	0	Length of CRV			
Call Reference Value (1 or 2 octets)							
0	Message Type						
Mandatory and Optional Information Elements (variable)							

These are the fields in a Q.931 header:

- *Protocol Discriminator (1 octet):* Identifies the Layer 3 protocol. If this is a Q.931 header, this value is always 08_{16}.
- *Length (1 octet):* Indicates the length of the next field, the CRV.
- *Call Reference Value (CRV) (1 or 2 octets):* used to uniquely identify each call on the user-network interface. This value is assigned at the beginning of a call, and this value becomes available for another call when the call is cleared.
- *Message Type (1 octet):* identifies the message type (*i.e.,*

SETUP, CONNECT, etc.). This determines what additional information is required and allowed.

- *Mandatory and Optional Information Elements (variable length)*: are options that are set depending on the Message Type.

Layer 3 Call Setup

These are the steps that occurs when an ISDN call is established. In the following example, there are three points where messages are sent and received; 1) the Caller, 2) the ISDN Switch, and 3) the Receiver.

- Caller sends a SETUP to the Switch.
- If the SETUP is OK, the switch sends a CALL PROCeeding to the Caller, and then a SETUP to the Receiver.
- The Receiver gets the SETUP. If it is OK, then it rings the phone and sends an ALERTING message to the Switch.
- The Switch forwards the ALERTING message to the Caller.
- When the receiver answers the call, is sends a CONNECT message to the Switch
- The Switch forwards the CONNECT message to the Caller.
- The Caller sends a CONNECT ACKnowledge message to the Switch
- The Switch forwards the CONNECT ACK message to the Receiver.
- Done. The connection is now up.

2

Medium Access Controlling of Sub Layer

MEDIUM ACCESS SUB LAYER

The MAC (Medium Access Control) sublayer is between the physical layer and the data link layer. The MAC sub layer is especially important in LANs, nearly all of which use a multi access (or broadcast) channel as the basis of their networks.

CHANNEL ALLOCATION

STATIC CHANNEL

FDM (Frequency-Division Multiplexing): Divide the bandwidth into equal sized portions so that each user can be assigned one portion. Under what circumstances FDM is efficient? When there is only a small and fixed number of users, and each of which has a heavy (buffered) load of traffic (*e.g.*, carriers' switching offices).

What's the problem with FDM?

- If fewer than users are currently interested in communication, some portions of spectrum will be wasted.
- If more than users want to communicate, some of them will be denied permission even if some users with allocated frequency hardly ever transmit anything.
- Even the number of users is and constant, when some users are quiescent, no one else can use their bandwidth so it is simply wasted.

- For bursty data traffic (peak traffic to mean traffic ratio of 1000:1), the allocated small subchannel will be idle most of the time but unable to handle the peak traffic.

LAN PROTOCOLS

ALOHA PROTOCOLS

The ALOHA system was used for ground-based radio broadcasting, but the basic idea is applicable to any system in which uncoordinated users are competing for the use of a single shared channel.

Pure ALOHA

Basic idea:

- Let users transmit whenever they have data to be sent.
- A sender can always find out whether or not its frame was destroyed by listening to the channel output (due to the feedback property of broad casting).
- If the frame was destroyed, the sender just waits a random amount of time and sends it again.

Systems in which multiple users share a common channel in a way that can lead to conflicts are known as contention systems.

A sketch of frame generation in an ALOHA system:

- Whenever two frames try to occupy the channel at the same time there will be a collision.
- What fraction of all transmitted frames escape collisions under these chaotic circumstances?

Assumptions and definitions:

- Infinite population: there are an infinite number of users (stations) in the system.
- *T*: the amount of time needed to transmit a standard, fixed-length frame.
- *S*: the mean number of frames generated within one *T*: Normally. What happens if ?

At equilibrium (a balanced situation), S represents the number of successful transmissions (or throughput) of the network.

- *G*: the mean number of frames transmitted within one T..

G includes the number of new frames and retransmissions and it represents the traffic load.

- , Where is the probability of a transmission being successful.

A frame will not suffer a collision if no other frames are sent within one frame time of its start. The vulnerable period in which the transmitted frame will be destroyed is. In an interval of, the mean number of frames transmitted is. The probability that frames are generated during a given period of time is (by the assumption of Poisson distribution): where is the mean number of frames transmitted within the given period of time. The probability that frame is generated during a given period of time is: The probability of no other traffic being initiated during the entire vulnerable period () is Using, we get At, (18% channel utilization).

Slotted ALOHA System

- Time is divided up into discrete intervals, each interval corresponding to one frame.
- A terminal is not permitted to send until the beginning of the next slot.

The vulnerable period is reduced in half (instead of), the number of transmitted frames in this period is (instead of), leading to Slotted ALOHA peaks at, with , twice that of pure ALOHA. The main reason for poor channel utilization of ALOHA (pure or slotted) is that all stations can transmit at will, without paying attention to what the other stations are doing. In LANs, it is possible for stations to detect what other stations are doing, and adapt their behaviour accordingly, achieving a much better channel utilization.

Carrier Sense Multiple Access Protocols

Protocols in which stations listen for a carrier (*i.e.*, a

transmission) and act accordingly are called carrier sense protocols.

Persistent and Non Persistent CSMA

1-persistent CSMA (Carrier Sense Multiple Access):

- To send data, a station first listens to the channel to see if anyone else is transmitting.
- If so, the station waits (keeps sensing it) until the channel becomes idle. Otherwise, it transmits a frame.
- If a collision occurs (how ?), the station waits a random amount of time and starts all over again.

It is called 1-persistent because the station transmits with a probability of 1 whenever it starts sensing the channel and finds the channel idle.

How could collisions happen in CSMA ? Whenever more than one station detect a idle channel and their transmission times overlap.

Discussions:

- What's the effect of signal propagation delay ?
  The longer the delay, the more the collisions, and the worse the performance of the protocol.
- How about zero propagation delay ?
  There still exist chances of collisions.
- Is this protocol any better than ALOHA (both pure and slotted) ?
  Yes, because both stations have the decency to desist from interfering with the third station's frame.

Nonpersistent CSMA

- To send data, a station first listens to the channel to see if anyone else is transmitting.
- If so, the station waits a random period of time (instead of keeping sensing until the end of the transmission) and repeats the algorithm. Otherwise, it transmits a frame.
- If a collision occurs, the station waits a random amount of time and starts all over again.

This protocol has better channel utilization and longer delays than 1-persistent CSMA.

P-persistent CSMA(applied to slotted channels):

- To send data, a station first listens to the channel to see if anyone else is transmitting.
- If the channel is idle, it transmits with a probability. With a probability it defers until the next slot.

If the next slot is also idle, it either transmits or defers again, with probabilities and.

This process is repeated until either the frame has been transmitted or another station has begun transmitting. In the latter case, it waits a random time and starts again.

- If a collision occurs, the station waits a random amount of time and starts all over again.
- If the channel is (initially) busy, it waits until the next slot and apply the above algorithm.

CSMA with Collision Detection

Persistent and non persistent CSMA protocols improve ALOHA by ensuring that no station begins to transmit when it senses the channel busy. CSMA/CD (Carrier Sense Multiple Access with Collision Detection) protocol further improves ALOHA by aborting transmissions as soon as a collision is detected.

The conceptual model:

- To send data, a station first listens to the channel to see if anyone else is transmitting.
- If so, the station waits until the end of the transmission (1-persistent) or wait a random period of time and repeats the algorithm (non persistent). Otherwise, it transmits a frame.
- If a collision occurs, the station will detect the collision, abort its transmission, waits a random amount of time, and starts all over again.

The model for CSMA/CD consists of alternating contention and transmission periods, with idle periods occurring when all stations are quiet. When two stations both begin transmitting at exactly the same time, how long will it take them to realise that there has been a collision. The minimum time to detect the collision is the time it takes the signal to propagate from one station to the other. How long could the transmitting station be sure it has seized the network (or ? where is time equal to the full cable propagation) The contention interval can be modeled as a slotted ALOHA system with slot width. Collision detection is an *analog* process the signal encoding must allow collisions to be detected Manchester encoding. It is worth noting that no MAC-sub layer protocol guarantees reliable delivery. Even in the absence of collisions, the receiver may not have copied the frame correctly due to various reasons (*e.g.*, lack of buffer space or a missed interrupt).

Collision-free Protocols

Can we avoid collision all together, even during the contention period ? Yes. But how? One assumption: there are stations, each with a unique address from 0 to "wired" into it. Which station gets the channel after a successful transmission ?

A Basic Bit-map Protocol

- Each contention period consists of exactly slots, with one slot time being at least.
- If station has a frame to send, it transmits 1 bit during the th slot; otherwise, it transmits 0 bit during the th slot.
- After all slots have passed by, stations begin transmitting in numerical order.
- After the last ready station has transmitted its frame, another -bit contention period is begun.

Protocols like this in which the desire to transmit is broadcast before the actual transmission are called reservation protocols.

Low load situation: the bit map repeats over and over. Assume one contention bit slot as one time unit, and a data frame consists of time units. For a low-numbered station, when it's ready to send, the "current" slot may be somewhere in the middle of the bit map.

Therefore, it has to wait slots (on the average) for the current scan to finish and another full slots for the following scan to complete before it may begin transmitting. For a high-numbered station, it will have to wait half a scan (bit slots) before starting to transmit. The mean waiting bit slots for all station is slots. The channel efficiency is at low load, but at high load.

Binary Countdown

A problem with the basic bit-map protocol is that overhead is 1 contention bit slot per station. We can do better than that by using binary station addresses.

- Each station has a binary address. All addresses are the same length.
- To transmit, a station broadcasts its address as a binary bit string, starting with high-order bit.
- The bits in each address position from different stations are BOOLEAN ORed together (so called Binary countdown).
- As soon as a station sees that a high-order bit position that is 0 in its address has been overwritten with a 1, it gives up.
- After the winning station has transmitted its frame, there is no information available telling how many other stations to send, so the algorithm begins all over with the next frame.

The channel efficiency of this method is.

Limited-contention Protocols

Two basic channel acquisition strategies studied:

- Contention methods. *E.g.*, ALOHA, CSMA.
- Collision-free methods. *E.g.*, basic bit map.

Two performance measures:

- Delay at low load. Contention methods are preferable.
- Channel efficiency at high load. Collision-free methods are preferable.

Could we combine the best properties of both the contention and collision-free protocols ? Yes. Such new protocols, called limited contention protocols, use a contention method at low loads, but use a collision-free technique at high loads.

Analysis of Symmetric Contention Protocols

Assumption: all stations attempt to acquire the channel with the same probability. The probability for a station to successfully acquire the channel during a given slot if there are stations contending for it: The optimal value of is so [probability of success with optimal]

Basic Idea

- Stations are divided into groups.
- Each group is allocated a slot for transmission.
- Members of one group compete for one slot only.

Special Cases

- Each group with only one member (*e.g.*, basic bit-map). Collision-free.
- Each group with two stations. The probability that both will try to transmit during a slot is, which for small is negligible.
- A single group containing all stations (*i.e.*, slotted ALOHA). Zero delay at low load but very high collisions at high load.

What we need is a way to assign stations to slots dynamically, with many stations per slot when the load is low and few station per slot when the load is high.

Adaptive Tree Walk Protocol

The algorithm devised by US Army for testing soldiers for syphilis during WW II:

- The Army took a blood sample from soldiers.
- A portion of each sample was poured into a single test tube. The mixed sample was then tested for antibodies.
- If none were found, all the soliders in the group were declared healthy.

- Otherwise, two new mixed samples were prepared, one for soldiers 1 through and one from the rest.
- The process was repeated recursively until the infected soldiers were determined.

Each bit slot (group) is associated with a particular node in the tree, with the root node corresponding to slot 0 for all stations in one group.

- Starting from the root node: all stations are permitted to try to acquire the channel.
- If a collision occurs, the search continues recursively with the left and right children of that node.
- If a bit slot goes idle or if there is exactly one station that transmits into it, the searching of its node can stop.

Is it worthwhile to dedicate slot 0 to the root node for all stations to compete ? At what level in the tree the search should begin ? The heavier the load, the deeper level the search should begin. Assumption: each station has a good estimate of the number of ready station, and the ready stations are uniformly distributed. The levels of the tree are numbered as follows: the level of the root node is numbered 0. For a level, the level below it is numbered as. Each node at level has a fraction of of the total stations below it. The number of ready stations below a specific node at level is. Therefore, the optimal level to begin searching the tree should be the one at which the mean number of contending stations per slot is 1, *i.e.,,* so.

IEEE STANDARDS

IEEE STANDARD 802.3 AND ETHERNET

This standard is for a 1-persistent CSMA/CD LAN:

- When a station wants to transmit, it listens to the cable.
- If the cable is busy, the station waits until it goes idle, otherwise it transmits immediately.
- If a collision occurs, all colliding stations terminate their transmission, wait a random time, and repeat the whole process all over again.

History

- Xerox Ethernet (2.94 Mbps)
- Standard Ethernet (10 Mbps)
- IEEE 802.3 (1 - 10 Mbps)

A typical example: A 10 Mbps baseband system using 50-ohm coaxial cable.

Cabling

Detecting cable breaks, bad taps, or loose connectors can be a major problem with both 10Base5 and 10Base2, which has driven systems using 10Base-T based on twisted pairs.

- *Connection device*: transceiver.
- Contact the cable.
- Handle carrier detection and collision detection.
- Issue invalid signals.

A transceiver cable (up to 50 m) connects the transceiver to an interface board in the computer. The interface board contains a controller chip that transmits frames to, and receives frames from, the transceiver. The controller is responsible for

- Assembling the data into the proper frame format,
- Computing checksums on outgoing frames and verifying them on incoming frames, and
- (Optionally) managing a pool of buffers for incoming frames, a queue of buffers for frames to be transmitted.

The controller contact the computer by means of interrupts, DMA, and I/O commands. Repeaters are used to connect multiple cables together. It receives, amplifies, and retransmits signals in both directions. Repeaters are physical layer devices. No two transceivers may be more than 2.5 km apart, and no path between any two transceivers may traverse more than four repeaters.

Manchester Encoding

None of the versions of 802.3 use straight binary encoding because it leads to ambiguities: it cannot tell the difference between an idle sender (0 volts) and a 0 bit (0 volts). What is needed is a way for receivers to unambiguously determine the start, end, or middle of each bit without reference to an external clock.

All 802.3 baseband systems use Manchester encoding due to its simplicity. The high signal is volts and the low signal is volts, giving a DC value of 0 volts.

The 802.3 MAC Sublayer Protocol

Preamble of 7 bytes, each with the bit pattern 10101010. For synchronization between the sender and the receiver. Start of frame byte contains 10101011 to denote the start of the frame.

Destination and source addresses, each with 2-6 bytes.

- *Ordinary address*: The high-order bit value is 0.
- *Multicast address*: The high-order bit value is 1.
- *Broadcast address*: All bits have a value of 1.
- *Local address*: Assigned by local network administrator, distinguished by the second high-order bit (46) value 0.
- *Global address ( )*: assigned by IEEE to ensure world wide uniqueness, distinguished by the second high-order bit value 1.

Length: 0 (46) - 1500 bytes. To make it easier to distinguish valid frames from garbage, 802.3 states that valid frames must be at least 64 bytes. Another more important reason for having a minimum length frame is to prevent a station from completing the transmission of a short frame before the first bit has even reached the far end of the cable, which it may collide with another frame, as illustrated in. After a collision, the station waits for a random time and try again. How the randomization is done ?

The binary exponential backoff algorithm: Time is divided into discrete slots whose length is equal to the worst case round trip propagation time ().

- After the first collision, each station waits either 0 or 1 slot time at random.
- After the second collision, each station waits either 0, 1, 2, or 3 slot times at random.
- After collisions, a random number between 0 and is chosen, and that number of slots is skipped.

- After 10 collisions have been reached, the randomization interval is frozen at 1023 slots.
- After 16 collisions, the controller gives up and reports failure.

What happens if the randomization interval for all collisions is always 1023 ? Think about the average delay when only a few stations collide. What happens if the randomization interval for all collisions is always 2 ? Think about the time needed to resolve the collision when 100 stations try to send at once. For reliable communication, the first contention slot following successful transmission can be reserved for the destination to acknowledge the source.

Switched 802.3 LANs

The heart of the system is a switch containing a high-speed (typically over 1 Gbps) backplane and room for multiple plug-in cards (typically 4 to 32), with one to eight connectors in each card.

- To transmit, a station outputs a standard 802.3 frame to a plug-in card in the switch.
- The plug-in card checks to see if the frame is destined for one of the other stations connected to the same card.

If so, the frame is copied there. If not, the frame is sent over the high-speed backplane to the destination station's card. What happens if two machines attached to the same plug-in card transmit frames at the same time ?

In case that all the ports on the card are wired together to form a local on-card LAN:

- Collisions on this on-card LAN will be detected and handled the same as any other collisions on a CSMA/DC network.
- Only one transmission per card is possible at any instant, but all the cards can be transmitting in parallel.

In case that each input port is buffered, so incoming frames are stored in the card's on-board RAM as they arrive:

- Once a frame has been completely received, the card

checks to see if the frame is destined for another port on the same card, or for a distant port. In the former case it can be transmitted directly to the destination. In the latter case, it must be transmitted over the backplane to the proper card.

- All input ports can receive (and transmit) frames at the same time, for parallel, full-duplex operation.

A port may be connected to a LAN (a 12-port Hub, as shown in. If all the input ports are connected to hubs, rather than to individual stations, the switch just becomes an 802.3 to 802.3 bridge (to be discussed later).

IEEE STANDARD 802.4

Two problems with 802.3:

- The worst case is unbounded: a station might have to wait arbitrarily long to send a frame. Unsuitable for factory automation applications (e.g, GM).
- Frames do not have priorities. Unsuitable for real time systems.

The Token bus

- Physically, it is a linear or tree-shaped cable onto which the stations are attached.

The 75-ohm broadband coaxial cable is used at the physical layer. Analog modulation schemes are used to transmit digital signals. Speeds of 1, 5, 10 Mbps are possible.

- Logically, the stations are organized into a ring, with each station knowing the address of the station to its "left" and "right".
  - When the logical ring is initialized, the highest numbered station may send the first frame.
  - Then, it passes to its immediate neighbour a special frame called a token.
  - The token propagates around the logical ring, with only the token holder being permitted to transmit.

Since only one station at a time holds the token, collisions do not occur. If there are stations and each station can hold the token for a maximum sec, no station will ever have to wait more than sec to get a chance. When a station is first powered on, it is not in the ring. Provisions are provided for adding to, and deleting stations from the ring.

The Token Bus MAC Sublayer Protocol

Token propagation direction: from high address to low address.

The Priority Scheme

- Each station conceptually consists of four substations, with each substation in one of the four traffic priority classes: 0, 2, 4, and 6 (the highest). As input comes into the MAC sublayer from above, the data are routed to one of the substations according to their priority.
- When a token comes in, it is passed internally to the priority 6 substation, which may transmit until its queue is empty or its timer expires and then pass the token to the next priority substation, and so on.
- Each station may hold the token for certain amount of time (quantum), then it must pass the token on (preemptive).

The priority 6 substation is guaranteed for a fraction of the total quantum (by setting its timer properly), the lower priorities will live with what is left over. For a network of 50 stations, if 1/3 of its bandwidth 10 Mbps is allocated to priority 6 traffic, then each station has a guaranteed kbps for priority 6 substation.

The Frame Format

Preamble field (1 byte) is used to synchronize the receiver's clock. Starting and ending delimiters fields contain analog encoding of symbols other than 0s and 1s. As a result, no length field is needed. Frame control field distinguishes data frames from control frames.

- For data frames, it carries the frame's priority and

an indicator for whether an acknowledgement is required.

- For control frames, it carries the frame's type: token passing, entering the ring, leaving the ring, and so on.

Destination and source addresses fields are the same as in 802.3. Data field may be up to 8182 bytes - five times the maximum 802.3 frame.

Logical Ring Maintenance

Each station interface contains the following infrastructures:

- Addresses of the predecessor and successor stations. Initialized after joining a ring.
- Two random bits used to distinguish 4 time slots for resolving collisions (combined with the binary countdown protocol). Regenerated periodically or after use.
- A number of timers.

Joining the Ring

- The token holder periodically (timer) broadcasts a frame which contains the holder's address and its successor's.
- Only stations with addresses in that range are allowed to bid to enter.
- If no one bids to enter within a slot time (), the token holder continues with its normal business.
- If exactly one station bids to enter, it is inserted into the ring, and becomes the token holder's successor.
- If two or more stations bid to enter, a collision occurs. The token holder runs an arbitration algorithm (a variation of binary countdown), starting with the broadcast of a frame. Only one station may enter at each solicitation.

Leaving the Ring

- Suppose the leaving station,, has successor, and predecessor.

- It leaves the ring by sending a frame telling it that henceforth its successor is instead of. The should also be informed that its new predecessor is.
- Stops transmitting.

Initializing the Ring

- When the first station comes on line, it notices that there is no traffic for a certain period (timer). Then it sends a frame.
- Not hearing any competitors contending for the token, it creates a token and sets up a ring containing only itself. If two or more stations are powered on simultaneously, an arbitration algorithm is used to resolve the collision. Only one of the stations may create a token.
- Periodically (timer), it solicits bids for new stations to join.

What happens if a station tries to pass the token to its successor that has gone down ?

- After passing the token, a station listens to see if its successor either transmits a frame or passes the token.
- If the successor does neither, the token is passed a second time.
- If that also fails, the station the successor has gone down, and transmits a frame specifying the address of its successor.
- When the failed station's successor sees this frame naming its predecessor, it responds by sending a frame to the station whose successor failed, naming itself as the new successor.
- If a station fails to pass the token to its successor and also fails to locate the successor's successor, which may also be down, it sends a frame to see if else is still alive so all alive stations will re-join the ring.

What happens if the token holder goes down and takes the token with it ?

- Each station has a timer that is reset whenever a frame appears on network.

- When this timer hits a threshold value, the station issues a frame to reinitialize the ring.

What happens if there are multiple tokens in the ring ?

- If a station holding the token notices a transmission from another station, it discards its token.
- If, by accident, all the tokens are discarded, the lack of activity will cause one or more stations to try to claim the token.

IEEE STANDARD 802.5: TOKEN RING

A ring network is not really a broadcast medium, but a collection of point-to-point links that happen to form a circle.

Main attractive features:

- Point-to-point links can run on different transmission media.
- Ring engineering is almost entirely digital (Ethernet has a substantial analog component for collision detection).
- A ring is fair and has a known upper bound on channel access.

The concept of "physical length" of a bit:

- If the data rate of the ring is Mbps, a bit is emitted every sec.
- With a typical signal propagation speed of 200 m/sec, each bit occupies metres on the ring.

For a 1-Mbps ring whose circumference is 1000 metres can contain only 5 bits on it at once. Each bit arriving at an interface is copied into a 1-bit buffer, inspected, possibly modified, and then copied out onto the ring again, causing a so called 1-bit delay at each interface.

In a token ring:

- A special bit pattern, called the token, circulates whenever all stations are idle.
- When a station wants to transmit, it is required to seize the token and remove it from the ring before transmitting.
- After a station has finished transmitting the last bit of its last frame, it must regenerate the token.

The ring must have a sufficient delay (the 1-bit delay plus the signal propagation delay) to contain a complete token to circulate when all stations are idle.

Ring interfaces have two operating modes:

- In listen mode, the input bits are copied to output. The input may be copied into the station if it is the destination.
- In transmit mode, which is entered only after the token has been seized, the interface breaks the connection between input and output, entering its own data onto the ring.

When the last bit of the frame has gone around and come back, the interface must switch back into listen mode. As bits have propagated around the ring and come back, they are removed from the ring by the sender. So there is no limit on the size of the frames.

Acknowledgement handling:

- The frame includes a 1-bit, initially zero.
- When the destination has received a frame, it inverts the bit.
- For broadcast, a more complicated scheme is needed. The network efficiency can approach 100% under conditions of heavy load.

802.5 standard:

- Shielded twisted pairs running at 1 or 4 Mbps.
- Signals are encoded using differential Manchester encoding.
- *Wire centre*: to improve the ring's reliability and maintainability.

The Token Ring MAC Sublayer Protocol

The basic operation:

- When no traffic on the ring, a 3-byte token circulates endlessly.
- When the token is seized, a specific 0 bit in the second byte is converted into 1. This action converts the first two bytes of the token into the start-of-frame sequence.

- The station then outputs the rest of a normal data frame.

A station may hold the token for the token-holding time (10 msec). Starting and ending delimiters mark the boundaries of the frame using invalid differential Machester patterns (HH and LL). Access control byte contains the token bit, and *Monitor bit, Priority bits,* and *Reservation bits*. Frame control byte distinguishes data frames from various control frames. Destination and source addresses are the same as in 802.3 and 802.4.

Data field may be as long as necessary but must be transmitted within a token holding time. Checksum field is also the same as 802.3 and 802.4. Frame status byte contains the and bits, which may be modified by the destination station. When the source station drains the frame from the ring, it examines the two bits:

- *And*: destination not present or not powered up.
- *And*: destination present but frame not accepted.
- *And*: destination present and frame copied.

Priority handling:

- The 3-byte token frame contains a field in the middle byte giving the priority of the token.
- When a station wants to transmit a priority frame, it must wait until it can capture a token with a priority less than or equal to.
- When a data frame goes by, a station can reserve the next token by writing the priority of the frame it want to send into the passing frame's *Reservation bits* if there is no higher priority already reserved there.
- When the current frame is finished, the next token is generated at the the priority reserved.

Ring Maintenance

Centralized monitoring: One of the stations acts as a monitor station which oversees the ring. If the monitor goes down, a contention protocol insures that another station is elected monitor.

Monitor Generation

- When the ring comes up or any station notices that there is no monitor, it transmits a control frame.
- If this frame circumnavigates the ring before any other frames are sent, the sender becomes the new monitor.

Monitor's Responsibilities

- *Checking whether the token is lost*: A timer is set to the longest possible tokenless interval, *i.e.,* each station transmitting for the full token-holding time. If this timer goes off, the monitor drains the ring and issues a new token.
- *Taking action when the ring breaks*: Locating breaks in the ring is not done by the monitor. Any station may transmit a frame to locate and delete its presumably dead neighbours, without human intervention.
- *Keeping the ring longer than 24 bits*: If the 1-bit delays in the stations plus the cable length add up to less than 24 bits (the length of a token), the monitor inserts extra delay bits so that a token can circulate.
- Cleaning the ring up when garbled frames appear.

When a garbled frame appears, the monitor can detect it by its invalid format or checksum, and then open the ring to drain it, issuing a new token when the ring has been cleaned up.

- *Watching out for orphan frames.* An orphan frame occurs when a station transmits a short frame in its entirety onto a long ring and then crashes or is powered down before the frame can be drained.

The monitor detects orphan frames by setting the *monitor* bit in the *Access control* byte whenever it passes through. If an incoming frame has this bit set, it is treated as an orphan (drained).

COMPARISON OF 802.3, 802.4, AND 802.5

Which LAN would you like to choose ?

Three LAN standards use roughly similar technology and get roughly similar performance.

Advanteges of 802.3 (Ethernet)

- The most widely used type.
- Simple algorithm.
- Stations can be installed on the fly, without taking the network down.
- A passive cable is used and modems are not required.
- The delay at low load is very low.

Limitations and Problems of 802.3 (Ethernet)

- It has a substantial analog component to detect collision.
- The minimum frame is 64 bytes, a substantial overhead when the data is just a single character.
- It is nondeterministic, without upper bound for delay.
- It has no priorities.
- The cable length is limited to 2.5 km because the round trip cable length determines the slot time.
- It is very difficult to run at high speed because when the speed increase, the frame transmission times drop but the contention interval does not (alway), resulting in low efficiency.
- At high load, collisions become a major problem (low throughput).
- It is not well suited to fibre optics due to the difficulty of installing taps.

Advantages of 802.4 (Token Bus)

- It uses highly reliable, off-the-shelf cable TV equipment.
- It is more deterministic than 802.3. (what about the repeated losses of the token at critical moments ?).
- It can handle short minimum frames.
- It supports priorities and provides a guaranteed fraction of the bandwidth to high-priority traffic.
- Excellent throughput and efficiency at high load (effectively TDM).
- Broadband cable can support multiple channels.

Limitations and Problems of 802.4 (Token Bus)

- Broadband systems use analog engineering (modems and amplifiers).
- Extremely complex protocol and substantial delay at low load (wait for the token).
- Poorly suited for fibre optic implementation.

Advantages of 802.5 (Token Ring)

- Point-to-point connections mean easy engineering and fully digital.
- Rings can be built using any transmission medium.
- The standard twisted pair is cheap and simple to install.
- The use of wire centres makes the token ring the only LAN that can detect and eliminate cable failures automatically.
- Priorities are possible (using not so fair scheme).
- Short frames are possible.
- The length of large frames is limited only by the token-holding time.
- Excellent throughput and efficiency at high load.

Limitations and Problems of 802.4 (Token Bus)

- The centralized monitor introduces a critical component.
- Large delay at low load.

The principle conclusion we can draw from these studies is that we can draw no conclusion from them. One inarguable general statement: an overloaded 802.3 LAN will collapse totally, but an overloaded token-based system will have an efficiency approaching 100 per cent. The convergence of three LANs is an unlikely event, so the issue of interconnecting (by bridges and gateways) different LANs is an important one, which will be discussed later.

IEEE STANDARD 802.6: DISTRIBUTED QUEUE DUAL BUS

For networks covering an entire city with thousands of

stations, IEEE defined one MAN, called DQDB (Distributed Queue Dual Bus), as standard 802.6.

- Two unidirectional buses.
- Each bus has a head-end, which generates a steady stream of 53-byte cells. Each cell travels downstream from the head-end, carring a 44-byte payload field. When it reaches the end, it falls off the bus.
- Each cell also holds two protocol bits, *Busy,* set to indicate that a cell is occupied, and *Request,* which can be set when a station wants to make a request.
- Data traffic to the right uses the upper bus (but the lower bus is used for making a request).
- Traffic to the left uses the lower bus (but the upper bus is used for making a request).

Stations in a DQDB queue up in the order they became ready to send and transmit in FIFO order. DQDB systems typically run for up to 160 km at speed 44.736 Mbps (T3). How does DQDB achieve FIFO order without having a central queue ?

IEEE STANDARD 802.2: LOGICAL LINK CONTROL

The LLC (Logical Link Control) layer offers three types of services to the network layer:

- Connectionless (type 1),
- Connection-oriented (type 2),
- And acknowledged connectless (type 3).

The LLC header is based on the older HDLC protocol.

FIBRE DISTRIBUTED DATA INTERFACE (FDDI)

FDDI stands for Fibre Distributed Data Interface. The FDDI standard is ANSI X3T9.5. The FDDI topology is ring with two counter rotating rings for reliability with no hubs. Cable type is fibre-optic. Connectors are specialized. The media access method is token passing. Multiple tokens may be used by the system. The maximum length is 100 kilometres. The maximum number of nodes on the network is 500.Speed is 100 Mbps. FDDI is normally used as a backbone to link other networks. A typical FDDI network can include servers, concentrators, and links to other networks. CDDI is a copper version of FDDI which uses category 5 cable. Obviously the distance is more limited than FDDI.

Devices called concentrators provide functions similar to hubs. Most concentrators use dual attachment station network cards but single attachment concentrators may be used to attach more workstations to the network.

FDDI token passing allows multiple frames to circulate around the ring at the same time. Priority levels of a data frame and token can be set to allow servers to send more data frames. Time sensitive data may also be given higher priority. The second ring in a FDDI network is a method of adjusting when there are breaks in the cable. The primary ring is normally used, but if the nearest downstream neighbour stops responding the data is sent on the secondary ring in attempt to reach the computer. Therefore a break in the cable will result in the secondary ring being used.

There are two network cards which are:

- Dual attachment stations (DAS) used for servers and concentrators are attached to both rings.
- Single Attachment stations (SAS) attached to one ring and used to attach workstations to concentrators.

A router or switch can link an FDDI network to a local area network (LAN). Normally FDDI is used to link LANs together since it covers long distances.

Protocol Structure: FDDI: Fibre Distributed Data Interface

2	6	6	0-30	Variable	4bytes
Frame control	Destination address	Source address	Route Information	Information	FCS

Frame control - The frame control structure is as follows:

C	L	F	F	Z	Z	Z	Z

- *C–Class bit*: 0 Asynchronous frame; 1 Synchronous frame/
- *L–Address length bit*: 0 16 bits (never); 1 48 bits (always).

- FF - Format bits.
- ZZZZ - Control bits.

Destination address - The address structure is as follows:

I/G	U/L	Address bits

Source address - The address structure is as follows:

I/G	RII	Address bits

- I/G - Individual/group address: 0 Group address; 1 Individual address.
- RII - Routing information indicator: 0 RI absent; 1 RI present.

Route Information: The structure of the route information is as follows:

3	5	1	6	1	16	16	16
RT	LTH	D	LF	R	RD1	RD2	RDn

- *RC*: Routing control (16 bits).
- *RDn:* Route descriptor (16 bits).
- *RT:* Routing type (3 bits).
- *LTH*: Length (5 bits).
- *D:* Direction bit (1 bit).
- *LF:* Largest frame (6 bits).
- *R:* Reserved (1 bit).

Information: The Information field may be LLC, MAC or SMT protocol.

- *FCS:* Frame check sequence.
- Related Protocols
- IEEE 802.5 , 802.2

FDDI FUNCTIONALITIES

In FDDI the primary cable that is used is the fibre optic cable but the technology can be used on copper wires also. The fibre optic cables have clear advantages over the copper cables. There is more security, and the fibre optic cables are more reliable than any other wire available. The data transfer in the fibre optic cable takes place without any electrical signals being transmitted.

This enhances the security because the electrical signals can usually be tapped and therefore a data breach can occur otherwise. Also the added advantage of not having the electrical signals is that the radio frequency and other electromagnetic waves are incapable of interfering with the fibre optic media. The data flow is undeterred and constant through a fibre optic cable. Long distances can be covered for data flow using the fibre optic cable using a single node.

FIBRE DISTRIBUTED DATA INTERFACE TYPES

There are two types of fibre distributed data interface mainly. The single mode interface and the multi mode interface. The mode here specifies the light or the single ray of light that is entering the fibre optic cable. The Multimode fibre uses the LED display to generate the light rays and the single mode uses the laser technology to generate the light rays.

The difference in both these methods is that multi mode as the name suggests allows many rays at one single point of time to pass and the single mode laser allows one ray at one time to pass through. However the angles at which the light reflects on the cable are all different so by the time they reach the nodes the time at which they arrive is different. In a single mode there is no such confusion so the data arrives at the node in a streamlined fashion.

The methodology which the multi mode uses is called modal dispersion and it is used in an environment which has limited boundaries. In comparison with the multi node the single node will be able to carry more data and deliver at a higher speed along with covering larger distances.

CONCLUSION

After the advent of FDDI internet has advanced to a great extent even with common day to day users. The internet service providers are able to provide better services to the people and are able to facilitate internet in a better fashion. Also since internet has advanced and the number of users has increased, more and more businesses have started e-commerce applications on the internet. Because the fibre distributed data interface is a safe and secure medium when it comes to cables the ecommerce transactions have found a reliable media. FDDI through single node transfers are widely adapted by MNC's for communication between different branches.

DATA LINK LAYER

DEFINITION

The data link layer is responsible for encoding *bits* into *packets* prior to transmission and then decoding the packets back into bits at the destination. Bits are the most basic unit of information in computing and communications. Packets are the fundamental unit of information transport in all modern computer networks, and increasingly in other communications networks as well.

The data link layer is also responsible for logical link control, media access control, hardware addressing, error detection and handling and defining physical layer standards. It provides reliable data transfer by transmitting packets with the necessary synchronization, error control and flow control. The data link layer is divided into two sublayers: the *media access control* (MAC) layer and the *logical link control* (LLC) layer. The former controls how computers on the network gain access to the data and obtain permission to transmit it; the latter controls packet synchronization, flow control and error checking.

The data link layer is where most LAN (local area network) and wireless LAN technologies are defined. Among the most popular technologies and protocols generally associated with this layer are Ethernet, Token Ring, FDDI (fibre distributed data interface), ATM (asynchronous transfer mode), SLIP (serial line Internet protocol), PPP (point-to-point protocol), HDLC (high level data link control) and ADCCP (advanced data communication control procedures).

The data link layer is often implemented in software as a driver for a network interface card (NIC). Because the data link and physical layers are so closely related, many types of hardware are also associated with the data link layer. For example, NICs typically implement a specific data link layer technology, so they are often called *Ethernet cards, Token Ring cards,* etc.

There are also several types of network interconnection devices that are said to operate at the data link layer in whole or in part, because they make decisions about what to do with data they receive by looking at data link layer packets. These devices include most bridges and switches, although switches also encompass functions performed by the network layer.

The second-lowest layer (layer 2) in the OSI Reference Model stack is the *data link layer,* often abbreviated "DLL" (though that abbreviation has other meanings as well in the computer world). The data link layer, also sometimes just called the *link layer,* is where many wired and wireless local area networking (LAN) technologies primarily function. For example, Ethernet, Token Ring, FDDI and 802.11 ("wireless Ethernet" or "Wi-Fi') are all sometimes called "data link layer technologies". The set of devices connected at the data link layer is what is commonly considered a simple "network", as opposed to an internetwork.

DATA LINK LAYER SUB LAYERS

The data link layer is often conceptually divided into two sublayers: *logical link control (LLC)* and *media access control (MAC).* This split is based on the architecture used in the IEEE 802 Project, which is the IEEE working group responsible for creating the standards that define many networking technologies (including all of the ones I mentioned above except FDDI). By separating LLC and MAC functions, interoperability of different network technologies is made easier, as explained in our earlier discussion of networking model concepts.

DATA LINK LAYER FUNCTIONS

The following are the key tasks performed at the data link layer:

- *Logical Link Control (LLC):* Logical link control refers

to the functions required for the establishment and control of logical links between local devices on a network.

As mentioned above, this is usually considered a DLL sublayer; it provides services to the network layer above it and hides the rest of the details of the data link layer to allow different technologies to work seamlessly with the higher layers. Most local area networking technologies use the IEEE 802.2 LLC protocol.

- *Media Access Control (MAC)*: This refers to the procedures used by devices to control access to the network medium. Since many networks use a shared medium (such as a single network cable, or a series of cables that are electrically connected into a single virtual medium) it is necessary to have rules for managing the medium to avoid conflicts. For example. Ethernet uses the CSMA/CD method of media access control, while Token Ring uses token passing.
- *Data Framing*: The data link layer is responsible for the final encapsulation of higher-level messages into *frames* that are sent over the network at the physical layer.
- *Addressing*: The data link layer is the lowest layer in the OSI model that is concerned with addressing: labeling information with a particular destination location. Each device on a network has a unique number, usually called a *hardware address* or *MAC address,* that is used by the data link layer protocol to ensure that data intended for a specific machine gets to it properly.
- *Error Detection and Handling*: The data link layer handles errors that occur at the lower levels of the network stack. For example, a cyclic redundancy check (CRC) field is often employed to allow the station receiving data to detect if it was received correctly.

ELEMENTARY DATA

ELEMENTARY DATA TYPES

What are the different kinds of data types that are available for use in programming? Data types fall under several categories and can be divided into the elementary data type, the structured data type, or the abstract data type. The elementary data types are the most basic of all. The structured data types are a composition of the elementary data types and a little more. The abstract data types basically have traits from both the elementary and the structured data types.

LEMENTARY DATA TYPES

Elementary data types are the basic data types. Basic numeric data like integers and floating point real numbers are considered to be elementary data types. The integer data type that you have been using is one of the many elementary data types in Visual Basic. Boolean or Logical data types are also of the elementary category. A Boolean value is either True or False, 1 or 0, respectively. Characters are elementary data types too. A character is a letter, a digit, or a special symbol used to represent a data element. Characters are usually strung together to form names.

Enumerations are considered to be an elementary data type. An enumeration is a set of values which can be represented by the set of positive integers. For example, you can make the type "Box Colour" which could take on the values of blue, green, red, orange, or yellow. The colours represent the integers from one to five. The programmer is the one who defines the values and the associated integers for it. A subrange is an elementary data type that has programmer specified ranges too. These subranges are restricted within a parent range. A subrange results in better type checking.

Pointers are elementary data types that contain a location of another data object or the null pointer. There are two fundamental pointer operations. Assignment sets the pointer variable to the address of some object. Dereferencing allows the pointer to be followed to the data object to which it points.

LINK PROTOCOLS

Often called layer 2 protocols, data link protocols exist in the protocol layer just above the physical layer relative to the OSI protocol model. Data link protocols provide communication between two devices. Because there are many different ways to connect devices, there are many different data link protocols.

The defining factors are,

- Dedicated point-to-point links between two devices, such as modem, bridges, or routers
- Shared media links in which multiple devices share the same cable (*i.e.*, Ethernet LAN)

The PPP (Point-to-Point Protocol) that people use to connect to the Internet via a dial-up modem is an example of a data link protocol. Because the link between two systems is point to point, the bits are always delivered from sender to receiver in order. Also, unlike shared-media LANs in which multiple stations attempt to use the network, there is no contention.

Data link protocols may provide any of the following services:

- *Framing:* Data is broken up into frames that are transmitted as independent units. If errors are detected in a frame, it is only necessary to retransmit that frame.
- *Session setup and termination:* For reliable services, session control messages are used by end systems to exchange status information about the session.
- *Error detection:* Determines whether a frame has been delivered accurately. A checksum is calculated on a frame by the sender, and the receiver must perform the same calculation and come up with the same checksum. If not, the frame is considered corrupted. If reliable services are being used, the frame is retransmitted. For nonreliable services, the frame is dropped and upper-layer protocols are relied on to handle the problem.
- *Addressing on a multipoint medium such as a LAN:* A computer's address is usually the hardwired address of the NIC (network interface card).

- *Flow control:* A technique that prevents the sender from sending more, overflowing the receiver with more data than it can handle.

Reliable services were essential in the days of dumb terminals that did not have the capabilities to perform error or frame checking. Today, end systems have their own processing power, so reliability services are not essential in the network itself. Instead, reliable services are executed on end systems. TCP is a reliable transport layer protocols that can replace network- level reliability services.

COMMON DATA LINK PROTOCOLS

The most common data link level protocols are listed here with a short description. Note that most of these data link protocol are used for WAN and Modem Connections. LLC is a LAN data link protocol.

- *SDLC (Synchronous Data Link Protocol):* This protocol was originally developed by IBM as part of IBM's SNA (Systems Network Architecture). It was used to connect remote devices to mainframe computers at central locations in either point-to-point (one-to-one) or point-to-multipoint (one-to-many) connections.
- *HDLC (High-level Data Link Control):* This protocol is based on SDLC and provides both a best-effort unreliable service and a reliable service. It is used with various serial interface protocols defined in the physical layer, such as EIA/TIA-232, V.24, V.35, and others.
- *SLIP (Serial Line Interface Protocol)*: SLIP is a data link control facility for transmitting IP packets, usually between an ISP (Internet service provider) and a home user over a dial-up link. SLIP has some limitations, including a lack of any error-detection and correction mechanisms. It is up to higher-layer protocols to perform these checks. Used over much of the same serial interfaces as HDLC.
- *PPP (Point-to-Point Protocol):* PPP provides the same

functionality as SLIP (*i.e.*, it is commonly used for Internet connections over dial-up lines); but it is a more robust protocol that can transport not only IP, but also other types of packets. Frames contain a field that identifies the type of protocol being carried (IP, IPX, and so on). It is used over much of the same serial interfaces as HDLC.

- *LAP (Link Access Procedure):* LAP has reliability service features and comes in three varieties. LAPB (LAP Balanced) is a protocol that provides point-to-point connections on X.25 packet-switched networks. LAPD (LAP D-Channel) provides the data link control over the D channel of an ISDN (Integrated Services Digital Network) connection. LAPF (LAP Frame-Mode Bearer Services) provides the data link for frame relay networks.
- *Frame Relay:* LAP used with X.25 is highly reliable, but it also has high overhead. Frame relay does away with the reliability services (*i.e.*, error-correction mechanisms are removed) to improve throughput.
- *LLC (Logical Link Control):* The IEEE (Institute of Electrical and Electronic Engineers) defines this protocol in its 802.x family of networks standards. The ANSI FDDI standard also uses this protocol. LLC is discussed further in the next section.

LAN DATA LINK CONTROL

The IEEE (Institute of Electrical and Electronics Engineers) has defined a number of LAN technologies in the data link layer, including Ethernet, Fast Ethernet, Gigabit Ethernet, and token ring. You can refer to the related entries page for more information. The actual data link layer is split into two sub layers, called the MAC (Medium Access Control) sub layer and the LLC (Logical Link Control) sub layer, as shown in Figure. The lower MAC layer defines the media access method, which can be CSMA/CD (carrier sense multiple access/collision detection), token ring, or other IEEE physical interface. The LLC sublayer provides a way for the network layer to communicate with one of these protocols. Data link layer devices include bridges and switches. Refer to "Bridges and Bridging" and "Switching and Switched Networks" for more information. Frame relay is a high-speed data link protocol. It uses LAPF (Link Access Procedure for Frame-Mode Bearer Services). See "Frame Relay" for more information. ATM (Asynchronous Transfer Mode) is a cell-based data link-level service. See "ATM (Asynchronous Transfer Mode)" for more information.

SLIDING WINDOW PROTOCOLS

Frames have sequence number 0 to maximum $2^n - 1$ (n bit field). At any moment, the sender maintains a list of sequence numbers it is permitted to send - these fall within the sending window. These are frames sent-but-no-ack and frames not-yet-sent. When new packet from Network layer comes in to send, it is given highest no, and upper edge of window advanced by 1. When ack comes in, lower edge of window advanced by 1. Receiver has receiving window - the frames it is permitted to accept.

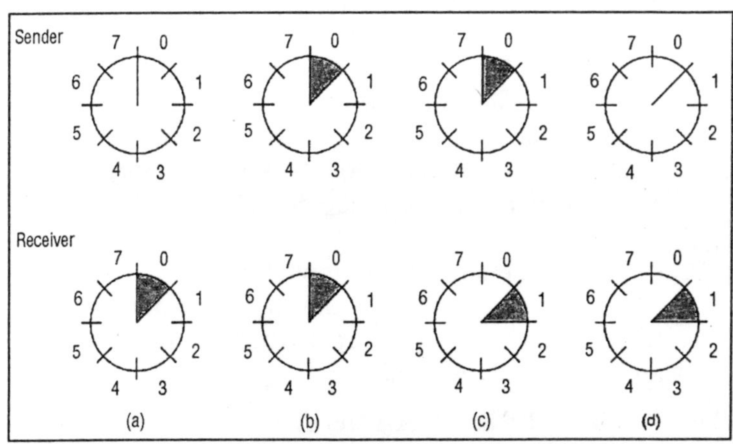

Sliding window size 1. Sequence nos. 0 to 7:

(a) At start. Receiver waits for 0.

(b) Sender sends 0.

(c) Receiver receives 0. Waits for 1.

(d) Sender got ack for 0. Hasn't got 1 from its Network layer yet.

More complex Data Link layer, as more freedom about the order in which it sends and receives frames. Sender may have n unacknowledged frames at any time (window size n). Needs n buffers to hold them all for possible re-transmit. If window grows to its maximum size, DA must shut off NA. This is all hidden from NB - still receives packets in exact same order.

- Sender window might grow as it receives more frames to send and still has ones un-ack'ed.
  Starts with nothing to send, then NA gives it frames to send.
  Later, window may shrink as frames are ack-ed and NA has no more.
- Receiver window constant size.
  Receiver window size 1 means will only accept them in order.
- Size n means will receive out of order (*e.g.* receive later ones after earlier frame is lost) and then must *buffer* them before sending to NB (must send to NB in order). *e.g.* DB has buffers to receive frames 0..7
- Receives 1..7 in varying orders. Still waiting on 0. Can't send frames to NB yet.
  0 got lost and was re-sent. Eventually gets 0.
  Can now send all of 0..7 to NB and re-use these slots.
  e.g. Consider frames numbered 0..7 but DB only has 2 buffers
- Currently the sliding window is over 4,5
  If get 4 can send it to NB and move window to 5,6
  If get 5 have to wait for 4, then send both, and advance window to 6,7

ERROR HANDLING

Error handling is important for both implementing new network protocols for and using them (through QUrlOperator). After processing an operation has been finished the network operation the QUrlOperator emits the finished() signal. This has as argument a pointer to the processed QNetworkOperation. If the state of this operation is QNetworkProtocol: StFailed, the operation contains some more information about this error. The following error codes are defined in QNetworkProtocol:

Error	Meaning
QNetworkProtocol: NoError	No error occurred
QNetworkProtocol: ErrValid	The URL you are operating on is not valid
QNetworkProtocol: ErrUnknownProtocol	There is no protocol implementation available for the protocol of the URL you are operating on (*e.g.* if the protocol is http and no http implementation has been registered)
QNetworkProtocol: ErrUnsupported	The operation is not supported by the protocol
QNetworkProtocol: ErrParse	Parse error of the URL
QNetworkProtocol: ErrLoginIncorrect	You needed to login but the username or password are wrong
QNetworkProtocol: ErrHostNotFound	The specified host (in the URL) couldn't be found
QNetworkProtocol: ErrListChildren	An error occurred while listing the children
QNetworkProtocol: ErrMkDir	An error occurred when creating a directory
QNetworkProtocol: ErrRemove	An error occurred while removing a child
QNetworkProtocol: ErrRename	An error occurred while renaming a child
QNetworkProtocol: ErrGet	An error occurred while getting (retrieving) data
QNetworkProtocol: ErrPut	An error occurred while putting (uploading) data
QNetworkProtocol: ErrFileNotExisting	A file which is needed by the operation doesn't exist
QNetworkProtocol: ErrPermissionDenied	The permission for doing the operation has been denied

- *QNetworkOperation*: ErrorCode() returns one of these codes or perhaps a different one if you use your an own network protocol im plementation which defines additional error codes.
- *QNetworkOperation*: ProtocolDetails() may also return a string which contains an error message then which might be suitable for display to the user.

If you implement your own network protocol, you must report any errors which occurred. First you always need to be able to access the QNetworkOperationwhich is being processed at the moment. This is done using Q Network Operation: operationInProgress(), which returns a pointer to the current network operation or 0 if no operation is processed at the moment.

Now if an error occurred and you need to handle it, do this:

```
if (operationInProgress())
{
operationInProgres ()³setErrorCode(error-code-
of-your-error); operationInProgress()³set
ProtocolDetails(detail);//optional emit
finished(operationInProgress());
return;
}
```

That's all. The connection to the QUrlOperator and so on is done automatically. Additionally, if the error was really bad so that no more operations can be done in the current state (*e.g.* if the host couldn't be found), call Q Network Protoco: clear Operation Stack () *before* emitting finished().

3

OSI Network Layer

OVERVIEW

DEFINITION

The seven layers in the OSI reference model, layer 3 belongs to the network layer. There are some important network layer protocols that you should know of. Protocol is nothing but a set of rules that determine how messages are being exchanged between different computers.

IPV4

IP stands for Internet Protocol while v4 indicates that it is the version 4. Here, version 4 refers to the fourth revision of the Internet Protocol that was later widely deployed. There exists an IPv4 header structure that is the basis for network layer transfer of packets. This is one of the most important network layer protocols.

IPV6

This is also an Internet Protocol that is of version 6. Though IPv4 is widely used these days, it is expected that this IPv6 is going to take over the rest of the attention. Hence, it is called the next generation protocol. There are just a few basic differences between both the protocols. The address space of IPv6 is larger than that of the IPv4.

CLNP

CLNP stands for Connectionless Network Protocol. The

service that this protocol renders is called CLNS. This routes the messages to their destination independently.

IPSEC

Internet Protocol Security is one such protocol that enables encryption and also authentication of every IP packet that moves in the data stream. Encryption and authentication are two techniques to ensure secure message transfer from the source to the destination.

ICMP

ICMP stands for Internet Control Message Protocol. This particular protocol is very important among all the network layer protocols. This is used by the operating systems of network computers to send error messages indicating that a particular service was not available or the connection to a router failed, etc.

POINT-TO-POINT NETWORK

DEFINITION

This type of network consists of many connections between individual pairs of machines. To go from the source to the destination, a packet of information on this type of network may have to first visit one or more intermediate machines. Often multiple routes, of different length are possible, so routing algorithms play an important role in point-to-point networks. As a general rule (although there are many exceptions), smaller, geographically localized networks tend to use broadcasting, whereas larger networks usually are point-to-point.

There are a number of different data link layer protocols that can be implemented on a point-to-point WAN. WAN data-link protocols used on point-to-point serial links provide the basic function of data delivery across that one link. The two most popular WAN data-link protocols are High-Level Data Link Control (HDLC) and PPP. Both of these protocols provide for the delivery of data across a single point-to-point serial link and deliver data on synchronous serial links. In addition, PPP also supports asynchronous serial links.

Each synchronous serial data-link protocol is frame-oriented, with each data-link protocol defining the beginning and end of the frame, the information and format of a header and trailer, and the location of the packet between the header and trailer. Data-link protocols also send idle frames. This is because synchronous WAN links require that the CSU/DSUs on each end of the link operate at the exact same speed. To accomplish this, the CSU/DSUs on each side of the WAN link agree to use a certain clock rate, or speed, to send and receive bits. After they agree to a particular speed, both CSU/DSUs try to operate at that speed.

One CSU/DSU is responsible for monitoring the clock rates between itself and the other CSU/DSU by noticing changes in the electrical signal received on the physical line. When a change occurs, the CSU/DSU monitoring the clock rates responds by adjusting its clock speed. If no traffic was sent across the link, there would be no electrical signal and clock synchronization would be lost. Therefore synchronous data-link protocols send idle frames when there is no end-user data to be sent over the link. The idle frames are called Receiver Ready. This need to monitor and adjust the clock rates for synchronous protocols requires more expensive hardware than asynchronous protocols. However, synchronous protocols allow more throughput over a serial link than asynchronous protocols. For links between routers, synchronous links are typically desired and used.

Almost all data-link protocols, including PPP and HDLC, perform error detection. These protocols use a field in the trailer called the frame check sequence (FCS) for this purpose. The FCS is used to verify whether bit errors occurred during transmission of the frame. If bit errors occurred, the frame is discarded. However, error recovery, which is the process that causes retransmission of the lost or errored frame, is not guaranteed. Error recovery can be performed by the data-link protocol or a higher-layer protocol, or it might not be performed at all.

PPP was defined much later than the original HDLC specifications. As a result, PPP includes many new features that are not implemented in HDLC. For this reason, PPP has become the most popular WAN data link layer protocol.

PPP uses a protocol that offers features regardless of the Layer 3 protocol used, and a protocol to support each Layer 3 protocol supported on the link. The PPP Link Control Protocol (LCP) provides the core features for PPP that operate regardless of the Layer 3 protocol used, while a series of PPP control protocols, such as IP Control Protocol (IPCP), provide features related to a specific Layer 3 protocol. Thus, PPP uses one LCP per link and one Control Protocol for each Layer 3 protocol defined on the link. If a router is configured for IPX, AppleTalk, and IP on a PPP serial link, the router configured for PPP encapsulation automatically tries to bring up the appropriate control protocols for each Layer 3 protocol. Cisco routers also use a PPP CP for supporting CDP traffic, called CDPCP.

LCP PROVIDES A VARIETY OF OPTIONAL FEATURES FOR PPP

- Error detection, which is provided by Link Quality Monitoring (LQM). The router can be configured to take down the link after a configured error rate has been exceeded. By taking down a link that has many errors, you can cause packets to use an alternative path that might not have as many errors but this is only useful when you have redundant routes in the network.
- Looped link detection, which is provided by magic numbers. Using different magic numbers, routers send messages to each other. If a router receives its own magic number, it knows that the frame it sent has been looped back. If configured to do so, the router can take down the interface through which the frame was sent, and effectively close the loop. This will improve convergence.
- Multilink support, which is provided by Multilink

PPP and allows PPP to load-balance fragments of packets across multiple links.

- Authentication, which can be provided by Password Authentication Protocol (PAP) or Challenge Handshake Authentication Protocol (CHAP) and allows for the exchange of names and passwords so that each device can verify the identity of the device on the other end of the link. CHAP is the preferred method because it uses a Message Digest 5 (MD5) one-way hash to encode the password while PAP sends passwords in clear-text

ROUTING

DEFINITION

Routing is a relay system by which packets are forwarded from one device to another. Each device in the network as well as the network itself has a logical address so it can be identified and reached individually or as part of a larger group of devices. For a router to act as an effective relay device, it must be able to understand the logical topology of the network and to communicate with its neighbouring devices. The router understands several different logical addressing schemes and regularly exchanges topology information with other devices in the network.

The mechanism of learning and maintaining awareness of the network topology is considered to be the routing function while the movement of traffic through the router is a separate function and is considered to be the switching function. Routing devices must perform both a routing and a switching function to be an effective relay device. A router receiving a packet from a host, the router will need to make a routing decision based on the protocol in use; the existence of the destination network address in its routing table; and the interface that is connected to the destination network.

After the decision has been made the router will switch the packet to the appropriate interface on the router to forward it out. If the destination logical network does not exist in the routing table, routing devices will discard the packet and to generate an Internet Control Message Protocol (ICMP) message to notify the sender of the event.

ROUTING TABLES

A routing table is a database repository that holds the router's routing information that represents each possible logical destination network that is known to the router. The entries for major networks are listed in ascending order and, most commonly, within each major network the subnetworks are listed in descending order. If the routing table entry points to an IP address, the router will perform a recursive lookup on that next-hop address until the router finds an interface to use. The router will switch the packet to the outbound interfaces buffer. The router will then determine the Layer 2 address that maps to the Layer 3 address. The packet will then be encapsulated in a Layer 2 frame appropriate for the type of encapsulation used by the outbound interface. The outbound interface will then place the packet on the medium and forward it to the next hop. The packet will continue this process until it reaches its destination. There are two ways in which a routing table can be populated: a route can be entered manually, this is called static routing, or a router can dynamically learning a route. Once a router learns a route, it is added to its route table.

Static Routing

A statically defined route is a route is manually entered into the router. The purpose of this is to add routes to a router's routing table. Thus, static routing consists of individual configuration commands that define a route to a router. A router can forward packets only to subnets in its routing table. The router always knows about directly connected routes. By adding static routes, a router can be told how to forward packets to subnets that are not attached to it.

A static route can be entered into the router in global configuration mode with the following command: Ip route destination_ip_address subnet_mask {ip-address | interface} [distance]. In the ip route command, the destination_ip_ address and subnet_mask is the IP address and subnet mask for the destination host. The ip-address parametre is the IP address of the next hop that can be used to reach the destination and interface is the router interface to use. The optional distance parametre specifies the administrative distance.

The advantages to using static routes in an internetwork are the administrator has total control of what is in the routers routing table and there is no network overhead for a routing protocol. The disadvantage of using only static routes is they do not scale well.

DYNAMIC ROUTING

Dynamic routing is a process in which a routing protocol will find the best path in a network and maintain that route. Once a route fails, the routing protocol will automatically find an alternate route to the destination. Routing protocols are easier to use than static routes. However, a routing protocol will consume more CPU cycles and network bandwidth than a static route.

ROUTING UPDATES

Routing updates can occur using the distance vector approach or the link-state approach.

- Distançe-vector protocols use a routine, periodic announcement that contains the entire contents of the routing table. These announcements are usually broadcasts and are propagated only to directly-connected, next-hop, devices. This allows the router to view the network from the neighbour's perspective and facilitates the addition of the router's metric to the 'distance' already stated by the neighbouring router. However, this approach uses considerable bandwidth at regular intervals on each link even if no topology changes have occurred.
- Link-state protocols use a triggered-update type of announcement that is generated only when there is

a topology change within the network. The link-state announcements only contain information about the link that changed and are propagated or flooded to all devices in the network. This approach saves bandwidth on each link because the announcements contain less information and is only sent when there is a topology change. In some link-state protocols, a periodic announcement is required to ensure that the topology database is synchronized among all routing devices.

VERIFYING ROUTING TABLES

You can use the show ip route privileged exec command to view an IP routing table. If the information that is displayed is not correct, you can force an update from the neighbouring devices with the clear ip route command. An optional keyword specifying an ip_address and subnet_mask, or the * (wildcard) character, can be used to further identify the routes to be refreshed.

ROUTING PROTOCOLS

There are two types of dynamic routing protocols: Interior Gateway Protocols (IGP) and External Gateway Protocols (EGP). IGPs are used to exchange routing information within an autonomous system (AS), which is a collection of routing domains under the same administrative control the same routing domain. An EGP, on the other hand, is used to exchange routing information between different ASs.

IGPs can be broken into two classes: distance-vector and link-state, and can also be broken into two categories: classful routing protocols and classless routing protocols.

DISTANCE-VECTOR ROUTING

Distance-vector routing is consists of two parts: distance and vector. Distance is the measure of how far it is to reach the destination and vector is the direction the packet must travel to reach that destination. The latter is determined by the next hop of the path. Distance-vector routing protocols will learn routes from its neighbours. This is called routing by rumor. Examples of distance-vector routing protocols are: Routing Information Protocol (RIP), Interior Gateway Routing Protocol (IGRP), and Enhanced Interior Gateway Routing Protocol (EIGRP).

ROUTE POISONING

Route poisoning is a feature that distance vector protocols use to reduce the chance of routing loops. Route poisoning begins when a router notices that a connected route is no longer valid. The router then advertises that route out all its interfaces and with a very large metric so that other routers consider the metric infinite and the route invalid. However, route poisoning does not solve the counting-to-infinity problem.

SPLIT HORIZON

As mentioned earlier, route poisoning does not solve the counting-to-infinity problem. Counting-to-infinity can occur when one router has a valid metric that points to an address that is reachable through an intermediate router while the intermediate router has an infinite-distance route to the same address. If routing table updates are sent by both routers at the same in time, the intermediate router will advertise that the route to the destination address is an infinite-distance route while the other router will advertise that the route has a valid metric. Because the two routers use the same update interval between updates, this process repeats itself with the next routing update, with the difference that the valid metric will be incremented by 1 each time until an infinite metric is reached, hence this phenomenon is called counting to infinity.

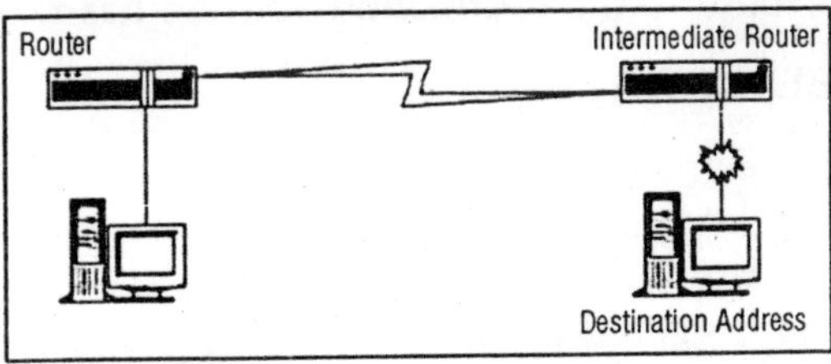

Fig. Count To Infinity

Split horizon solves the counting-to-infinity problem by preventing a router from sending routing updates out the same interface on which it learnt the route. Thus, in Figure the router would have learnt the route to the destination address across the link from the intermediate router. With split horizon, that router cannot then send advertisements about the route to the destination address out across the same link. Therefore the intermediate router will not receive the valid metric from the route to the destination address from the other router ad the count to infinity problem will not occur, solving the count-to-infinity problem on a single link.

SPLIT HORIZON WITH POISON REVERSE

Split horizon with poison reverse, or simply poison reverse combines the two features. When a route fails the router uses route poisoning, *i.e.*, the router advertises an infinite-metric route about that subnet out all interfaces, including interfaces previously prevented by split horizon. This ensures that all routers know for sure that the route has failed, while split horizon prevents counting to infinity.

HOLD-DOWN TIMER

Split horizon solves the counting-to-infinity problem over a single link but the counting to infinity problem can also occur in networks with multiple or redundant paths because there are more than one path to a router. In such networks, the hold-down timer feature prevents the counting-to-infinity problem. With the Hold-down timer feature, a router ignores any information about an alternative route to a destination address for a time equal to the hold-down timer once it has learnt that a route to the destination address has failed.

TRIGGERED UPDATES

Distance vector protocols typically send updates based on a regular update interval. However, most looping problems occur when a route fails. Therefore, some distance vector protocols send triggered updates as soon as a route fails. This causes the information about the route whose status has changed to be forwarded more quickly and also starts the hold-down timers more quickly on the neighbouring routers.

LINK-STATE ROUTING

Link-state routing differs from distance-vector routing in that each router knows the exact topology of the network. This reduces the number of bad routing decisions that can be made because every router in the process has an identical view of the network. Each router in the network will report on its state, the directly connected links, and the state of each link. The router will then propagate this information to all routers in the network. Each router that receives this information will take a snapshot of the information. This ensures all routers in the process have the same view of the network, allowing each router to make its own routing decisions based upon the same information.

In addition, link-state routing protocols generate routing updates only when there is a change in the network topology. When a link, *i.e.*, a point on a route, changes state, a link-state advertisement (LSA) concerning that link is created by the device that detected the change and propagated to all neighbouring devices using a multicast address. Each routing device takes a copy of the LSA, updates its topological database and forwards the LSA to all neighbouring devices. An LSA is generated for each link on a router. Each LSA will include an identifier for the link, the state of the link, and a metric for the link. With the use of LSAs, linkstate protocols reduces routing bandwidth usage.

Examples of link-state routing protocols are: Open Shortest Path First (OSPF) and Integrated Intermediate System to Intermediate System (IS-IS). Another protocol, Enhanced Interior Gateway Routing Protocol (EIGRP) is considered a hybrid protocol because it contains traits of both distance-vector and link-state routing protocols. Most link-state routing protocols require a hierarchical design, especially to support proper address summarization. The hierarchical approach, such as creating multiple logical areas for OSPF, reduces the need to flood an LSA to all devices in the routing domain. The use of areas restricts the flooding to the logical boundary of the area rather than to all devices in the OSPF domain. In other words, a change in one area should only cause routing table recalculation in that area, not in the entire domain.

CLASSFUL ROUTING

Classful routing is used in routing packets based upon the class of IP address. IP addresses are divided into five classes: Class A, Class B, Class C, Class D, and Class E. Class A, Class B and Class C are used to private and public network addressing; Class D is used for multicast broadcasting; and Class E is reserved by the Internet Assigned Numbers Authority (IANA) for future use.

Classful routing is a consequence of the fact that routing masks are not advertised in the periodic, routine, routing advertisements generated by distance vector routing protocols. In a classful environment, the receiving device must know the routing mask associated with any advertised subnets or those subnets cannot be advertised to it.

There are two ways this information can be gained:

- Share the same routing mask as the advertising device.
- If the routing mask does not match, this device must summarize the received route a classful boundary and send the default routing mask in its own advertisements.

Classful routing protocols, such as Routing Information Protocol version 1 (RIPv1) and Interior Gateway Routing Protocol (IGRP), exchange routes to subnetworks within the same network if network administrator configured all of the subntworks in the major network have the same routing mask. When routes are exchanged with foreign networks, subnetwork information from this network cannot be included because the routing mask of the other network is not known. As a result, the subnetwork information from this network must be summarized to a classful boundary using a default routing mask prior to inclusion in the routing update. The creation of a classful summary route at major network boundaries is handled automatically by classful routing protocols. However, summarization at other points within the major network address is not allowed by classful routing protocols.

BASIC SWITCHING FUNCTIONS

In order to forward a packet that has arrived at a router interface, the router must perform a switching function.

This switching function has four steps:

- A packet transiting the router will be accepted into the router if the frame header contains the MAC address of one of the router's NIC cards. If properly addressed, the frame and its content will be buffered occurs in memory pending further processing.
- The switching process checks the destination logical network portion of the packet header against the network/subnetwork entries in the routing table. If the search is successful, the switching process associates the destination network with a next-hop logical device and an outbound interface.
- For the next device in the relay chain. The lookup is performed in an Address Resolution Protocol (ARP) table for LAN interfaces or a map table for WAN interfaces.
- Once the physical address of the next-hop device is known, the frame header is overwritten, and the frame is then moved to the outbound interface for transmission onto the media. As the frame is placed on the media, the outbound interface adds the CRC character and ending delimiters to the frame. These characters will need to be validated at the arriving interface on the next-hop relay device

CONVERGENCE

In a routed network, the routing process in each router must maintain a loop-free, single path to each possible destination logical network. When all of the routing tables are synchronized and each contains a usable route to each destination network, the network is described as being 'converged'. Convergence is the time it takes for all routers to agree on the network topology after a change in the network.

Convergence efforts are different within different routing protocols. There are at least two different detection methods used by all routing protocols. The first method is used by the Physical Layer (Layer 1) and the Data Link Layer (Layer2) protocols. When the network interface on the router does not receive three consecutive keepalives, the link will be considered down. The second method is that when the routing protocol at the Network/Transport Layer (Layer 3) fails to receive three consecutive Hello messages, the link will be considered down.

Routing protocols have timers that are used to stop network loops from occurring on a network when a link failure has been detected. Hold-down timers are used to give the network stability while new route calculations are being performed. They also allow all the routers a chance to learn about the failed route to avoid routing loops and counting to infinity problems. Since a network cannot converge during this holddown period, this can cause a delay in the routing process of the network. Because of this slow convergence time, link-state routing protocols do not use hold-down timers.

TESTING AND TROUBLESHOOTING ROUTES

There are two tools that can be used for testing and troubleshooting routes or reachability. These are: ping and traceroute.

CONGESTION CONTROL

DEFINITION

The throttle module provides a congestion control throttling mechanism for automatically detecting a surge in incoming traffic. If the site gets linked to by a popular website, or otherwise comes under a "Denial of Service" (DoS) attack, your webserver might become overwhelmed. This mechanism performance by temporarily disabling CPU-intensive functionality. For example, in the site theme, you might choose to disable pictures when the site is too busy (reducing bandwidth), or in modules, you might choose to disable some complicated logic (reducing CPU utilization).

The congestion control throttle can be automatically enabled when the number of anonymous users currently visiting the site exceeds the specified threshold. The congestion control throttle can be automatically enabled when the number of authenticated users currently visiting the site exceeds the specified threshold.

You can,

- Enable throttle for modules at administer >> module.
- Enable throttle for blocks at administer >> block.
- Drupal 5: administer throttle at administer >> Site configuration >> throttle
- Drupal 6: administer throttle at administer >> settings >> throttle.

In Asynchronous Transfer Mode (ATM) networks, congestion control schemes may be based on fields within the ATM cell header (CLP, EFCI within the PTI) or may be based on a more sophisticated mechanism between the ATM end-system and ATM switches. The ATM Forum has developed a mechanism based on rate control for Available Bit Rate (ABR)-type traffic. In Frame Relay networks, congestion is handled by the FECN, BECN and DE bits.

WHAT CAUSES CONGESTION

The assumption that statistical multiplexing can be used to improve the link utilization is that the users do not reach their peak rate values simultaneously, but since the traffic demands are stochastic and cannot be predicted, congestion is unavoidable. Whenever the total input rate is greater than the output link capacity, congestion occurs. When the network becomes congested, the queue lengths may become very large in a short time, resulting in buffer overflows and cell loss. Congestion control is therefore necessary to ensure that users get the negotiated Quality of Service (QoS).

END-TO-END VERSUS LINK-BY LINK CONTROL

A network can control congestion over an entire connection path or by sub-links. With end-to-end control, the network measures the minimum available bandwidth along the connection and communicates the amount of bandwidth to the application, which then transmits at the appropriate rate. Each link in the network simply forwards the data as fast as it receives it.

Under the link-to-link technique, each link along the network connection controls its traffic flow independently. Each link buffers data as needed to adjust the incoming speed to the outgoing speed.

RATE-BASED VERSUS CREDIT-BASED CONTROL

The rate-based traffic-flow technique constantly tells the application what transmission rate (the currently allowed rate) the sending device should use. For example, the network can tell an application that it can send 1000 cells per second. If the network becomes congested, it reduces this rate and notifies the application; when the network is no longer congested, the rate is increased.

The credit-based technique is slightly different. Here, the network indicates to the sending device the amount of buffer space (credits) available in the network. For example, the application may be allowed to transmit 100 cells, after which it must wait.

The network periodically replenishes the application's credits. If the network becomes congested, the application gets fewer credits and they're replenished less often. This forces the application to slow the sending of data. When the congestion clears, the number of credits is increased and replenished fast enough that the application can transmit at full speed.

INTEGRATED CONGESTION CONTROL

The integrated proposal currently under consideration by the ATM Forum provides for an end-to-end, rate-based scheme as the default method, with the link-by-link scheme as an option where more precise control is needed. Because most existing ATM equipment already offers the default method, users should soon have a standards based ABR congestion-control scheme.

INTERNETWORKING

WHAT IS AN INTERNETWORK

An *internetwork* is a collection of individual networks, connected by intermediate networking devices, that functions as a single large network.

Internetworking refers to the industry, products, and procedures that meet the challenge of creating and administering internetworks. Figure illustrates some different kinds of network technologies that can be interconnected by routers and other networking devices to create an internetwork.

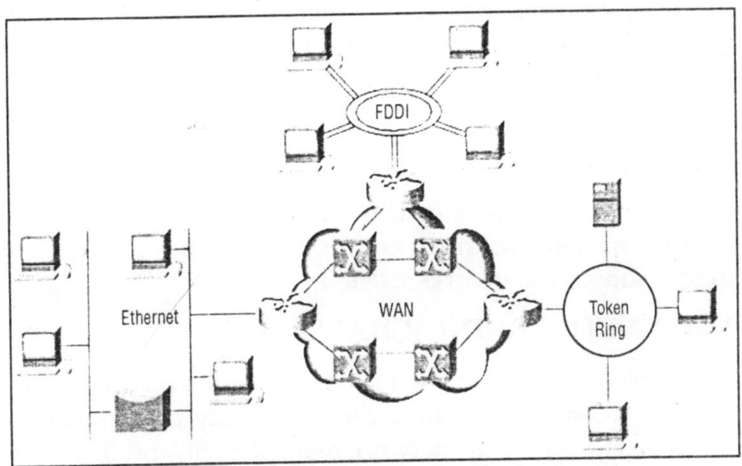

Fig. Different Network Technologies
Can Be Connected to Create an Internetwork

HISTORY OF INTERNETWORKING

The first networks were time-sharing networks that used mainframes and attached terminals. Such environments were implemented by both IBM's Systems Network Architecture (SNA) and Digital's network architecture.

- *Local-area networks (LANs):* Evolved around the PC revolution. LANs enabled multiple users in a relatively small geographical area to exchange files and messages, as well as access shared resources such as file servers and printers.
- *Wide-area networks (WANs):* Interconnect LANs with geographically dispersed users to create connectivity. Some of the technologies used for connecting LANs include T1, T3, ATM, ISDN, ADSL, Frame Relay, radio links, and others. New methods of connecting dispersed LANs are appearing everyday.

Today, high-speed LANs and switched internetworks are becoming widely used, largely because they operate at very high speeds and support such high-bandwidth applications as multimedia and videoconferencing.

Internetworking evolved as a solution to three key problems: Isolated LANs, duplication of resources, and a lack of network management. Isolated LANs made electronic communication between different offices or departments impossible. Duplication of resources meant that the same hardware and software had to be supplied to each office or department, as did separate support staff. This lack of network management meant that no centralized method of managing and troubleshooting networks existed.

INTERNETWORKING CHALLENGES

Implementing a functional internetwork is no simple task. Many challenges must be faced, especially in the areas of connectivity, reliability, network management, and flexibility. Each area is key in establishing an efficient and effective internetwork. The challenge when connecting various systems is to support communication among disparate technologies. Different sites, for example, may use different types of media operating at varying speeds, or may even include different types of systems that need to communicate. Because companies rely heavily on data communication, internetworks must provide a certain level of reliability. This is an unpredictable world, so many large internetworks include redundancy to allow for communication even when problems occur.

Furthermore, network management must provide centralized support and troubleshooting capabilities in an internetwork. Configuration, security, performance, and other issues must be adequately addressed for the internetwork to function smoothly. Security within an internetwork is essential. Many people think of network security from the perspective of protecting the private network from outside attacks. However, it is just as important to protect the network from internal attacks, especially because most security breaches come from inside. Networks must also be secured so that the internal network cannot be used as a tool to attack other external sites.

Early in the year 2000, many major web sites were the victims of distributed denial of service (DDOS) attacks. These attacks were possible because a great number of private networks currently connected with the Internet were not properly secured. These private networks were used as tools for the attackers.

OPEN SYSTEM INTERCONNECTION REFERENCE MODEL

The *Open System Interconnection (OSI) reference model* describes how information from a software application in one computer moves through a network medium to a software application in another computer. The OSI reference model is a conceptual model composed of seven layers, each specifying particular network functions. The model was developed by the International Organization for Standardization (ISO) in 1984, and it is now considered the primary architectural model for intercomputer communications. The OSI model divides the tasks involved with moving information between networked computers into seven smaller, more manageable task groups. A task or group of tasks is then assigned to each of the seven OSI layers. Each layer is reasonably self-contained so that the tasks assigned to each layer can be implemented independently. This enables the solutions offered by one layer to be updated without adversely affecting the other layers. The following list details the seven layers of the Open System Interconnection (OSI) reference model:

- *Layer* 7: Application
- *Layer* 6: Presentation
- *Layer* 5: Session
- *Layer* 4: Transport
- *Layer* 3: Network
- *Layer* 2: Data link
- *Layer* 1: Physical

Note A handy way to remember the seven layers is the sentence "All people seem to need data processing." The beginning letter of each word corresponds to a layer.

- *All*: Application layer
- *People*: Presentation layer
- *Seem*: Session layer
- *To*: Transport layer
- *Need*: Network layer
- *Data*: Data link layer
- *Processing*—Physical layer

CHARACTERISTICS OF OSI LAYERS

The seven layers of the OSI reference model can be divided into two categories: upper layers and lower layers.

The *upper layers* of the OSI model deal with application issues and generally are implemented only in software. The highest layer, the application layer, is closest to the end user. Both users and application layer processes interact with software applications that contain a communications component. The term upper layer is sometimes used to refer to any layer above another layer in the OSI model.

The *lower layers* of the OSI model handle data transport issues. The physical layer and the data link layer are implemented in hardware and software. The lowest layer, the physical layer, is closest to the physical network medium (the network cabling, for example) and is responsible for actually placing information on the medium. Figure illustrates the division between the upper and lower OSI layers.

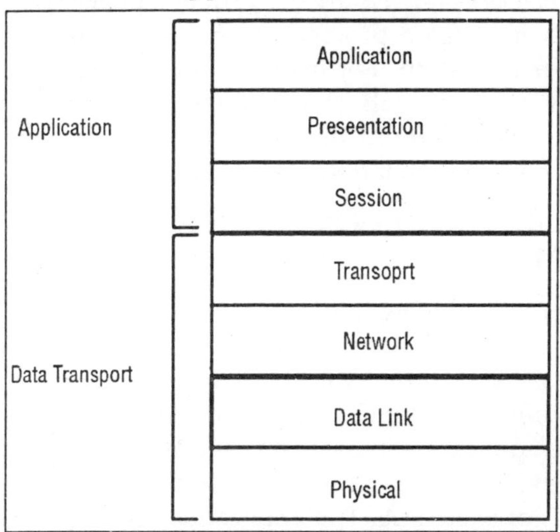

Fig. Two Sets of Layers Make Up the OSI Layers

PROTOCOLS

The OSI model provides a conceptual framework for communication between computers, but the model itself is not a method of communication. Actual communication is made possible by using communication protocols. In the context of data networking, a *protocol* is a formal set of rules and conventions that governs how computers exchange information over a network medium. A protocol implements the functions of one or more of the OSI layers.

A wide variety of communication protocols exist. Some of these protocols include LAN protocols, WAN protocols, network protocols, and routing protocols. *LAN protocols* operate at the physical and data link layers of the OSI model and define communication over the various LAN media. *WAN protocols* operate at the lowest three layers of the OSI model and define communication over the various wide-area media. *Routing protocols* are network layer protocols that are responsible for exchanging information between routers so that the routers can select the proper path for network traffic. Finally, *network protocols* are the various upper-layer protocols that exist in a given protocol suite. Many protocols rely on others for operation. For example, many routing protocols use network protocols to exchange information between routers. This concept of building upon the layers already in existence is the foundation of the OSI model.

OSI MODEL AND COMMUNICATION BETWEEN SYSTEMS

Information being transferred from a software application in one computer system to a software application in another must pass through the OSI layers. For example, if a software application in System A has information to transmit to a software application in System B, the application programme in System A will pass its information to the application layer (Layer 7) of System A. The application layer then passes the information to the presentation layer (Layer 6), which relays the data to the session layer (Layer 5), and so on down to the physical layer (Layer 1). At the physical layer, the information is placed on the physical network medium and is sent across the medium to System B. The physical layer of System B removes the information from the physical medium, and then its physical layer passes the information up to the data link layer (Layer 2), which passes it to the network layer (Layer 3), and so on, until it reaches the application layer (Layer 7) of System B. Finally, the application layer of System B passes the information to the recipient application programme to complete the communication process.

Interaction Between OSI Model Layers

A given layer in the OSI model generally communicates with three other OSI layers: the layer directly above it, the layer directly below it, and its peer layer in other networked computer systems. The data link layer in System A, for example, communicates with the network layer of System A, the physical layer of System A, and the data link layer in System B. Figure illustrates this example.

OSI Model Layers Communicate with Other Layers

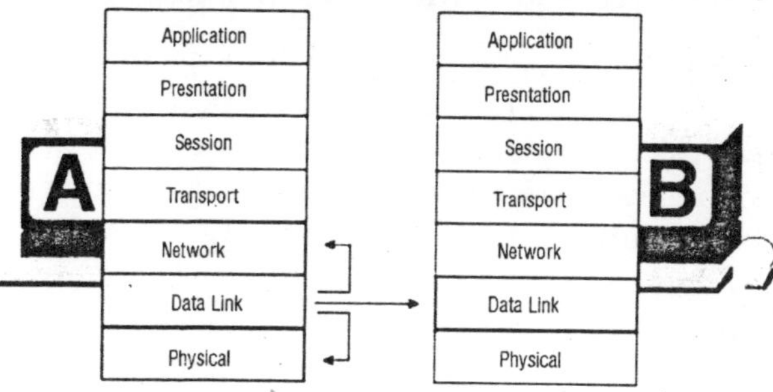

OSI Layer Services

One OSI layer communicates with another layer to make use of the services provided by the second layer. The services provided by adjacent layers help a given OSI layer communicate with its peer layer in other computer systems. Three basic elements are involved in layer services: the service user, the service provider, and the service access point (SAP). In this context, the *service user* is the OSI layer that requests services from an adjacent OSI layer. The *service provider* is the OSI layer that provides services to service users. OSI layers can provide services to multiple service users. The SAP is a conceptual location at which one OSI layer can request the services of another OSI layer. Figure Illustrates how these three elements interact at the network and data link layers.

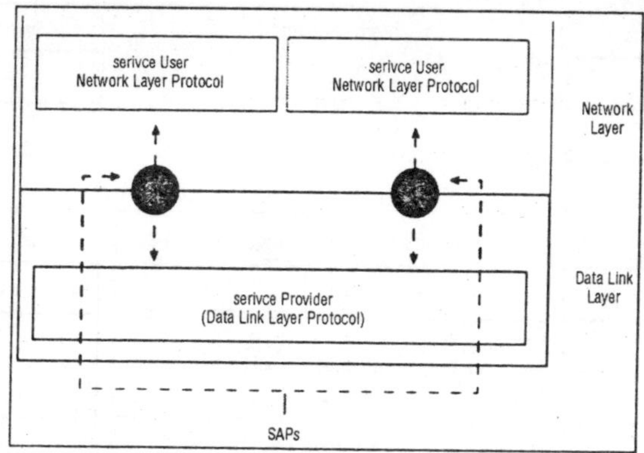

Fig: Service Users, Providers, and SAPs Interact at the Network and Data Link Layers

OSI Model Layers and Information Exchange

The seven OSI layers use various forms of control information to communicate with their peer layers in other computer systems. This *control information* consists of specific requests and instructions that are exchanged between peer OSI layers. Control information typically takes one of two forms: headers and trailers. *Headers* are prepended to data that has been passed down from upper layers. *Trailers* are appended to data that has been passed down from upper layers. An OSI layer is not required to attach a header or a trailer to data from upper layers.

Headers, trailers, and data are relative concepts, depending on the layer that analyses the information unit. At the network layer, for example, an information unit consists of a Layer 3 header and data. At the data link layer, however, all the information passed down by the network layer (the Layer 3 header and the data) is treated as data.

In other words, the data portion of an information unit at a given OSI layer potentially can contain headers, trailers, and data from all the higher layers. This is known as *encapsulation*. Figure shows how the header and data from one layer are encapsulated into the header of the next lowest layer.

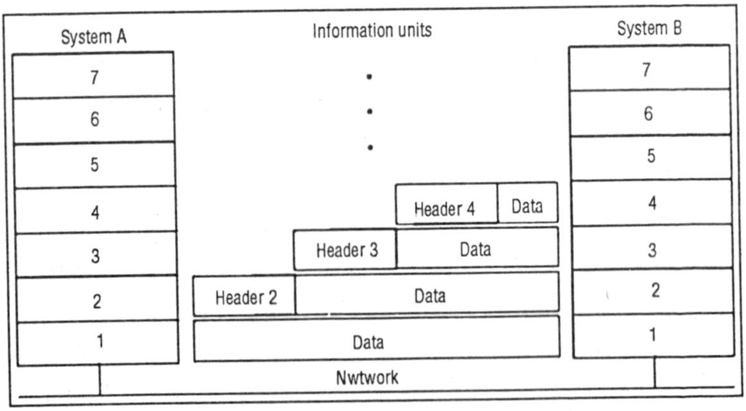

Fig. Headers and Data Can Be Encapsulated During Information Exchange

Information Exchange Process

The information exchange process occurs between peer OSI layers. Each layer in the source system adds control information to data, and each layer in the destination system analyses and removes the control information from that data.

If System A has data from a software application to send to System B, the data is passed to the application layer. The application layer in System A then communicates any control information required by the application layer in System B by prepending a header to the data. The resulting information unit (a header and the data) is passed to the presentation layer, which prepends its own header containing control information intended for the presentation layer in System B. The information unit grows in size as each layer prepends its own header (and, in some cases, a trailer) that contains control information to be used by its peer layer in System B. At the physical layer, the entire information unit is placed onto the network medium.

The physical layer in System B receives the information unit and passes it to the data link layer. The data link layer in System B then reads the control information contained in the header prepended by the data link layer in System A. The header is then removed, and the remainder of the information unit is passed to the network layer. Each layer performs the same actions: The layer reads the header from its peer layer, strips it off, and passes the remaining information unit to the next highest layer. After the application layer performs these actions, the data is passed to the recipient software application in System B, in exactly the form in which it was transmitted by the application in System A.

OSI MODEL PHYSICAL LAYER

The physical layer defines the electrical, mechanical, procedural, and functional specifications for activating, maintaining, and deactivating the physical link between communicating network systems. Physical layer specifications define characteristics such as voltage levels, timing of voltage changes, physical data rates, maximum transmission distances, and physical connectors. Physical layer implementations can be categorized as either LAN or WAN specifications.

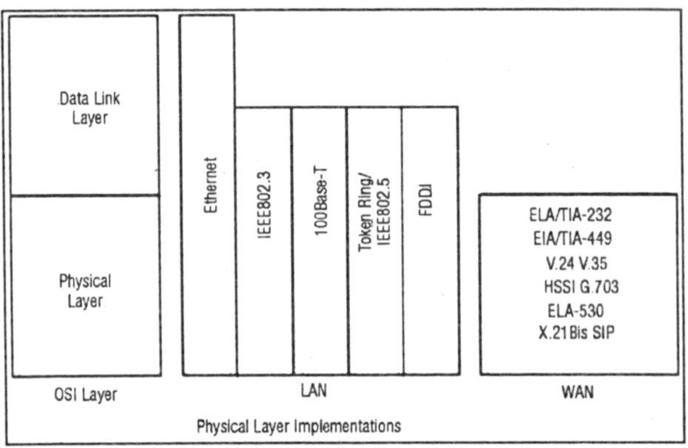

Fig. Physical Layer Implementations

OSI MODEL DATA LINK LAYER

The data link layer provides reliable transit of data across a physical network link. Different data link layer specifications define different network and protocol characteristics, including physical addressing, network topology, error notification, sequencing of frames, and flow control. Physical addressing (as opposed to network addressing) defines how devices are addressed at the data link layer.

Network topology consists of the data link layer specifications that often define how devices are to be physically connected, such as in a bus or a ring topology. Error notification alerts upper-layer protocols that a transmission error has occurred, and the sequencing of data frames reorders frames that are transmitted out of sequence. Finally, flow control moderates the transmission of data so that the receiving device is not overwhelmed with more traffic than it can handle at one time.

The Institute of Electrical and Electronics Engineers (IEEE) has subdivided the data link layer into two sublayers: Logical Link Control (LLC) and Media Access Control (MAC). Figure illustrates the IEEE sublayers of the data link layer.

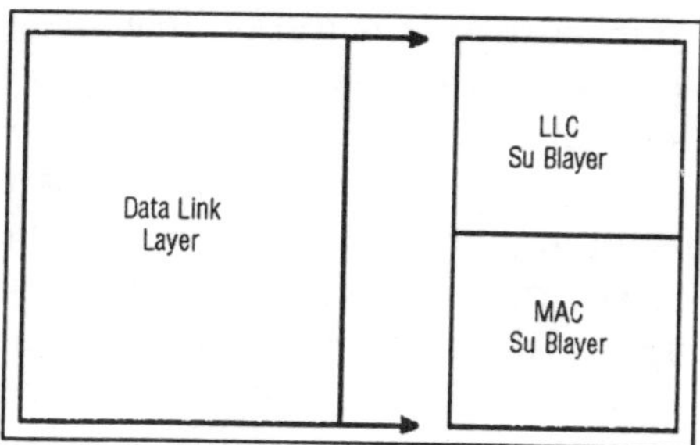

Fig. The Data Link Layer Contains Two Sublayers

The *Logical Link Control (LLC)* sublayer of the data link layer manages communications between devices over a single link of a network. LLC is defined in the IEEE 802.2 specification and supports both connectionless and connection-oriented services used by higher-layer protocols. IEEE 802.2 defines a number of fields in data link layer frames that enable multiple higher-layer protocols to share a single physical data link. The *Media Access Control (MAC)* sublayer of the data link layer manages protocol access to the physical network medium. The IEEE MAC specification defines MAC addresses, which enable multiple devices to uniquely identify one another at the data link layer.

OSI MODEL NETWORK LAYER

The network layer defines the network address, which differs from the MAC address. Some network layer implementations, such as the Internet Protocol (IP), define network addresses in a way that route selection can be determined systematically by comparing the source network address with the destination network address and applying the subnet mask. Because this layer defines the logical network layout, routers can use this layer to determine how to forward packets. Because of this, much of the design and configuration work for internetworks happens at Layer 3, the network layer.

OSI MODEL TRANSPORT LAYER

The transport layer accepts data from the session layer and segments the data for transport across the network.

Generally, the transport layer is responsible for making sure that the data is delivered error-free and in the proper sequence. Flow control generally occurs at the transport layer.

Flow control manages data transmission between devices so that the transmitting device does not send more data than the receiving device can process. Multiplexing enables data from several applications to be transmitted onto a single physical link. Virtual circuits are established, maintained, and terminated by the transport layer. Error checking involves creating various mechanisms for detecting transmission errors, while error recovery involves acting, such as requesting that data be retransmitted, to resolve any errors that occur. The transport protocols used on the Internet are TCP and UDP.

OSI MODEL SESSION LAYER

The session layer establishes, manages, and terminates communication sessions. Communication sessions consist of service requests and service responses that occur between applications located in different network devices. These requests and responses are coordinated by protocols implemented at the session layer. Some examples of session-layer implementations include Zone Information Protocol (ZIP), the AppleTalk protocol that coordinates the name binding process; and Session Control Protocol (SCP), the DECnet Phase IV session layer protocol.

OSI MODEL PRESENTATION LAYER

The presentation layer provides a variety of coding and conversion functions that are applied to application layer data. These functions ensure that information sent from the application layer of one system would be readable by the application layer of another system. Some examples of presentation layer coding and conversion schemes include common data representation formats, conversion of character representation formats, common data compression schemes, and common data encryption schemes.

Common data representation formats, or the use of standard image, sound, and video formats, enable the interchange of application data between different types of computer systems. Conversion schemes are used to exchange information with systems by using different text and data representations, such as EBCDIC and ASCII. Standard data compression schemes enable data that is compressed at the source device to be properly decompressed at the destination. Standard data encryption schemes enable data encrypted at the source device to be properly deciphered at the destination.

Presentation layer implementations are not typically associated with a particular protocol stack. Some well-known standards for video include QuickTime and Motion Picture Experts Group (MPEG). QuickTime is an Apple Computer specification for video and audio, and MPEG is a standard for video compression and coding.

Among the well-known graphic image formats are Graphics Interchange Format (GIF), Joint Photographic Experts Group (JPEG), and Tagged Image File Format (TIFF). GIF is a standard for compressing and coding graphic images. JPEG is another compression and coding standard for graphic images, and TIFF is a standard coding format for graphic images.

OSI MODEL APPLICATION LAYER

The application layer is the OSI layer closest to the end user, which means that both the OSI application layer and the user interact directly with the software application.

This layer interacts with software applications that implement a communicating component. Such application programmes fall outside the scope of the OSI model. Application layer functions typically include identifying communication partners, determining resource availability, and synchronizing communication. When identifying communication partners, the application layer determines the identity and availability of communication partners for an application with data to transmit.

When determining resource availability, the application layer must decide whether sufficient network resources for the requested communication exist. In synchronizing communication, all communication between applications requires cooperation that is managed by the application layer.

Some examples of application layer implementations include Telnet, File Transfer Protocol (FTP), and Simple Mail Transfer Protocol (SMTP).

INFORMATION FORMATS

The data and control information that is transmitted through internetworks takes a variety of forms. The terms used to refer to these information formats are not used consistently in the internetworking industry but sometimes are used interchangeably. Common information formats include frames, packets, datagrams, segments, messages, cells, and data units.

A frame is an information unit whose source and destination are data link layer entities. A frame is composed of the data link layer header (and possibly a trailer) and upper-layer data. The header and trailer contain control information intended for the data link layer entity in the destination system.

Data from upper-layer entities is encapsulated in the data link layer header and trailer. Figure illustrates the basic components of a data link layer frame.

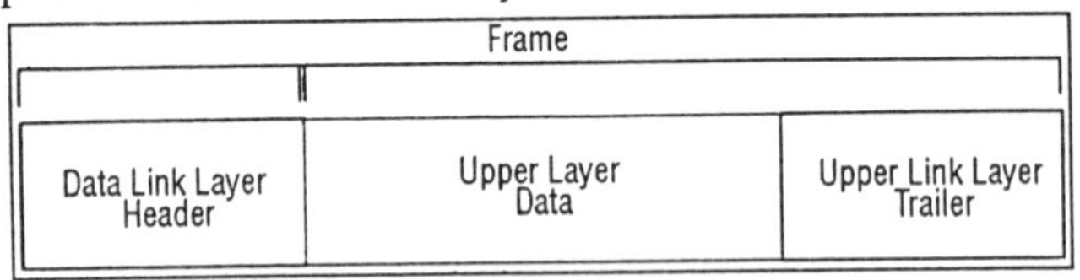

Fig. Data from Upper-Layer Entities Makes Up the Data Link Layer Frame

A *packet* is an information unit whose source and destination are network layer entities. A packet is composed of the network layer header (and possibly a trailer) and upper-layer data. The header and trailer contain control information intended for the network layer entity in the destination system. Data from upper-layer entities is encapsulated in the network layer header and trailer. Figure illustrates the basic components of a network layer packet.

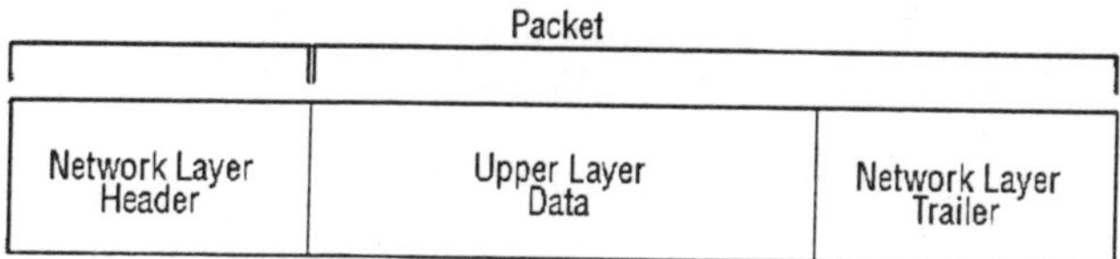

Fig. Three Basic Components Make Up a Network Layer Packet

The term *datagram* usually refers to an information unit whose source and destination are network layer entities that use connectionless network service. The term *segment* usually refers to an information unit whose source and destination are transport layer entities. A *message* is an information unit whose source and destination entities exist above the network layer (often at the application layer).

A *cell* is an information unit of a fixed size whose source and destination are data link layer entities. Cells are used in switched environments, such as Asynchronous Transfer Mode (ATM) and Switched Multimegabit Data Service (SMDS) networks. A cell is composed of the header and payload. The header contains control information intended for the destination data link layer entity and is typically 5 bytes long. The payload contains upper-layer data that is encapsulated in the cell header and is typically 48 bytes long. The length of the header and the payload fields always are the same for each cell. Figure depicts the components of a typical cell.

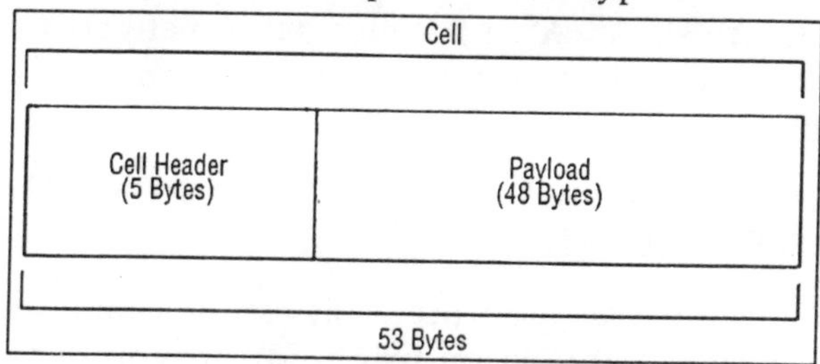

Fig. Two Components Make Up a Typical Cell

Data unit is a generic term that refers to a variety of information units. Some common data units are service data units (SDUs), protocol data units, and bridge protocol data units (BPDUs). SDUs are information units from upper-layer protocols that define a service request to a lower-layer protocol. PDU is OSI terminology for a packet. BPDUs are used by the spanning-tree algorithm as hello messages.

ISO HIERARCHY OF NETWORKS

Large networks typically are organized as hierarchies. A hierarchical organization provides such advantages as ease of management, flexibility, and a reduction in unnecessary traffic. Thus, the International Organization for Standardization (ISO) has adopted a number of terminology conventions for addressing network entities. Key terms defined in this section include end system (ES), intermediate system (IS), area, and autonomous system (AS).

An *ES* is a network device that does not perform routing or other traffic forwarding functions. Typical ESs include such devices as terminals, personal computers, and printers. An *IS* is a network device that performs routing or other traffic-forwarding functions.

Typical ISs include such devices as routers, switches, and bridges. Two types of IS networks exist: intradomain IS and interdomain IS. An intradomain IS communicates within a single autonomous system, while an interdomain IS communicates within and between autonomous systems. An *area* is a logical group of network segments and their attached devices. Areas are subdivisions of autonomous systems (AS's). An AS is a collection of networks under a common administration that share a common routing strategy.

CONNECTION-ORIENTED AND CONNECTIONLESS NETWORK SERVICES

In general, transport protocols can be characterized as being either connection-oriented or connectionless. Connection-oriented services must first establish a connection with the desired service before passing any data. A connectionless service can send the data without any need to establish a connection first. In general, connection-oriented services provide some level of delivery guarantee, whereas connectionless services do not.

Connection-oriented service involves three phases: connection establishment, data transfer, and connection termination. During connection establishment, the end nodes may reserve resources for the connection. The end nodes also may negotiate and establish certain criteria for the transfer, such as a window size used in TCP connections. This resource reservation is one of the things exploited in some denial of service (DOS) attacks.

An attacking system will send many requests for establishing a connection but then will never complete the connection.

The attacked computer is then left with resources allocated for many never-completed connections. Then, when an end node tries to complete an actual connection, there are not enough resources for the valid connection.

The data transfer phase occurs when the actual data is transmitted over the connection. During data transfer, most connection-oriented services will monitor for lost packets and handle resending them. The protocol is generally also responsible for putting the packets in the right sequence before passing the data up the protocol stack. When the transfer of data is complete, the end nodes terminate the connection and release resources reserved for the connection.

Connection-oriented network services have more overhead than connectionless ones. Connection-oriented services must negotiate a connection, transfer data, and tear down the connection, whereas a connectionless transfer can simply send the data without the added overhead of creating and tearing down a connection. Each has its place in internetworks.

INTERNETWORK ADDRESSING

Internetwork addresses identify devices separately or as members of a group. Addressing schemes vary depending on the protocol family and the OSI layer. Three types of internetwork addresses are commonly used: data link layer addresses, Media Access Control (MAC) addresses, and network layer addresses.

DATA LINK LAYER ADDRESSES

A *data link layer address* uniquely identifies each physical network connection of a network device. Data-link addresses sometimes are referred to as *physical* or *hardware addresses*. Data-link addresses usually exist within a flat address space and have a pre-established and typically fixed relationship to a specific device.

End systems generally have only one physical network connection and thus have only one data-link address. Routers and other internetworking devices typically have multiple physical network connections and therefore have multiple data-link addresses. Figure illustrates how each interface on a device is uniquely identified by a data-link address.

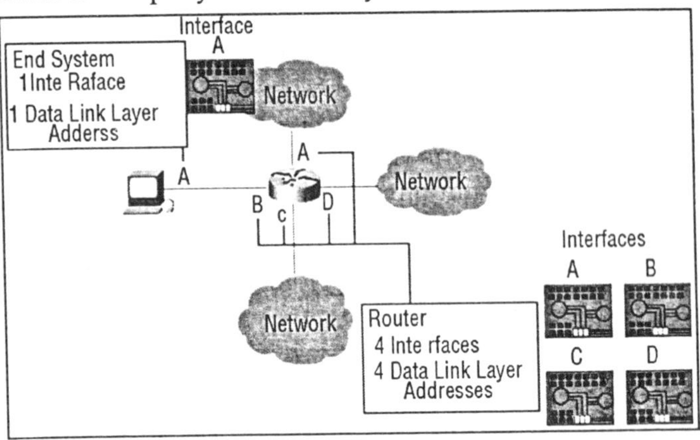

Fig. Each Interface on a Device is Uniquely Identified by a Data-Link Address.

MAC ADDRESSES

Media Access Control (MAC) addresses consist of a subset of data link layer addresses. MAC addresses identify network entities in LANs that implement the IEEE MAC addresses of the data link layer.

As with most data-link addresses, MAC addresses are unique for each LAN interface. Figure illustrates the relationship between MAC addresses, data-link addresses, and the IEEE sublayers of the data link layer.

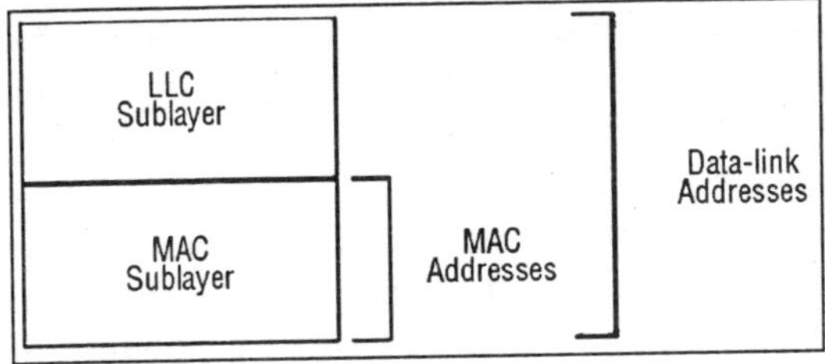

Fig. MAC Addresses, Data-Link Addresses, and the IEEE Sublayers of the Data Link Layer Are All Related

MAC addresses are 48 bits in length and are expressed as 12 hexadecimal digits. The first 6 hexadecimal digits, which are administered by the IEEE, identify the manufacturer or vendor and thus comprise the Organizationally Unique Identifier (OUI). The last 6 hexadecimal digits comprise the interface serial number, or another value administered by the specific vendor. MAC addresses sometimes are called *burned-in addresses (BIAs)* because they are burned into read-only memory (ROM) and are copied into random-access memory (RAM) when the interface card initializes. Figure illustrates the MAC address format.

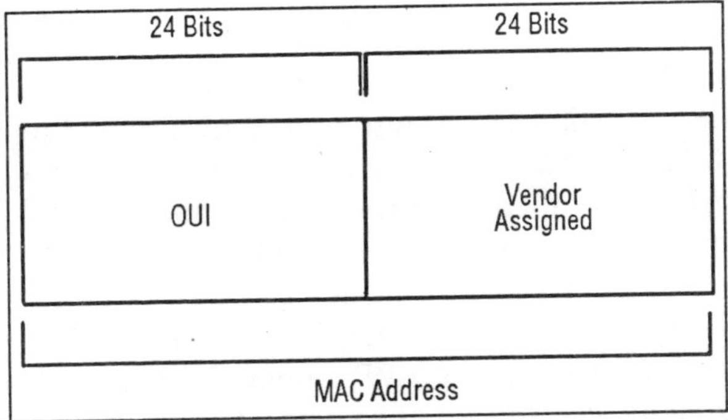

Fig. The MAC Address Contains a Unique Format of Hexadecimal Digits

MAPPING ADDRESSES

Because internetworks generally use network addresses to route traffic around the network, there is a need to map network addresses to MAC addresses. When the network layer has determined the destination station's network address, it must forward the information over a physical network using a MAC address. Different protocol suites use different methods to perform this mapping, but the most popular is Address Resolution Protocol (ARP).

Different protocol suites use different methods for determining the MAC address of a device. The following three methods are used most often. Address Resolution Protocol (ARP) maps network addresses to MAC addresses. The Hello protocol enables network devices to learn the MAC addresses of other network devices. MAC addresses either are embedded in the network layer address or are generated by an algorithm.

Address Resolution Protocol (ARP) is the method used in the TCP/IP suite. When a network device needs to send data to another device on the same network, it knows the source and destination network addresses for the data transfer. It must somehow map the destination address to a MAC address before forwarding the data. First, the sending station will check its ARP table to see if it has already discovered this destination station's MAC address.

If it has not, it will send a broadcast on the network with the destination station's IP address contained in the broadcast. Every station on the network receives the broadcast and compares the embedded IP address to its own. Only the station with the matching IP address replies to the sending station with a packet containing the MAC address for the station. The first station then adds this information to its ARP table for future reference and proceeds to transfer the data.

When the destination device lies on a remote network, one beyond a router, the process is the same except that the sending station sends the ARP request for the MAC address of its default gateway. It then forwards the information to that device.

The default gateway will then forward the information over whatever networks necessary to deliver the packet to the network on which the destination device resides. The router on the destination device's network then uses ARP to obtain the MAC of the actual destination device and delivers the packet.

The Hello protocol is a network layer protocol that enables network devices to identify one another and indicate that they are still functional. When a new end system powers up, for example, it broadcasts hello messages onto the network. Devices on the network then return hello replies, and hello messages are also sent at specific intervals to indicate that they are still functional. Network devices can learn the MAC addresses of other devices by examining Hello protocol packets.

Three protocols use predictable MAC addresses. In these protocol suites, MAC addresses are predictable because the network layer either embeds the MAC address in the network layer address or uses an algorithm to determine the MAC address. The three protocols are Xerox Network Systems (XNS), Novell Internetwork Packet Exchange (IPX), and DECnet Phase IV.

NETWORK LAYER ADDRESSES

A *network layer address* identifies an entity at the network layer of the OSI layers. Network addresses usually exist within a hierarchical address space and sometimes are called *virtual* or *logical addresses.*

The relationship between a network address and a device is logical and unfixed; it typically is based either on physical network characteristics (the device is on a particular network segment) or on groupings that have no physical basis (the device is part of an AppleTalk zone). End systems require one network layer address for each network layer protocol that they support. (This assumes that the device has only one physical network connection.) Routers and other internetworking devices require one network layer address per physical network connection for each network layer protocol supported.

For example, a router with three interfaces each running AppleTalk, TCP/IP, and OSI must have three network layer addresses for each interface. The router therefore has nine network layer addresses. Figure illustrates how each network interface must be assigned a network address for each protocol supported.

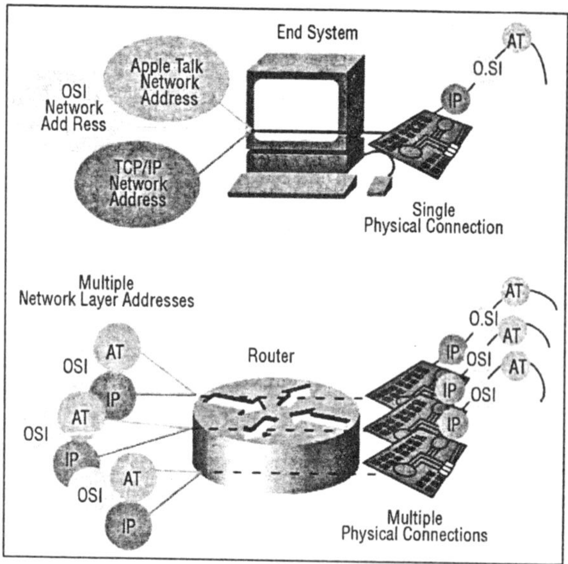

Fig. Each Network Interface Must Be Assigned a Network Address for Each Protocol Supported

HIERARCHICAL VERSUS FLAT ADDRESS SPACE

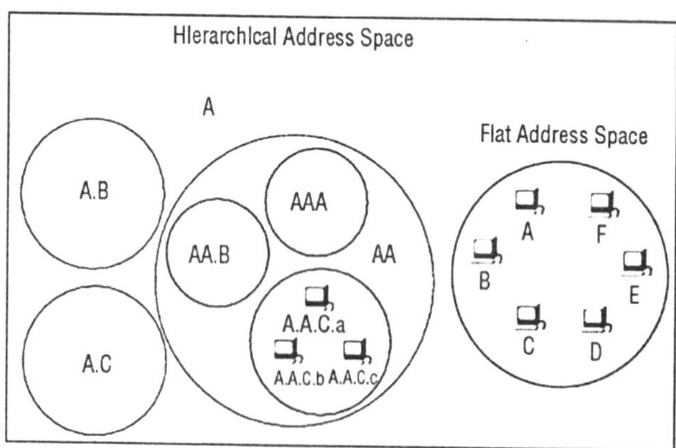

Fig. Hierarchical and Flat Address Spaces Differ in Comparison Operations

Internetwork address space typically takes one of two forms: hierarchical address space or flat address space. A *hierarchical address space* is organized into numerous subgroups, each successively narrowing an address until it points to a single device (in a manner similar to street addresses). A *flat address space* is organized into a single group (in a manner similar to U.S. Social Security numbers).

Hierarchical addressing offers certain advantages over flat-addressing schemes. Address sorting and recall is simplified using comparison operations. For example, "Ireland" in a street address eliminates any other country as a possible location. Figure illustrates the difference between hierarchical and flat address spaces.

ADDRESS ASSIGNMENTS

Addresses are assigned to devices as one of two types: static and dynamic. *Static addresses* are assigned by a network administrator according to a preconceived internetwork addressing plan. A static address does not change until the network administrator manually changes it. *Dynamic addresses* are obtained by devices when they attach to a network, by means of some protocol-specific process. A device using a dynamic address often has a different address each time that it connects to the network. Some networks use a server to assign addresses. Server-assigned addresses are recycled for reuse as devices disconnect.

A device is therefore likely to have a different address each time that it connects to the network.

ADDRESSES VERSUS NAMES

Internetwork devices usually have both a name and an address associated with them. Internetwork names typically are location-independent and remain associated with a device wherever that device moves (for example, from one building to another). Internetwork addresses usually are location-dependent and change when a device is moved (although MAC addresses are an exception to this rule). As with network addresses being mapped to MAC addresses, names are usually mapped to network addresses through some protocol. The Internet uses Domain Name System (DNS) to map the name of a device to its IP address. For example, it's easier for you to remember www.cisco.com instead of some IP address. Therefore, you type www.cisco.com into your browser when you want to access Cisco's web site. Your computer performs a DNS lookup of the IP address for Cisco's web server and then communicates with it using the network address.

FLOW CONTROL BASICS

Flow control is a function that prevents network congestion by ensuring that transmitting devices do not overwhelm receiving devices with data. A high-speed computer, for example, may generate traffic faster than the network can transfer it, or faster than the destination device can receive and process it. The three commonly used methods for handling network congestion are buffering, transmitting source-quench messages, and windowing.

Buffering is used by network devices to temporarily store bursts of excess data in memory until they can be processed. Occasional data bursts are easily handled by buffering. Excess data bursts can exhaust memory, however, forcing the device to discard any additional datagrams that arrive.

Source-quench messages are used by receiving devices to help prevent their buffers from overflowing. The receiving device sends source-quench messages to request that the source reduce its current rate of data transmission. First, the receiving device begins discarding received data due to overflowing buffers. Second, the receiving device begins sending source-quench messages to the transmitting device at the rate of one message for each packet dropped. The source device receives the source-quench messages and lowers the data rate until it stops receiving the messages. Finally, the source device then gradually increases the data rate as long as no further source-quench requests are received.

Windowing is a flow-control scheme in which the source device requires an acknowledgment from the destination after a certain number of packets have been transmitted. With a window size of 3, the source requires an acknowledgment after sending three packets, as follows. First, the source device sends three packets to the destination device. Then, after receiving the three packets, the destination device sends an acknowledgment to the source. The source receives the acknowledgment and sends three more packets. If the destination does not receive one or more of the packets for some reason, such as overflowing buffers, it does not receive enough packets to send an acknowledgment. The source then retransmits the packets at a reduced transmission rate.

ERROR-CHECKING BASICS

Error-checking schemes determine whether transmitted data has become corrupt or otherwise damaged while traveling from the source to the destination. Error checking is implemented at several of the OSI layers.

One common error-checking scheme is the cyclic redundancy check (CRC), which detects and discards corrupted data. Error-correction functions (such as data retransmission) are left to higher-layer protocols. A CRC value is generated by a calculation that is performed at the source device.

The destination device compares this value to its own calculation to determine whether errors occurred during transmission. First, the source device performs a predetermined set of calculations over the contents of the packet to be sent. Then, the source places the calculated value in the packet and sends the packet to the destination. The destination performs the same predetermined set of calculations over the contents of the packet and then compares its computed value with that contained in the packet. If the values are equal, the packet is considered valid. If the values are unequal, the packet contains errors and is discarded.

MULTIPLEXING BASICS

Multiplexing is a process in which multiple data channels are combined into a single data or physical channel at the source. Multiplexing can be implemented at any of the OSI layers. Conversely, *demultiplexing*is the process of separating multiplexed data channels at the destination. One example of multiplexing is when data from multiple applications is multiplexed into a single lower-layer data packet. Figure illustrates this example.

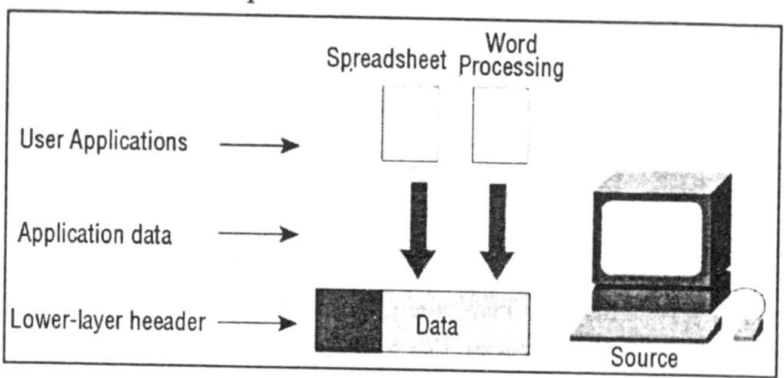

Fig. Multiple Applications Can Be Multiplexed into a Single Lower-Layer Data Packet

Another example of multiplexing is when data from multiple devices is combined into a single physical channel (using a device called a multiplexer). Figure illustrates this example.

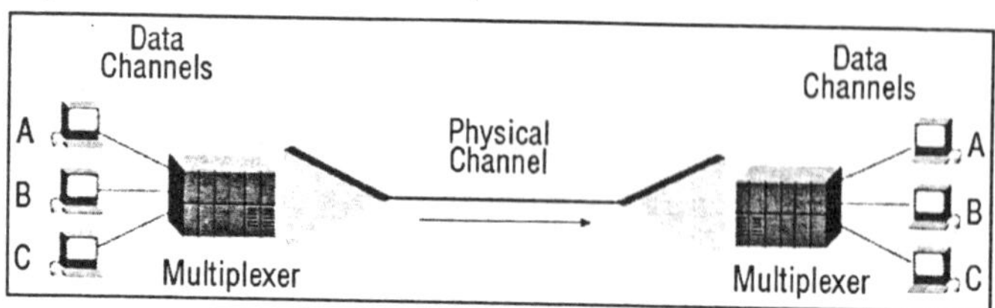

Fig. Multiple Devices Can Be Multiplexed into a Single Physical Channel

A *multiplexer* is a physical layer device that combines multiple data streams into one or more output channels at the source. Multiplexers demultiplex the channels into multiple data streams at the remote end and thus maximize the use of the bandwidth of the physical medium by enabling it to be shared by multiple traffic sources.

Some methods used for multiplexing data are time-division multiplexing (TDM), asynchronous time-division multiplexing (ATDM), frequency-division multiplexing (FDM), and statistical multiplexing.

In TDM, information from each data channel is allocated bandwidth based on preassigned time slots, regardless of whether there is data to transmit. In ATDM, information from data channels is allocated bandwidth as needed by using dynamically assigned time slots. In FDM, information from each data channel is allocated bandwidth based on the signal frequency of the traffic. In statistical multiplexing, bandwidth is dynamically allocated to any data channels that have information to transmit.

STANDARDS ORGANIZATIONS

A wide variety of organizations contribute to internetworking standards by providing forums for discussion, turning informal discussion into formal specifications, and proliferating specifications after they are standardized. Most standards organizations create formal standards by using specific processes: organizing ideas, discussing the approach, developing draft standards, voting on all or certain aspects of the standards, and then formally releasing the completed standard to the public.

Some of the best-known standards organizations that contribute to internetworking standards include these:

- *International Organization for Standardization (ISO)*: ISO is an international standards organization responsible for a wide range of standards, including many that are relevant to networking. Its best-known contribution is the development of the OSI reference model and the OSI protocol suite.
- *American National Standards Institute (ANSI)*: ANSI, which is also a member of the ISO, is the coordinating body for voluntary standards groups within the United States. ANSI developed the Fibre Distributed Data Interface (FDDI) and other communications standards.
- *Electronic Industries Association (EIA)*: EIA specifies electrical transmission standards, including those used in networking. The EIA developed the widely used EIA/TIA-232 standard (formerly known as RS-232).
- *Institute of Electrical and Electronic Engineers (IEEE)*: IEEE

is a professional organization that defines networking and other standards. The IEEE developed the widely used LAN standards IEEE 802.3 and IEEE 802.5.

- *International Telecommunication Union Telecommuni-cation Standardization Sector (ITU-T)*: Formerly called the Committee for International Telegraph and Telephone (CCITT), ITU-T is now an international organization that develops communication standards. The ITU-T developed X.25 and other communications standards.
- *Internet Activities Board (IAB)*: IAB is a group of internetwork researchers who discuss issues pertinent to the Internet and set Internet policies through decisions and task forces. The IAB designates some Request For Comments (RFC) documents as Internet standards, including Transmission Control Protocol/Internet Protocol (TCP/IP) and the Simple Network Management Protocol (SNMP).

SUMMARY

This chapter introduced the building blocks on which internetworks are built. Under-standing where complex pieces of internetworks fit into the OSI model will help you understand the concepts better. Internetworks are complex systems that, when viewed as a whole, are too much to understand. Only by breaking the network down into the conceptual pieces can it be easily understood. As you read and experience internetworks, try to think of them in terms of OSI layers and conceptual pieces. Understanding the interaction between various layers and protocols makes designing, configuring, and diagnosing internetworks possible. Without understanding of the building blocks, you cannot understand the interaction between them.

REVIEW QUESTIONS

Q: What are the layers of the OSI model?

A: Application, presentation, session, transport, network, data link, physical. Remember the sentence "All people seem to need data processing."

Q: *Which layer determines path selection in an internetwork?*

A: Layer 3, the network layer.

Q: *What types of things are defined at the physical layer?*

A: Voltage levels, time of voltage changes, physical data rates, maximum transmission distances, physical connectors, and type of media.

Q: *What is one method of mapping network addresses to MAC addresses?*

A: ARP, Hello, predictable.

Q: *Which includes more overhead, connection-oriented or connectionless services?*

A: Connection-oriented.

ADVANCE TCP/IP

The original design for the Internet required every organization to have one or more unique IP network numbers. In the early to mid-1990s, it became apparent that the Internet was growing so fast that all IP network numbers would be used. One solution to this problem was to increase the size of the IP address by developing IP Version 6 (IPv6). IPv6 has a much larger address structure than IPv4, allowing for trillions of IPv6 networks.

Three other IP functions have been introduced to reduce the need for IPv4 registered network numbers. These include Network Address Translation (NAT), along with a feature called private IP addressing, which allows organizations to use unregistered IP network numbers internally and still communicate well with the Internet; and Classless Interdomain Routing (CIDR), which allows Internet service providers (ISPs) to reduce the wasting of IP addresses by assigning a company a subset of a network number rather than the entire network.

TCP/IP ROUTING

You can also route traffic to your logical partitions

through your iSeries™ server with various routing techniques. This solution is not difficult to configure on your iSeries but depending on the topology of your network, it may not be practical to implement. Consider the following figure:

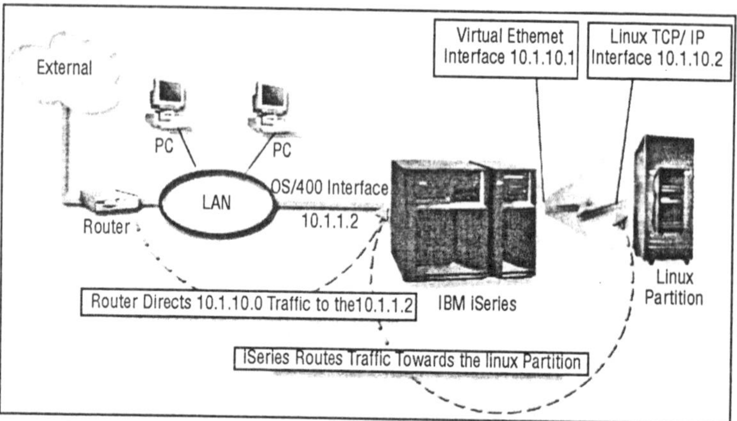

The existing TCP/IP interface (10.1.1.2) connects to the LAN. The LAN is connected to remote networks with a router. The Linux™ TCP/IP interface is addressed as 10.1.10.2 and the virtual Ethernet TCP/IP interface as 10.1.10.1. In OS/400®, if you turn on IP Datagram Forwarding, the iSeries will route the IP packets to and from the logical partition. When you define your Linux TCP/IP connection, the router address must be 10.1.10.1.

The difficulty of this type of routing is getting the IP packets to the iSeries. In this scenario, you could define a route on the router so that it passes packets destined to the 10.1.10.0 network to the 10.1.1.2 interface. That works great for remote network clients. It would also work for the local LAN clients (clients connected to the same LAN as the iSeries) if they recognize that same router as their next hop. If they do not, then each client must have a route that directs 10.1.10.0 traffic to the iSeries 10.1.1.2 interface; therein starts the impracticability of this method. If you have hundreds of LAN clients, then you have to define hundreds of routes.

To configure a setup similar to this, use the following instructions:

- During the configuration of your logical partition,

make sure you selected to create virtual Ethernet. See Configure a logical partitionfor more information.

- Create an Ethernet line description for virtual Ethernet. Note the port of the hardware resource, because you will need it when you set up TCP/IP in your logical partition. In the case of the above example, assume the hardware resource is CMN05 with a port of 0 and although arbitrary, the line description name is VETH0. CRTLINETH LIND (VETH0) RSRCNAME (CMN05) LINESPEED (1G) DUPLEX(*FULL)
- Add a TCP/IP Interface for your virtual line description. Following the example, you could use: ADDTCPIFC INTNETADR('10.1.10.1') LIND ('VETH0') SUBNETMASK ('255.255.255.0')
- Start your new TCP/IP interface using the command STRTCPIFC INTNETADR (*yourIPaddress*) or STRTCPIFC INTNETADR('10.1.10.1') for the example.
- On your logical partition, set up networking using the instructions or tools provided by your Linux distribution. Be sure to use the correct IP address, subnet mask, port, and gateway IP address.
- During the TCP/IP setup in Linux, you will need to know your net or network device. If you are running a 32-bit kernel version of 2.4.9 or less, the network device is VETH plus the port number from when you configured an Ethernet line description. If you are running a 64-bit kernel or a 32-bit kernel greater than or equal to 2.4.10, the network device is ETH plus the port number. See Create an Ethernet line description for virtual Ethernet for more information.

  In the example:
  - The interface IP address is 10.1.10.2
  - The subnet mask is 255.255.255.0
  - The gateway IP address is 10.1.10.1
  - The network device is VETH0 or ETH0 depending on the kernel version.

- Turn on IP datagram forwarding. This allows the OS/400 TCP/IP interfaces to pass IP packets between each other. CHGTCPA IPDTGFWD(*YES)

PRIVATE IP ADDRESSING

Most organizations have a number of computers that will never be connected to the Internet. These computers do not need globally unique IP addresses but must be unique within the organization's network. Thus, an organization could use any network number(s) it wanted, regardless of whether those network number(s) are in use on the Internet or not. However, a set of IP addresses from Class A, Class B and Class C has been set aside for use in private networks and has been defined in RFC 1918. This RFC defines a set of networks that not be assigned to any organization as a registered network number to be used on the Internet. These network numbers allow organizations to use unregistered network numbers that are not used by anyone else in the public Internet. However, no organization is allowed to advertise these networks using a routing protocol on the Internet.

NETWORK ADDRESS TRANSLATION (NAT)

The advantage of using private IP addresses is that it allows an organization to use private addressing in a network, and use the Internet at the same time, by implementing Network Address Translation (NAT). NAT is defined in RFC 1631 and allows a host that does not have a valid registered IP address to communicate with other hosts through the Internet. Essentially, NAT allows hosts that use private addresses or addresses assigned to another organization, *i.e.* addresses that are not Internet-ready, to continue to be used and still allows communication with hosts across the Internet. NAT accomplishes this by using a valid registered IP address to represent the private address to the rest of the Internet. The NAT function changes the private IP addresses to publicly registered IP addresses inside each IP packet that is transmitted to a host on the Internet.

VARIATIONS OF NAT

The IOS software supports several variations of NAT. These include Static NAT; Dynamic NAT; and Overloading NAT with Port Address Translation (PAT)

STATIC NAT

In Static NAT, the IP addresses are statically mapped to each other. Thus, the NAT router simply configures a one-to-one mapping between the private address and the registered address that is used on its behalf. Supporting two IP hosts in the private network requires a second static one-to-one mapping using a second IP address in the public address range, depending on the number of addresses supported by the registered IP address.

DYNAMIC NAT

Dynamic NAT is similar to static NAT in that the NAT router creates a one-to-one mapping between an inside local and inside global address and changes the IP addresses in packets as they exit and enter the inside network. However, the mapping of an inside local address to an inside global address happens dynamically.

Dynamic NAT accomplishes this by setting up a pool of possible inside global addresses and defining criteria for the set of inside local IP addresses whose traffic should be translated with NAT.

With dynamic NAT, you can configure the NAT router with more IP addresses in the inside local address list than in the inside global address pool. When the number of registered public IP addresses is defined in the inside global address pool, the router allocates addresses from the pool until all are allocated.

If a new packet arrives, and it needs a NAT entry, but all the pooled IP addresses are already allocated, the router discards the packet. The user must try again until a NAT entry times out, at which point the NAT function works for the next host that sends a packet. This can be overcome through the use of Port Address Translation (PAT).

NAT WITH PORT ADDRESS TRANSLATION (PAT) [

In some networks, most, if not all, IP hosts need to reach the Internet. If that network uses private IP addresses, the NAT router needs a very large set of registered IP addresses. If you use static NAT, each private IP host that needs Internet access needs a publicly registered IP address.

Dynamic NAT lessens the problem, but if a large percentage of the IP hosts in the network need Internet access throughout normal business hours, a large number of registered IP addresses would also be required. These problems can be overcome through overloading with port address translation.

Overloading allows NAT to scale to support many clients with only a few public IP addresses. To support lots of inside local IP addresses with only a few inside global, publicly registered IP addresses, NAT overload uses Port Address Translation (PAT), translating the IP address as well as translating the port number.

When NAT creates the dynamic mapping, it selects not only an inside global IP address but also a unique port number to use with that address.

The NAT router keeps a NAT table entry for every unique combination of inside local IP address and port, with translation to the inside global address and a unique port number associated with the inside global address. And because the port number field has 16 bits, NAT overload can use more than 65,000 port numbers, allowing it to scale well without needing many registered IP addresses.

TRANSLATING OVERLAPPING ADDRESSES

NAT can also be used in organizations that do not use private addressing but use a network number registered to another company. If one organization uses a network number that is registered to another organization, and both organizations are connected to the Internet, NAT can be used to translate both the source and the destination IP addresses. However, both the source and the destination addresses must be changed as the packet passes through the NAT router.

CONFIGURING NAT

There are a number of commands that can be used to configure the different variations of NAT.

Configuring Static NAT

Static NAT configuration requires that each static mapping between a local, or private, address and a global, or public, address must be configured. Then, each interface needs to be identified as either an inside or outside interface. The ip nat inside source static command is used to create a static mapping.

The inside keyword indicates that NAT translates addresses for hosts on the inside part of the network. The source keyword indicates that NAT translates the source IP address of packets coming into its inside interfaces. The static keyword indicates that the parametres define a static entry. If two hosts require Internet access, two ip nat inside commands must be used.

The ip nat inside and ip nat outside interface subcommands identify which interfaces are "inside" and which are "outside" respectively.

Two show commands list the most important information about static NAT.

These commands are:

- Show ip nat translations, which lists the static NAT entries; and the
- Sow ip nat statistics, which lists statistics, including the number of currently active translation table entries and the number of hits, which increments for every packet for which NAT must translate addresses.

Configuring Dynamic NAT

Dynamic NAT configuration differs from static NAT but it also has some similarities. It requires that each interface be identified as either an inside or outside interface but the static mapping is not required. In addition, a pool of inside global addresses needs to be defined. The ip nat inside source command is used to identify which inside local IP addresses need to have their addresses translated.

The ip nat pool command defines the set of IP addresses to be used as inside global addresses. The two show commands used to trouble shoot static NAT can also be used to troubleshoot dynamic NAT. In addition to these you can use the debug ip nat command. This command causes the router to issue a message every time a packet has its address translated for NAT.

CONFIGURING NAT OVERLOAD AND PAT

The ip nat inside source overload command is used to configure NAT overload. The overload parametre is required to enable overload. Without this parametre, the router does not perform overload, but dynamic NAT. You can use the show ip nat translations to troubleshoot NAT overload.

INTERNET CONTROL MESSAGE PROTOCOL (ICMP)

ICMP is a TCP/IP protocol designed to help manage and control the operation of a TCP/IP network. The ICMP protocol provides a wide variety of information about a network's status and is considered part of TCP/IP's network layer. ICMP can provide useful information for troubleshooting TCP/IP. ICMP uses messages to accomplish its tasks. Many of these messages are used in even the smallest IP network.

FTP AND TFTP

File Transfer Protocol (FTP) and Trivial File Transfer Protocol (TFTP) are two popular file transfer protocols used in TCP/IP networks. Most end users use FTP, but Cisco router and switch administrators often use TFTP.

FTP is a TCP-based application that has many options and features, including the capability to change directories, list files using wildcard characters, transfer multiple files with a single command, and use a variety of character sets or file formats. When a user, called a FTP client, attempts to connect to an FTP server, a TCP connection is established to the FTP server's well-known port 21. The user is required to enter a username and password, which the server uses to authenticate the files available to that user for read and write permissions. This security is based on the file security on the server's platform.

All the commands used to control the transfer of a file are sent across this connection. At this point, the user has a variety of commands available to enable settings for transfer, change directories, list files, etc.

However, whenever a get (mget for multiple files) or put (or mput for multiple files) command is entered, or the equivalent button is clicked on the user interface, a file is transferred. The data is transferred over a separate FTP data connection, another TCP connection, established to well-known port 20. This prevents a file transfer from impacting on the control connection.

Trivial File Transfer Protocol (TFTP) is a more basic file transfer protocol that use a small set of features, takes little memory to load, and little time to programme. TFTP uses User Datagram Protocol (UDP), so there is no connection establishment and no error recovery by the transport layer. However, TFTP uses application layer recovery by embedding a small header between the UDP header and the data.

This header includes codes along with a numbering scheme that numbers 512-byte blocks of data. The TFTP application uses these block numbers to acknowledge receipt and resend the data. TFTP sends one block and waits on an acknowledgment before sending another block.

MTU AND FRAGMENTATION

TCP/IP defines a maximum length for an IP packet. The term used to describe that maximum length is maximum transmission unit (MTU). The MTU varies based on configuration and the interface's characteristics. By default, a computer calculates an interface's MTU based on the maximum size of the data portion of the data-link frame. IP hosts, including routers, cannot forward a packet out an interface if the packet is longer than the MTU.

Therefore, if a router's interface MTU is smaller than a packet that must be forwarded, the router fragments the packet into smaller packets, each of which is less than or equal to the MTU value.

The fragmented packets are reassembled by the endpoint host. The IP header contains fields that are used for reassembling the fragments. This includes an ID value that is the same in each fragmented packet, as well as an offset value that defines which part of the original packet is held in each fragment.

Therefore fragmented packets can be reassembled in the correct order. Two configuration commands can be used to change the IP MTU size on an interface.

These are:

- Mtu, which sets the MTU for all Layer 3 protocols; and
- Ip mtu, which sets the MTU for IP only.

If both mtu and ip mtu are configured on an interface, the ip mtu setting takes precedence. However, if the mtu command is configured after ip mtu is configured, the ip mtu value is reset to the mtu value.

DATA IN ETHERNET TCP/IP PACKET

Are you confused about Ethernet communications? Many of us are. Here is a quick summary. Ethernet is the base physical layer communications.

Ethernet is the pipe. In the pipe we have TCP/IP packets usually referred to as TCP. Data in a TCP packet is specific to an application. Usually it has a very highly structured data like your e-mail or browser data.

Other times the data in a TCP packet is very specific to a device. For example, a manufacturer of weigh scales may put the weigh data in a TCP/IP packet in a format like "125.56 grams".

Unfortunately, many HMIs, Programmable Controllers and other devices aren't able to open a TCP/IP packet like this and process the data. They need it much more highly structured.

Application Diagram

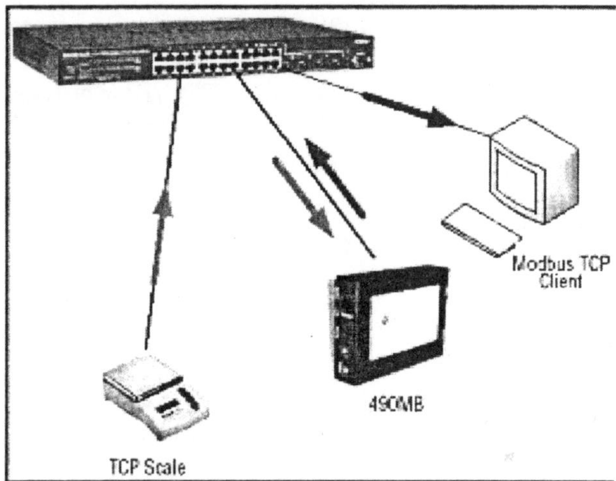

Fig. TCP/IP Scale Data to a Modbus TCP Client

Features

- Specifically designed for Barcode Readers, Weigh scales and other TCP/IP devices
- TCP/IP Client or Server Operation
- Accepts up to 6 TCP/IP connections in Server Mode
- In Server mode, any device can send data to the Modbus TCP Client
- In Server mode, all data from the Modbus TCP Client is sent to the TCP/IP device
- Simple, easy-to-use Configuration Using Any Browser
- Fully Compatible with Rockwell and Modicon Modbus TCP Modules
- Based on standard, off-the-shelf Technology
- ODVA Conformance Testing Pending

Benefits

- An Optimized Solution for Transferring your TCP/IP data to a Control Logix PLC
- Compatible with any TCP/IP device

- Transfer data to multiple TCP/IP devices from your Modbus TCP Client
- Receive data to multiple TCP/IP devices from your Modbus TCP Client
- Seamlessly Integrate your TCP/IP devices with Modicon and Rockwell Automation PLCs
- Proven and reliable hardware platform
- Transfer data with Little or No Latency

IP PACKET

INTRODUCTION

Firewalls are a key part of keeping networked computers safe and secure. All computers deserve the protection of a firewall, whether it's the thousands of servers and desktops that compose the network of a Fortune 500 company, a traveling salesperson's laptop connecting to the wireless network of a coffee shop, or your grandmother's new PC with a dial-up connection to the Internet.

This article covers the design, deployment, and use of both network and host-based firewalls (also called personal firewalls). Although home users have traditionally used only host-based firewalls, recent trends in security exploits highlight the importance of using both types of firewalls together.

Traditional firewall architectures protect only the perimetre of a network. However, once an attacker penetrates that perimetre, internal systems are completely unprotected. Hybrid worms, in particular, have penetrated corporate networks through e-mail systems, and then have spread quickly to unprotected internal systems. Applying host-based firewalls to all systems, including those behind the corporate firewall, should now be standard practice.

THE NATURE OF TODAY'S ATTACKERS

If a worm or a virus does find a security vulnerability and compromises your system, it can do one of several things. To begin with, it will almost always start looking for other systems to attack so that it can spread itself further. In this case, you become one of the bad guys—because the worm or virus is using your computer to attack other systems on your internal network and the Internet, wasting your computing resources and bandwidth.

Even though the worm or virus won't know what to do with your confidential data, chances are good that it will open a new back door into your system to allow someone else to further abuse your computer and compromise your privacy. Worms and viruses have dramatically increased the need for network security of all kinds—especially the need for host-based firewalls.

Individuals still launch some attacks, though, and these are generally the most dangerous. The least worrisome attackers focus on crashing computers and networks by using Denial of Service (DoS) attacks.

Others might be looking for confidential data that they can abuse for profit, such as sales contacts, financial data, or customer account information. Still others might be amassing hundreds or thousands of computers from which to launch a distributed attack against a single network on the Internet.

THE FIREWALL TO THE RESCUE

In the physical world, businesses rely on several layers of security. First, they rely on their country's government and military forces to keep order. Then, they trust their local police to patrol the streets and respond to any crimes that occur.

They further supplement these public security mechanisms by using locks on doors and windows, employee badges, and security systems. If all these defences fail and a business is a victim of a crime, the business's insurance agency absorbs part of the impact by compensating the business for a portion of the loss.

Unfortunately, the state of networking today lacks these multiple levels of protection. Federal and local governments do what they can to slow network crime, but they're far from 100 per cent effective. Beyond prevention, law enforcement generally only responds to the most serious network intrusions.

The average Internet-connected home or business is attacked dozens of times per day, and no police force is equipped to handle that volume of complaints. Losses from computer crime are hard to quantify and predict, and as a result most business insurance policies do little to compensate for the losses that result from a successful attack.

The one aspect of physical security, however, that isn't missing from network security is the equivalent of door locks, employee badges, and security systems: firewalls. Just as you lock your car and home, you need to protect your computers and networks.

Firewalls are these locks, and just like in the physical world, they come in different shapes and sizes to suit different needs. The famous Jargon Dictionary has a great definition for *firewall:* "a dedicated gateway machine with special security precautions on it, used to service outside network connections and dial-in lines." Firewalls serve two useful purposes: they filter what traffic comes into your network from the outside world, and they control what computers on your network may send there.

It's important to understand one thing, however. No firewall—whether a small, free host-based firewall or a multiple-thousand-dollar enterprise firewall array—will make your computers impervious to attack. Firewalls, like locks and walls and moats and dragons, create barriers to attack—they get in the way of someone trying to take control. By making it difficult for attackers to get into your computer, by making them invest lots of time, you become less attractive. Firewalls very effectively block most bad guys from compromising an individual computer.

But it's impossible to fully prevent every intrusion: All software has bugs, and someone might find an obscure bug in your firewall that allows them to pass through. In a nutshell, there's no such thing as absolute security. How much you invest in firewalls should be a function of how much you have to lose if an attack is successful.

TYPES OF FIREWALLS

There are two main types of firewalls: network firewalls and host-based firewalls. Network firewalls, such as the software-based Microsoft's Internet Security and Acceleration (ISA) Server or the hardware-based Nortel Networks Alteon Switched Firewall System, protect the perimetre of a network by watching traffic that enters and leaves.

Host-based firewalls, such as Internet Connection Firewall (ICF—included with Windows XP and Windows Server 2003), protect an individual computer regardless of the network it's connected to. You might need one or the other—but most businesses require a combination of both to meet their security requirements.

HOW A FIREWALL WORKS

The sections that follow provide background information about network traffic and how firewalls filter traffic. This information applies to all types of firewalls.

BASIC TCP/IP FLOW

This section describes how TCP/IP packages its information, to show how firewalls decide to allow or deny traffic. TCP/IP traffic is broken into packets, and firewalls must examine each packet to determine whether to drop it or forward it to the destination. Figure shows a simplified breakdown of a packet with the following three key sections: the IP header, the TCP or UDP header, and the actual contents of the packet. The IP header contains the IP addresses of the source, which is the sender, and the destination, which is the receiver.

The TCP or UDP header contains the source port of the sender and the destination port of the receiver to identify the applications that are sending and receiving the traffic. In addition, TCP headers contain additional information such as sequence numbers, acknowledgment numbers, and the conversation state. The destination TCP or UDP ports define the locations for delivery of the data on the server when the packet reaches its destination.

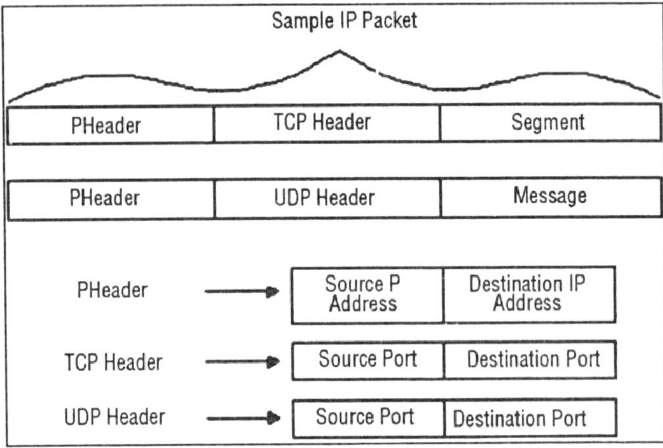

Fig. An IP packet contains a header useful to firewalls.

It's important to appreciate the communication flow of a TCP/IP conversation when configuring the firewall. When a browser, for example, sends an HTTP request to a Web server, the request contains the identity of the client computer, the source IP address, and the source port that the request went out on. The source port of the client identifies the client application that sent the request—in this case, the browser. When the Web server sends a response, it uses the client's source port as the destination port in the response. The client operating system recognizes the port number as belonging to a session the browser application started, and gives the data to the browser.

PACKET FILTERING

The primary purpose of a firewall is to filter traffic. Firewalls inspect packets as they pass through, and based on the criteria that the administrator has defined, the firewall allows or denies each packet.

Firewalls block everything that you haven't specifically allowed. Routers with filtering capabilities are a simplified example of a firewall. Administrators often configure them to allow all outbound connections from the internal network, but to block all incoming traffic. So, a user on the internal network would be able to download e-mail without a problem, but an administrator would need to customise the router configuration to connect to your home PC from work by using Remote Desktop. Other applications that might require special firewall configuration are WebCam servers, collaboration software, and multiplayer online games.

You use packet filters to instruct a firewall to drop traffic that meets certain criteria. For example, you could create a filter that would drop all ping requests. You can also configure filters with more complex exceptions to a rule. For example, a filter might assist with troubleshooting the firewall by allowing the firewall to respond to ping requests coming from a monitoring station's IP address. By default, Microsoft ISA Server doesn't respond to ping queries on its external interface. You would need to create a packet filter on the ISA Server computer for it to respond to a ping request.

The following are the main TCP/IP attributes used in implementing filtering rules:

- Source IP addresses
- Destination IP addresses
- IP protocol
- Source TCP and UDP ports
- Destination TCP and UDP ports
- The interface where the packet arrives
- The interface where the packet is destined

If you've configured the firewall to allow all traffic by default, you can use filters to block specific traffic. If you've configured the firewall to deny all traffic, filters allow only specific traffic through. A common packet-filtering configuration is to allow inbound DNS requests from the public Internet so that a DNS service can respond.

Developers have designed most applications to work properly with both routers and host-based firewalls, but some might require you to configure your firewall to allow the application to communicate. Fortunately, firewalls are very common, and any application that requires a firewall should include information about how to configure your firewall. Host-based firewalls are easier to configure than network firewalls and generally include a wizard to walk you through the configuration process. Many host-based firewalls automatically prompt you the first time any application attempts to use the Internet—whether the connection is inbound or outbound. While using a host-based firewall, you might even notice applications that you didn't know accessed the Internet, such as Microsoft Word.

Figure shows the filter configuration screen for ICF:

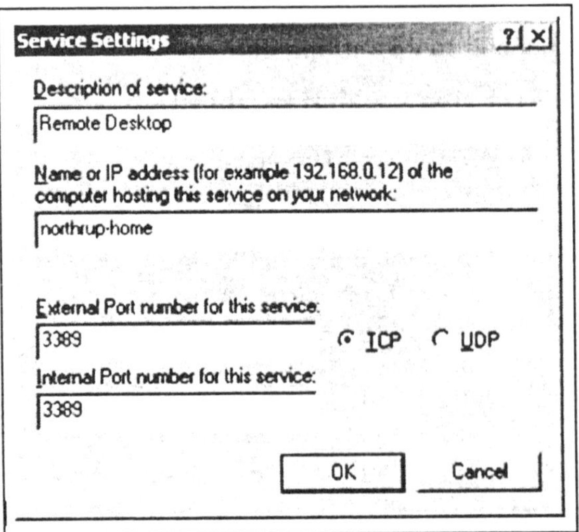

Fig. ICF Allows Custom Filters to be Created.

FILTERING AND DESTINATION

Some types of firewalls can filter traffic based on source or destination IP address. IP addresses are the telephone numbers of the Internet: They're the unique, numeric label that identifies a single host's location. Filtering based on source or destination address is useful because it enables you to allow or deny traffic based on the computers or networks that are sending or receiving the traffic.

This is useful in two ways. First, you can configure firewalls to block specific Web sites. Blocking Web sites by name is a form of destination filtering. Second, firewalls can allow or deny traffic based on the computer sending the request. This allows administrators to disable instant messaging from the computer in one organization, while allowing the same protocol from a different set of computers.

Source filtering also allows you to give greater access to users on internal networks than those on external networks. It's common to use a firewall to block all requests sent to an internal e-mail server except those requests from users on the internal network. You can also use source filtering to block all requests from a specific address—for example, to block traffic from an IP address identified as having attacked the network.

APPLICATION-LAYER FILTERING

Application-layer firewalls can understand the traffic flowing through them and allow or deny traffic based on the content. Host-based firewalls designed to block objectionable Web content based on keywords contained in the Web pages are a form of application-layer firewall. You also use application-layer firewalls to inspect packets bound for an internal Web server to ensure the request isn't really an attack in disguise.

Currently, the ability to inspect a packet's contents is one of the best ways to distinguish between firewall products. ICF lacks this feature. However, most business-oriented firewalls do include this capability.

ISA Server is also an application-level proxy that's able to read data within packets for a particular application and perform an action based on a rule set. In addition, ISA Server comes with predefined application filters that inspect each packet and block, redirect, or modify the data within the packet. For instance, you can implement Web-routing rules that tell the ISA Server computer to redirect an HTTP request to a certain internal IIS server, based on the URL in the packet. Another example is the DNS intrusion-detection filter. This filter blocks packets that aren't valid DNS requests, or that fit common types of DNS attacks. You can invoke application filtering on ISA Server when Web Publishing or Server Publishing is configured.

LOGGING

Firewalls don't prevent attacks; they simply reduce the

likelihood of a break-in. When you deploy a firewall, you'll still get just as many attacks as you always did—you just won't have to worry about them as much. All firewalls provide some capability for logging these attacks for later, manual review. This allows administrators to watch for attacks that are out-of-the-ordinary. It's also useful for forensics purposes. If an attacker does manage to defeat your firewall, you can refer to the firewall's log and gather information to determine how the attacker carried out the attack. This log can be useful to law enforcement officials, if they're involved in a related investigation.

INTRUSION DETECTION

Intrusion detection is an advanced firewall feature, and many firewalls (such as ICF) lack this feature. Intrusion detection systems (IDSs) can identify attack signatures or patterns, generate alarms to alert the operations staff, and cause the routers to terminate the connection with the hostile sources. These systems can also prevent DoS attacks. A DoS attack occurs when a user sends fragments of TCP requests, masked as legitimate TCP requests, or sends requests from a bad IP source. The server can't handle so many requests and displays a DoS message to legitimate site users. IDSs provide real-time monitoring of network traffic and implement the "prevent, detect, and react" approach to security.

Although IDSs are necessary to meet security requirements for many businesses and some home users, their use has downsides that you should take into account:

- IDSs are processing-intensive and can affect the performance of your site.
- IDSs are expensive.
- IDSs can sometimes mistake normal network traffic for a hostile attack and cause unnecessary alarms. These unnecessary alarms can be so frequent that they cause operational staff to ignore genuine alarms.

There are a number of third-party tools available for intrusion detection. For example, you can use Cisco's Intrusion Detection System (IDS) or ISS's RealSecure for real-time network traffic monitoring. IDSs are still in the process of being enhanced and developed.

ANTIVIRUS

The term "virus" is used to describe self-replicating computer programmes that propagate themselves between files on a computer, and even between computers. Viruses usually, but not always, do something malicious, such as overwrite files or waste your bandwidth by sending copies of themselves to everyone in your address book.

Antivirus capabilities are a feature of some network and host-based firewalls. Network firewalls might inspect all incoming e-mail traffic for virus-infected attachments, and filter them out. Host-based firewalls might change the configuration of the user's e-mail client so that the e-mail client sends all requests through the host-based firewall.

Firewalls are certainly not the only way to protect yourself from viruses, and if the firewall you choose doesn't have antivirus features, you'll need to complement it with antivirus software. The best way to protect your organization against viruses is to use a good-quality commercial antivirus package. These scanners examine the files, folders, mail messages, and Web pages on your computers, looking for the distinctive patterns of viral code. When the scanner detects something that looks like a virus, it quarantines the suspect object and warns you about what it found. If your organization uses Outlook as its mail client, be sure to install the Outlook Security Update, which gives you a great deal of protection against e-mail-borne viruses. (Note that this update's functionality is built into Outlook 2002, which comes as part of Office XP.) TechNet has a great summary page that's continually updated to reflect newly emergent viruses. While you're reading it, reflect on the fact that most e-mail-carried viruses spread because people do things they shouldn't, such as launch attachments from unknown sources.

VPNS AND ENCRYPTION

Port forwarding is sufficient for publishing a Web site

through your firewall. However, it's not sufficient if you want to connect two Internet-connected networks that are both protected by firewalls. For this, you should use a Virtual Private Network (VPN). A VPN is the extension of a private network that encompasses encapsulated, encrypted, and authenticated links across shared or public networks. VPN connections can provide remote access and routed connections to private networks over the Internet. Accessing the corporate network requires administrators to enforce strong authentication to validate identity as well as provide strong encryption to prevent users from communicating data "in the clear."

VPNs aren't strictly a firewall feature, and many businesses implement them by using completely separate, dedicated VPN devices. However, network architects generally place network firewalls at the perimetre of the network, just like a VPN. Both firewalls and VPNs are designed to improve network security, so it's logical that VPN capabilities have become a feature of many firewalls.

If you're using a Windows 2000 Server or Windows Server 2003 system as your network firewall, you already have VPN capabilities built into the base platform. All recent Windows platforms provide the authentication and encryption infrastructure to enable secure connectivity.

With the Windows 2000 Server and Windows Server 2003 built-in VPN server and Windows XP VPN client, organizations can take advantage of a secure standards-based VPN directly "out of the box." Because Microsoft supports VPN standards such as L2TP/IPSec and smart card authentication, organizations have access to the encryption, authentication, and interoperability that best meet their VPN security needs.

Although organizations often use VPNs to encrypt traffic over the Internet between users and the corporate network, they can also implement encryption between any Windows 2000, Windows Server 2003, and Windows XP machine. Since Microsoft has full standards-based support for the IPSec security extensions, organizations can provide robust encryption of all network traffic, without requiring cumbersome changes to deployed applications, servers, or network hardware.

HOST-BASED FIREWALLS

Host-based firewalls are software firewalls installed on each individual system. Depending on the software you choose, a host-based firewall can offer features beyond those of network firewalls, such as protecting your computer from spyware (a component of some free software that tracks your Web browsing habits) and Trojan horses (a programme that claims to do one thing, but does another, malicious thing, such as recording your passwords). If you travel with a laptop, a host-based firewall is a necessity—you need protection wherever you connect to the Internet, and your hardware firewall can protect you only at home.

Why would you buy third-party firewall software when Windows XP includes ICF for free? ICF is designed to provide basic intrusion prevention, but doesn't include the rich features of a third-party firewall application. Most third-party firewalls protect you from software that could violate your privacy or allow an attacker to misuse your computer—features not found in ICF.

Also, you can install third-party firewall programmes on systems that have older versions of Windows. Note that firewall software doesn't replace antivirus software. You should use both.

Popular host-based firewall products include ZoneAlarm, Tiny Personal Firewall, Agnitum Outpost Firewall, Kerio Personal Firewall, and Internet Security Systems' BlackICE PC Protection. Most host-based firewall software is available in free or trial versions, so it won't cost you anything to download these packages and determine whether they meet your needs better than ICF.

NETWORK FIREWALLS

Network firewalls protect an entire network by guarding the perimetre of that network. Network firewalls forward traffic to and from computers on an internal network, and filter that traffic based on the criteria the administrator has set. Network firewalls come in two flavours: hardware firewalls and software firewalls. Hardware-based network firewalls are generally cheaper than software-based network firewalls, and are the right choice for home users and many small businesses. Software-based network firewalls often have a larger feature set than hardware-based firewalls, and might fit the needs of larger organizations. Software-based firewalls can also run on the same server as other services, such as e-mail and file sharing, allowing small organizations to make better use of existing servers. Network firewalls often include additional features that aren't necessary for host-based firewalls, as described in the following sections.

PROXY SERVICES

If you have or are planning to have a home or small office network, you'll have to create a gateway from your firewall to the rest of the network. If you're implementing a software firewall on a specific computer, this means that you'll need at least two network cards in that machine. You attach one network card to the public interface (such as a DSL or cable modem), and You attach the other network card to your internal network. You then have to configure the computer to allow traffic on one side of the network to communicate with the other. ICS allows you to do this in both Windows 2000and Windows XP.

However, at this stage in the game, many small office users decide to buy a dedicated residential gateway. These units plug directly into the DSL router or cable modem and provide the functionality of a firewall and network hub. You need to configure a residential gateway to act in the stead of the computer running ICS when contacting the ISP. For example, if you had a static IP address, you would have to assign that IP address to the gateway instead of your computer. You could either assign a new IP address to your computer, or, more likely, instruct the computer to ask the gateway for an IP address.

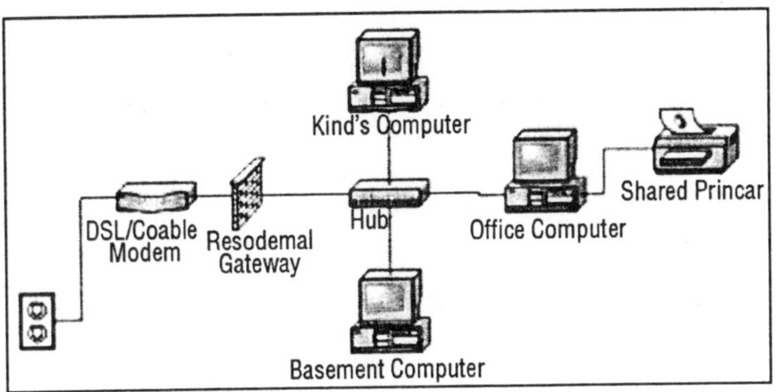

Fig A Full-fledged Small Office Network Complete with a Residential Gateway

If a small business is using the 192.168.0.0 network ID for its intranet and its ISP has granted it the public address of w1.x1.y1.z1, then Network Address Translation (NAT) maps all private addresses on 192.168.0.0 to the IP address of w1.x1.y1.z1. If NAT maps multiple private addresses to a single public address, it uses dynamically chosen TCP and UDP ports to distinguish one intranet location from another.

Note: The use of w1.x1.y1.z1 and w2.x2.y2.z2 is intended to represent valid public IP addresses assigned by an ISP.

Figure shows an example of using NAT to transparently connect an intranet to the Internet:

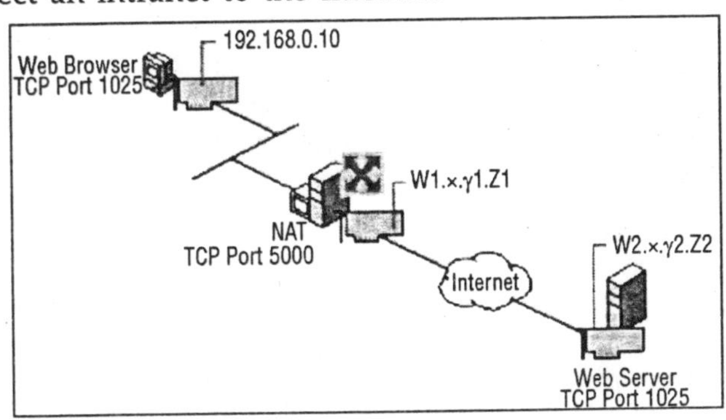

Fig. Using NAT to Connect an Intranet to the Internet

If a private user at 192.168.0.10 uses a Web browser to connect to the Web server at w2.x2.y2.z2, the user's computer creates an IP packet with the following information:

- Destination IP address: w2.x2.y2.z2
- Source IP address: 192.168.0.10
- Destination port: TCP port 80
- Source port: TCP port 5000

The private user's computer then forwards this packet to the NAT server, which translates the addresses of the outgoing packet to the following:

- Destination IP address: w2.x2.y2.z2
- Source IP address: w1.x1.y1.z1
- Destination port: TCP port 80
- Source port: TCP port 1025

The NAT server keeps the mapping of {192.168.0.10, TCP 1025} to {w1.x1.y1.z1, TCP 5000} in a table. The NAT server then sends the translated packet over the Internet to the Web server. The Web server sends the response back to the NAT server. When the NAT server receives the packet, the packet contains the following public address information:

- Destination IP address: w1.x1.y1.z1
- Source IP address: w2.x2.y2.z2
- Destination port: TCP port 1025
- Source port: TCP port 80

The NAT server checks its translation table and maps the public addresses to private addresses and forwards the packet to the computer at 192.168.0.10.

The forwarded packet contains the following address information:

- Destination IP address: 192.168.0.10
- Source IP address: w2.x2.y2.z2
- Destination port: TCP port 5000
- Source port: TCP port 80

For outgoing packets from the NAT server, the NAT server maps the source IP address (a private address) to the ISP allocated address (a public address), and maps the TCP/UDP port numbers to a different TCP/UDP port number.

For incoming packets to the NAT server, the NAT server maps the destination IP address (a public address) to the original intranet address (a private address), and maps the TCP/UDP port numbers back to their original TCP/UDP port numbers.

Note: NAT properly translates packets that contain the IP address only in the IP header. NAT might not properly translate packets that contain the IP address within the IP payload.

REVERSE PROXY SERVICES

Most proxy servers offer services beyond the standard functionality discussed above. Reverse proxy enables the firewall to provide secure access to an internal Web server (not exposing it to the outside) by redirecting external HTTP (application proxy) requests to a single designated machine. This isn't suitable for multi server Web hosting (reverse hosting—described next—takes care of this), but it can be quite valuable when working with a single site. Reverse hosting allows the firewall to redirect HTTP (application proxy) requests to multiple internal Web servers. One method/way is to provide access to multiple servers as sub webs of one large aggregate Web site or as multiple independent Web servers. More flexible than reverse proxy but equally secure, this method enables you to abstract the physical architecture of your Web sites by mapping multiple servers to a single logical one. Both options allow the firewall to offer caching functionality, which can improve responsiveness.

Server proxy provides the same functionality as reverse proxy and reverse hosting, but unlike these features, it works with protocols other than HTTP to provide secure access from the Internet to internal resources such as internal mail or SQL Server. To an outside user, the proxy server appears to be the mail or SQL Server. Basically, server proxy responds to external requests on behalf of the internal servers, which simply have to run the proxy client that redirects the listen directive on a given port to a proxy server. The security benefit is obvious: Placing servers behind a proxy prevents direct tampering from the outside and fools would-be attackers into thinking that the proxy server is the box containing the information they want.

Reverse proxy can be very useful. For instance, suppose you need to allow a Web server to query an internal database.

There are several ways to do this. You could replicate the database to the outside (if it's not too large), but this puts the contents' integrity at risk. It might make more sense to move the Web and database servers behind the firewall and use reverse proxy or reverse hosting to get at the site. This option is very secure, although the overhead of running multiple Web servers behind the proxy might tax the proxy's ability to service Web requests from internal clients.

FIREWALLS

Firewalls used to be only for large corporate networks—but then again, Internet connections used to be only for large networks, too. Now that high-speed, always-on Internet connectivity is becoming more and more common, so too are attacks against connected computers. Firewalls help protect you against such attacks by screening out many types of malicious traffic. In addition, firewalls can help keep your computer from participating in attacks on others without your knowledge. The good news is that consumer-level firewalls provide good security without requiring that you be a computer security expert.

It used to be true that if you had a computer or two in a small office, the biggest risk you faced was losing data due to a fire, hardware failure, or other catastrophe. Although those risks are still with us, the blessing of always-on, high-speed Internet connectivity has exposed us to new threats, as well as intensifying some older ones. The good news is that, with the right tools, you can do a great deal to safeguard your computer systems against malicious attacks, viruses, and other bad stuff. Some of these tools come included with various versions of Windows. Others come from third-party vendors, such as Symantec, McAfee, and others. It's not necessarily important that you use a particular brand of tool; it's more important that you have the right tools, no matter who makes them.

Once you decide you need a firewall for your small office or home office, the first step in setting up a firewall is simple: Decide whether a hardware or a software solution will work best for your needs. Firewall products come in many different forms, from freely available software for your computer to tamper-resistant industrial units. Whether you buy a certified firewall or not, no matter what kind of firewall you buy, all firewalls provide the same basic feature: control of inbound and outbound traffic.

When making this decision, you should be asking the following questions:

- *Are my computers all running Windows XP or Windows Server 2003*: If so, you already have a built-in firewall, ICF, so you might not need to buy anything additional.
- *Do I want to share my Internet connection between multiple computers*: If you do, you either have, or will have, your computers networked together. In that case, you can use Windows' Internet Connection Sharing (ICS) feature to share the connection. ICS is included with Windows 2000, Windows XP, and Windows Server 2003.
- *Do I want to be able to share my connection without using one computer as a firewall*: Perhaps you want to share your Internet connection, but you don't want to have to use one particular computer as the gateway—ICS only works when the computer running it is powered up and on the network. Instead, you can buy an inexpensive appliance that acts as a gateway for sharing connections—these so-called "Internet access routers" or "residential gateways" almost always include basic firewall functionality.

For maximum security, you can install a hardware firewall to protect your small office network, and then combine it with ICF or another host-based firewall. You can configure host-based firewalls for individual machines so that each machine on your network can have different network permissions, if that's what you need. In addition, host-based firewalls can alert you when software on a machine that has a firewall is sending out data when it shouldn't. Hardware-based firewalls are typically very flexible and powerful; once you get them set up, you can leave them alone and let them work to silently protect you. Of course, getting them set up in the first place can be a difficult exercise!

Combining the two types can give you tighter security than using either one alone. For maximum security, the most reliable way for small office users to protect a network is to purchase a router with firewall capabilities. These routers do more than act as a firewall—they network multiple computers, allow them to share a single Internet connection, and might even support wireless networking. If you have more than one computer and an always-on broadband connection, a router/firewall gives you the benefits of a small office network and connects every computer to the Internet.

The router is generally a separate device from the cable or DSL modem—it's important to understand that most cable and DSL modems offer your small office network no protection whatsoever. If you didn't choose to pay extra for security features, you probably don't have any. If you're unsure about your modem, ask your ISP what level of protection your modem provides. Using a router with firewall capabilities has several advantages over using host-based firewall software. Host-based firewalls can protect only one computer at a time, and configuring a host-based firewall for every computer on your small office network can be a nuisance. Host-based firewalls are completely unable to protect other types of devices connected to your network, such as a game system or personal television viewer. Finally, if you use multiple operating systems on your computer or experiment with beta operating systems, it's easy to forget to install a host-based firewall for every OS.

If you decide to use a hardware firewall, select one that has enough network ports to allow you to connect all computers and other network devices directly to it. As shown in Figure, wiring a firewall into your network is as simple as adding an answering machine to your phone line. Simply unplug the Ethernet connection between your cable/DSL modem and your PC, and plug it into the firewall. Then connect your computer and other network devices into your firewall. Configuring a hardware firewall isn't as simple—we'll discuss that later.

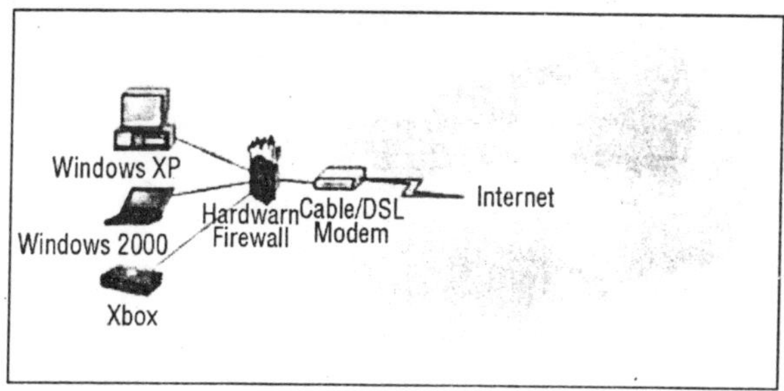

Fig. Wiring a Firewall Into a Network

The following are some of the popular hardware firewall products available: Linksys Routers, NETGEAR Routers, and SMC Routers. Home and small office computers that are directly connected to the Internet require the added security of a firewall.

The least expensive way to do this is to enable both ICF and ICS on a system, and allow all networked computers to connect through that system.

You can enable ICS on only one Internet connection on your network, and you should protect this connection by enabling ICF. ICF can check only the communications that cross the Internet connection on which it's enabled. The following types of network topologies, which Figures show, are safe and the most recommended:

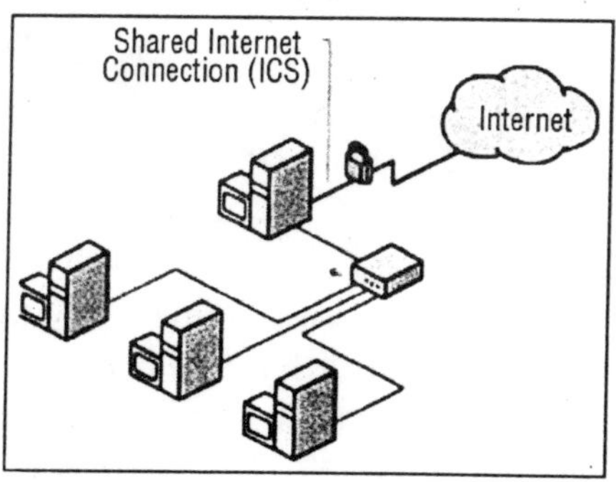

Fig. An Example of Using ICS to Connect a LAN to the Internet.

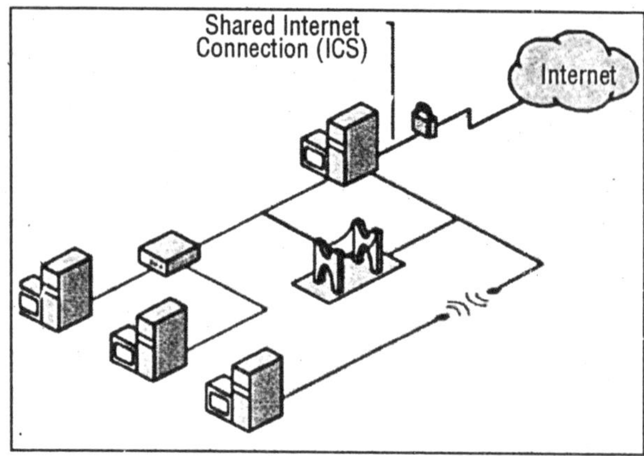

Fig. An Example of Using ICS to Connect Multiple Networks to the Internet.

You should avoid topologies with multiple Internet connections. If you must have multiple direct Internet connections on your network, you should ensure that ICF is enabled on each direct Internet connection in order to protect your network, as shown in Figure. However, because ICF works on a per-connection basis, this topology is still not a recommended topology because there's no central point of administration through which you can ensure the continuous protection of all Internet connections.

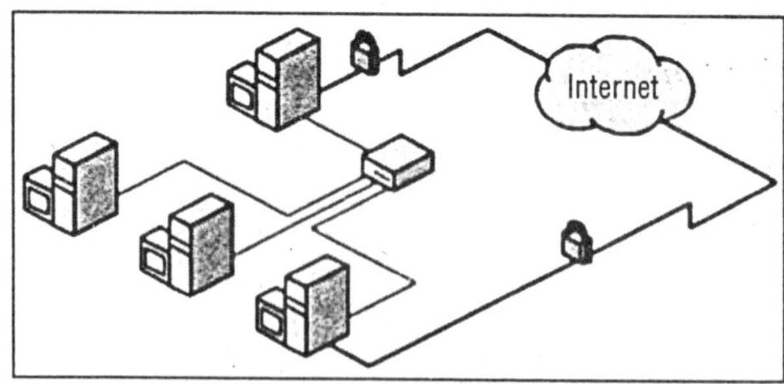

Fig. Multiple Internet Connections are More Difficult to Secure.

Likewise, as shown in below figure, providing Internet connectivity to your network by connecting your network hub directly to the Internet causes similar vulnerabilities and isn't a recommended topology.

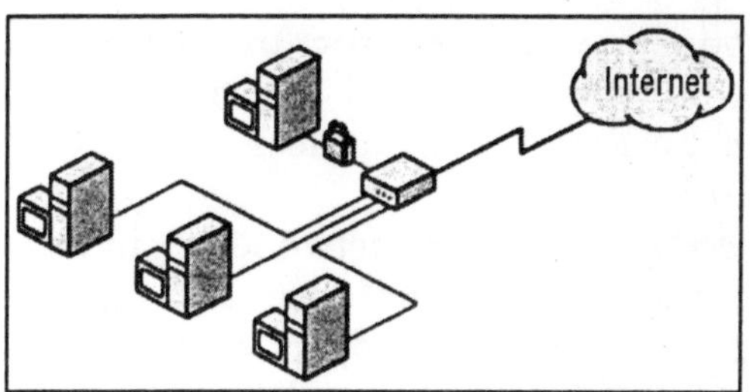

Fig. LAN Systems are Not Protected Unless all Traffic Passes Through ICF.

Enabling ICF on this type of network topology disrupts some network communications and provides protection only for the computer on which it's enabled. The other computers have direct connections to the Internet through the hub and aren't protected.

FIREWALLS FOR ENTERPRISES

Organizations of all sizes want secure network connectivity to their business data and applications. The need to connect and collaborate with partners, customers, and remote/mobile employees anytime and anywhere has expanded network connectivity requirements beyond traditional wired local area networks (LANs) to include dial-up remote access, VPNs, and wireless networks. To enable greater access to the network and higher productivity, customers must address issues around security, management complexity, and cost. With Windows Server 2003, Windows 2000, Windows XP, and a carefully designed firewall architecture, administrators can provide secure and integrated network connectivity to business-critical applications and data.

When addressing secure network connectivity, administrators need to consider the following:

- *Security*: Employees not only work from corporate offices, but also from branch offices, home offices, or the road. Providing remote connectivity requires solutions that are secure, standards-based, and manageable.
- *Management complexity*: Many vendors offer dedicated product solutions with little integration with other

products and infrastructure. Setting up wireless clients with centralized authentication and policies can be a challenge unless there are integrated solutions.

- *Lowering cost*: Secure networking can be expensive if there are multiple products and technologies with separate licensing, support contracts, and training. For example, a secure VPN implementation might require a separate certificate authority for PKI, a separate authentication model, client-side software, and additional server gateways and firewalls.

By addressing these key secure connectivity challenges, organizations can achieve greater employee productivity, decrease costs, and improve business integration.

HOST-BASED FIREWALLS ON CORPORATE NETWORKS

Corporate networks also employ layers of defence. Often there will be some traffic screening at the router connecting the network to the Internet, one or more enterprise-class firewalls, virus scanning engines on the e-mail servers, and some kind of intrusion detection mechanism.

An interesting consideration is whether host-based firewalls make sense in corporate networks. Enterprise firewalls and host-based firewalls operate at different defensive layers: Enterprise firewalls protect entire networks, whereas host-based firewalls protect individual hosts; so in one sense, combining the two seems appropriate. Host-based firewalls, however, block certain corporate network activity: For instance, some organizations periodically scan corporate clients for conformance to password policies; host-based firewalls interfere with this operation. Firewalls like ICF that block all incoming connections interfere with LAN-based applications that need to send notices to client computers (printer status messages and Exchange new mail notification are two examples). Your organization's security policy needs to describe whether host-based firewalls are permitted and how they should be configured. ICF in Windows XP obeys Network Location Awareness, and you can disable it via

Windows Server 2003 Active Directory (AD) Group Policy. Mobile users don't have to remember to enable or disable ICF as they roam about. They can leave ICF enabled, being protected while at home or traveling. At the office, Group Policy can disable ICF whenever a computer is attached to the corporate network.

USING A DEMILITARIZED ZONE

Most organizations use their Internet connection to expose services to the public Internet. At a minimum, SMTP services are exposed to allow inbound e-mail. You can use filtering and port forwarding to allow this traffic through a firewall, but many organizations require a DMZ to further protect the internal network. This section discusses how to secure your DMZ—the area in which you typically place your servers that expose public services to provide the best security.

A DMZ consists of front-end servers, back-end servers, and firewalls. The firewalls protect the front-end servers from the public network and filter traffic between the corporate network and back-end servers. A DMZ provides a multilayer protection system between the Internet and the internal network of an organization.

To provide protection, the DMZ comprises:

- A firewall that protects the front-end servers from Internet traffic.
- A set of "security-hardened" servers that support the services the application provides. You set up these servers so that dangerous Internet services, such as file sharing and Telnet, are disabled.
- A firewall that separates the back-end servers from the corporate networks and enables communication between the back-end servers and a few servers within the corporate network.

A DMZ is an important element for securing a site. You need to take additional security measures to protect data the back-end servers store. You can also store extremely sensitive data or data that's needed elsewhere in your enterprise outside the DMZ, although doing so has negative performance implications and runs the risk, however small, of opening your corporate network to hacking. At the very least, a DMZ requires a router. A more sophisticated design would include two routers and a firewall. How complex your configuration needs to be depends on factors such as:

- How much security you need
- What sort of connectivity your system maintains to other networks (internal—corporate network; external—Internet)
- How many servers you need to protect

Figure below show DMZ configurations common in corporate environments today. Both provide excellent protection for the internal network. Figure shows a simpler configuration; the configuration that Figure shows protects the DMZ servers with the same security features used to protect the internal network, controlling DMZ access from the trusted and untrusted sides of the firewall. It's more complex but more secure.

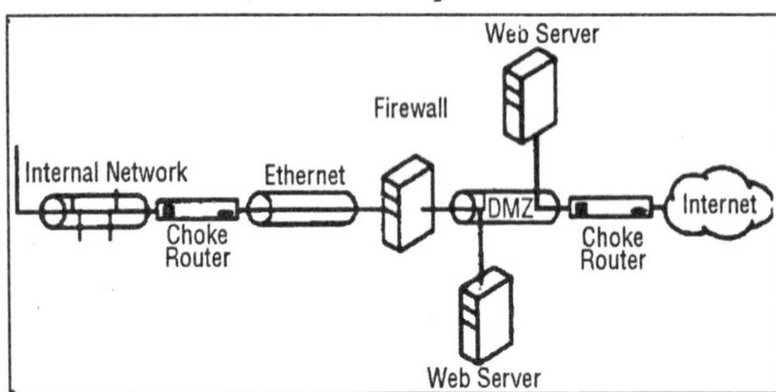

Fig. A Simple DMZ Configuration

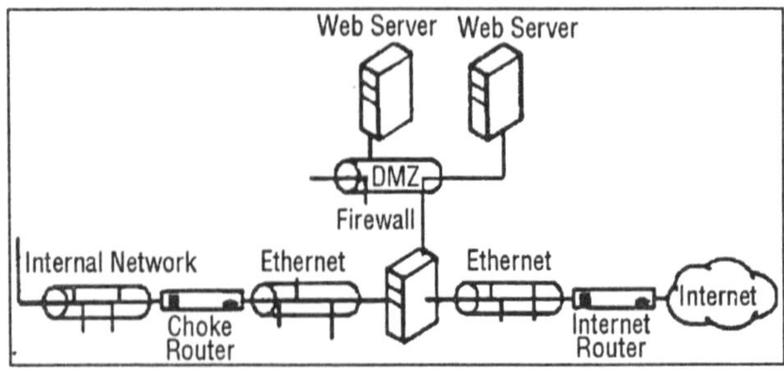

Fig. DMZ Configuration Controlling DMZ Access from the Trusted and Untrusted Sides of the Firewall

After DMZ topology, the most important step in securing the environment is controlling its traffic. You need to determine who's allowed to connect and who isn't, and then enforce those rules, usually with routers and firewalls. Routers can provide packet filtering, which controls traffic flow between two nodes, but this tends to decrease router performance, so you have to be careful not to overuse it. Check your router utilization before and after.

You must give particular attention to each server in the DMZ to ensure they're capable of withstanding malicious attacks. You can harden the exposed servers by using the Security Tools and Checklists for your servers' operating systems. You can also implement low-level filtering policies and close selective ports. For example, you should configure a host-based firewall on systems in a DMZ.

STANDARD DMZ WEB SITE ARCHITECTURES

If you're going to implement an e-commerce or enterprise application, you have to be concerned with the security of your systems and data to ensure that people who shouldn't be accessing data can't get at it and to ensure that your system will be available despite attempts at a DoS attack. For enterprise applications, the main worry is unscrupulous employees—so security is typically enforced by using Windows and AD authentication and authorization.

But malicious attackers can also attack e-commerce applications from outside your company via the Internet. And since it's not practical to give every anonymous customer their own Windows logon ID, you'll need to use a different sort of authentication. Because the network is the Internet, instead of an intranet that you control, you'll also have to prepare your servers to make other sorts of attacks impossible or ineffective. Finally, you'll have to be especially careful protecting customer data, such as credit card numbers.

If you plan to host the site at your corporate facilities, you'll need to use a DMZ. The Internet-facing firewall must provide access to services such as HTTP, HTTPS, FTP, and SMTP mail. If you're collocating your servers at a hosting provider's network, a single Internet-facing firewall might be sufficient. However, you'll also need to use a VPN to securely manage the site from your corporate network. Figure shows a typical architecture for hosting a large-scale e-commerce site using an enterprise's existing Internet connection.

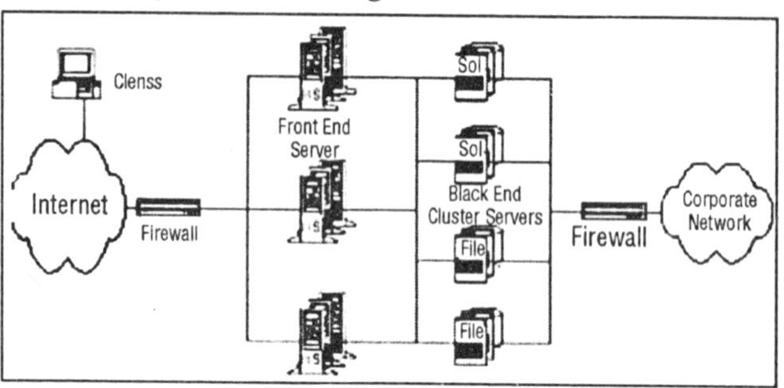

Fig. A Typical self-hosted e-commerce Web architecture

In general, here's what happens: Clients access the application over the Internet. Requests pass through a firewall, which filters out packets sent to the wrong address or wrong ports. The external firewall filters these requests, ensuring they originate from a valid address and are destined for a valid address and port number. If the firewall is an application-layer firewall, it will verify that the name of the page requested is valid and the request is well-formed. A Web server running IIS handles the requests, typically by using an ASP.NET page, and requests information from the database servers as needed. The Web servers may make requests to resources located within the corporate network. The DMZ's internal firewall—a final layer of protection for the internal network—filters these requests. This additional protection is critical since the risk of an attacker compromising externally facing Web servers is much higher than other internal servers, and an attacker might leverage them as a launching point for further attacks against the internal network.

MULTILAYER FIREWALL WEB SITE ARCHITECTURES

Many organizations have security requirements that necessitate placing a firewall between the front-end Web servers and the back-end database servers. Figure shows an example architecture that meets those requirements, and provides redundancy, while minimizing cost by using multi homed redundant firewalls. In this architecture, requests the Web servers send to the database servers must pass through the redundant firewalls.

The firewalls can verify the source and destination of the address, and validate that it's a legitimate request. This example architecture is placed at an Internet data centre where administrators perform management of the systems remotely. Therefore, the firewalls have VPN capability, allowing administrators to securely access the Web and database servers from the corporate network.

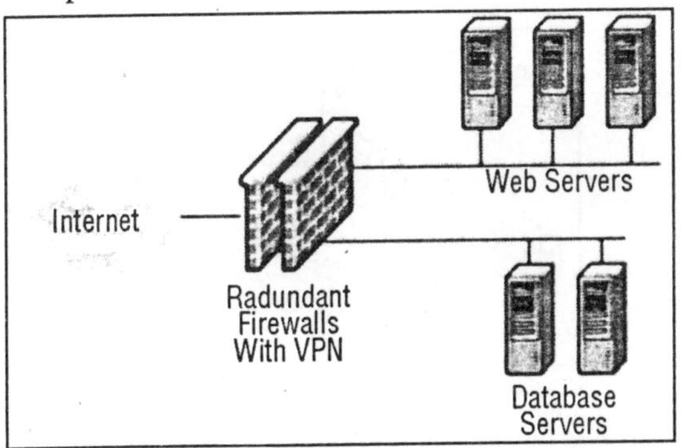

Fig. Firewall Placement in the Internet Data Centre Architecture

The firewalls in this architecture must support packet filtering, stateful inspection, application-level filtering, and VPNs. Further, they must be capable of supporting a sufficient number of connections and throughput to handle inbound requests from Web users, outbound responses to clients, requests between the Web and database servers, and connections across the VPN for system management. A typical production architecture would include another network connected to the firewalls or directly to the servers for backing up data.

FIREWALL PRODUCTS

This section provides an overview of some key firewall products and categories.

Internet Connection Firewall

ICF is host-based firewall software that you use to set restrictions on what traffic is allowed to enter your computer. ICF protects your computer against external threats by allowing safe network traffic to pass through the firewall into your network, while denying the entrance of unsafe traffic.

If you configure ICF on a system that uses ICS, that protection is extended to all traffic passing through the system. If your network uses ICS to provide shared Internet access to multiple computers, you should enable ICF on the shared Internet connection, as Figure shows:

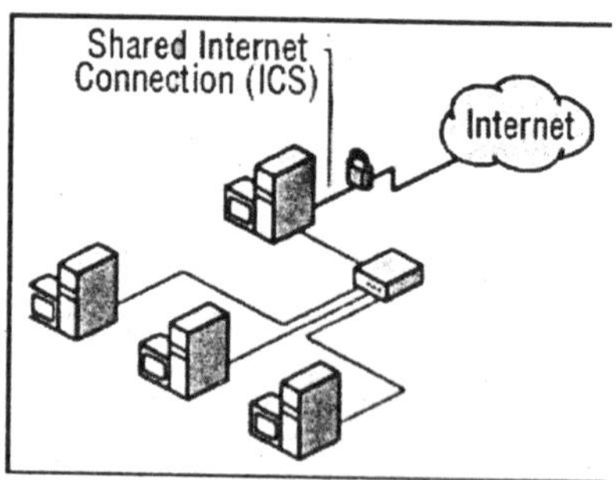

Fig. Enabling ICF on an ICS-enabled System Increases the Security of the Entire Network.

Although it's critical to enable ICF on the Internet connection of any computer that's connected directly to the Internet, you should enable ICF on all network interfaces to protect against attacks originating from the internal network. ICF can provide protection to a single computer connected to the Internet with a cable modem. To check to see whether ICF is enabled on Windows Server 2003, or to enable ICF, see To enable or disable ICF. For information about using ICF, seeProtecting your home or small office network using Internet Connection Firewall.

HOW ICF WORKS

ICF is considered a stateful firewall. To prevent unsolicited traffic from the public side of the connection from entering the private side, ICF keeps a table of all communications that have originated from the ICF computer. When used in conjunction with ICS, ICF tracks all traffic that has originated from the ICF/ICS computer and all traffic that has originated from private network computers. ICF compares all inbound traffic from the Internet against entries in the table. ICF allows inbound Internet traffic to reach the computers in your network only when there's a matching entry in the table that shows that the communication exchange originated from your computer or private network.

To thwart common hacking attempts (such as port scanning), the firewall drops communications that originate from the Internet. Rather than sending you notifications about firewall activity, ICF silently discards unsolicited communications, because frequently sending such notifications could become a distraction. Instead, ICF creates a security log to track this activity. For more information, see Internet Connection Firewall security log.

You can configure services to allow the ICF computer to forward unsolicited traffic from the Internet to the private network. For example, if you're hosting an HTTP Web server service, and the HTTP service is enabled on your ICF computer, the ICF computer forwards unsolicited HTTP traffic. ICF requires a set of operational information, known as a service definition, to allow it to forward unsolicited Internet traffic to the Web server on your private network. Service definitions for ICF work on a per-connection basis. If your network has multiple firewall connections, you should configure service definitions on all firewall connections. For information about service definitions, see Service definitions for Internet Connection Firewall and Internet Connection Sharing. For information about adding and editing service definitions, see To manage service definitions for ICF or ICS.

Note

Microsoft includes ICS and ICF only with Windows XP; Windows Server 2003, Standard Edition; and the 32-bit version of Windows Server 2003, Enterprise Edition. These features aren't included with Windows Server 2003, Web Edition; the

32-bit version of Windows Server 2003, Datacentre Edition; or the 64-bit versions of the Windows Server 2003 family.

For those who live and breathe TCP/IP, ICF's engine uses addresses, ports, sequence numbers, and flags in its state table. For TCP, the outgoing request must have only the SYN flag turned on; incoming replies must have only the ACK and SYN flags turned on; the next outgoing packet must have only the ACK flag turned on. If this sequence is violated, ICF terminates the connection. Also, ICF drops any incoming packet (including ACK-SYN) that it can't associate with (using addresses, ports, and sequence numbers) a previous outgoing ACK. ICF also drops any incoming unsolicited SYN unless it matches a user-defined exception . When ICF discards packets, it does so silently; it never returns an RST.

ICF "forgets" about a particular state between the client and a server when:

- It sees a special connection-termination sequence for TCP-based communications (ACK-FIN, ACK, ACK-FIN, and ACK)
- A period of inactivity (a "timeout") for UDP-based communications

Essentially, ICF allows in only that which is a reply to a previous request that went out. ICF blocks and discards all other incoming traffic. It seems simple, but it's an extremely effective method for protecting a computer. Even enterprise-class firewalls operate using the same basic principle. This method means that ICF blocks the following kinds (among others) of potentially dangerous communications:

Scans

Attackers often scan computers looking for vulnerabilities, especially the popular well-known cable-modem subnets. Because incoming scans are "unsolicited" (*i.e.*, don't match something in ICF's traffic memory), ICF blocks them.

File Sharing and Anonymous Connections

Windows networking is intended to allow easy file sharing between computers; you use anonymous connections for discovering a computer's name and list of available file shares. Of course, on the Internet you really don't want to do this; ICF prohibits these kinds of connections.

By default, turning on ICF automatically blocks all communications originating from foreign computers to all ports on your computer. This essentially renders your computer invisible to port scanners, hacking tools that repetitively try different ports on a network address to see how a particular machine might be attacked. Hackers frequently run port scanners against DSL and cable-modem services to see whether they can find any unsecured machines; with ICF running, the port scanners never see your machine.

If you want to enable Internet users to communicate with your machine (as you might if you're running a Web server or using a popular peer-to-peer programme), you can choose to allow communications to specified ports by clicking on the Settings button on the Advanced tab in the properties window of your public network connection. Although the Code Red and Nimda viruses demonstrate the importance of patching services even when they're not exposed through the firewall, once you open up a port to the outside world, it's imperative you apply and keep up-to-date with any patches for that service. Windows Update provides an easy way to ensure that you're up-to-date with Windows XP services.

If you're hosting a service that you want other computers to have access to, you need to let ICF know that it's OK for computers to access it. The classic example is a Web server. ICF is easily configurable for any services that you might be running on your computer and comes preconfigured with definitions for common protocols and services such as HTTP, FTP, and SMTP. Even if the service or programmes that you want to expose aren't on the default list, you can add them by defining the internal and external TCP ports that they utilize.

ICF AND NOTIFICATION MESSAGES

Because ICF inspects all incoming communications, some programmes, especially e-mail programmes, might behave differently when ICF is enabled. Some e-mail programmes periodically poll their e-mail server for new mail, and some e-mail programmes wait for notification from the e-mail server.

Outlook Express, for example, automatically checks for new e-mail when its timer tells it to do so. When new e-mail is present, Outlook Express prompts the user with a new e-mail notification. ICF won't affect the behaviour of this programme because the request for new e-mail notification originates from inside the firewall. The firewall makes an entry in a table noting the outbound communication. When the mail server acknowledges the new e-mail response, the firewall finds an associated entry in the table and allows the communication to pass, and then the user receives notification that a new e-mail message has arrived.

Outlook 2000, however, is connected to a Microsoft Exchange server that uses a remote procedure call (RPC) to send new e-mail notifications to clients. Outlook 2000 doesn't automatically check for new e-mail when it's connected to an Exchange server. The Exchange server notifies Outlook 2000 when new e-mail arrives. Because the Exchange server—which is outside the firewall—not Outlook 2000—which is inside the firewall— initiates the RPC notification, ICF can't find the corresponding entry in the table, and it doesn't allow the RPC messages to cross from the Internet into the network. ICF drops the RPC notification message. Users can send and receive e-mail, but need to manually check for new e-mail.

ADVANCED ICF SETTINGS

The ICF security-logging feature provides a way to create a security log of firewall activity. ICF is capable of logging both traffic that's permitted and traffic that's rejected. For example, the firewall, by default, doesn't allow incoming echo requests from the Internet. If the Internet Control Message Protocol (ICMP) Allow incoming echo request isn't enabled, then the inbound request fails, and ICF generates a log entry that notes the failed inbound attempt. For information about ICMP, see Internet Control Message Protocol (ICMP). ICMP allows you to modify the behaviour of the firewall by enabling various ICMP options, such as Allow incoming echo request, Allow incoming time stamp request, Allow incoming router request, and Allow redirect. The ICMP tab provides brief descriptions of these options. For navigation and instructions for ICMP, see Enable Internet Control Message Protocols.

You can set the allowable size of the security log to prevent the potential overflow that DoS attacks could cause. ICF generates event-log entries into the Extended Log File Format as established by the World Wide Web Consortium (W3C). For more information about ICF security logging, see Internet Connection Firewall security log file overview.

OTHER HOST-BASED FIREWALLS

If you're not running Windows XP, or if you want to have greater control (and awareness) of what your firewall is doing on your behalf, a separate host-based firewall software package might serve you better. There are a variety of good products available that enhance your computer's security. For example, Zone Alarm by Zone Labs not only filters incoming connections, but also filters outgoing connections by programme. That means that you can specify which programmes on your computer should be able to communicate over the Internet and which, if any, should be prevented from doing so.

INTERNET SECURITY SERVER

ISA Server is part of the Microsoft.NET Enterprise Server family, which comprises a comprehensive set of server applications for quickly building, deploying, and managing scalable and integrated Web-based solutions and services. Designed with mission-critical performance and integration in mind, the.NET Enterprise Servers are built from the ground up for interoperability using open Web standards such as XML. The.NET Enterprise Servers, along with the Windows 2000 operating system, supply the foundation for the.NET platform, which enables the third-generation Internet: where software is delivered as a service; is accessible by any device, at any time and any place; and is fully programmable and customizable. Microsoft explicitly designed the.NET platform to enable the rapid development, integration, and orchestration of any group of Web services and applications into a single comprehensive solution.

ISA Server is an extensible enterprise firewall and Web-cache server that integrates with Windows 2000 for policy-based security, acceleration, and management of Internetworking. ISA Server provides two tightly integrated modes: a multilayer firewall and a high-performance Web-cache server. The firewall provides filtering at the packet, circuit, and application layers; stateful inspection to examine data crossing the firewall; control of access policy; and routing of traffic. The cache improves network performance and the user experience by storing frequently requested Web content. You can deploy the firewall and cache on dedicated servers separately, or integrated on the same box. Sophisticated management tools simplify policy definition, traffic routing, server publishing, and monitoring. ISA Server builds on Windows 2000 security, directory, VPN, and bandwidth control. Whether deployed as a set of separate firewall and cache servers or in integrated mode, ISA Server can enhance network security, enforce consistent Internet usage policy, accelerate Internet access, and maximize employee productivity for organizations of all sizes.

ISA Server 2000 Enterprise Edition is Microsoft's scalable enterprise firewall and Web-caching server. Microsoft designed ISA Server Enterprise Edition to meet the performance, management, and scalability needs of high-volume Internet traffic environments with centralized server management, multiple levels of access policy, and fault tolerance. ISA Server Enterprise Edition provides fast, secure, and scalable Internet connectivity for mission-critical environments.

Administrators must secure the network access points of corporate networks against hackers and unauthorized access. Blocking traffic and shutting down ports aren't sufficient or feasible in an Internet-connected organization. Having security solutions that "look inside" network traffic to validate application-specific requests mitigates risks. ISA Server

Enterprise Edition provides organizations with the stateful-packet inspection and application-layer firewall protection required to protect against today's sophisticated attacks. With ISA Server Enterprise Edition's application-level filtering technology, you can mitigate attacks such as Code Red and Nimda at the firewall before they enter company networks.

ISA Server Enterprise Edition integrates with Microsoft Management Console (MMC) and AD to provide a single directory to validate and manage all access requests for application data or services. This enables consolidation of access control and authorization policy in a centrally managed, replicated, and secure repository. ISA Server Enterprise Edition is also designed to work best with Exchange 2000 and IIS to provide fast and secure access to e-mail and Web content.

MULTILAYER FIREWALL SECURITY

A firewall can enhance security through various methods, including packet filtering, circuit-level filtering, and application filtering. Advanced enterprise firewalls, such as that provided with ISA Server Enterprise Edition, combine all three of these methods to provide protection at multiple network layers.

CIRCUIT-LEVEL FILTERING

At the circuit level, the ISA Server Firewall service works with virtually all Internet applications and protocols—such as Telnet, mail, news, Microsoft Windows Media technologies, RealAudio, and Internet Relay Chat (IRC)—and other client applications. The Firewall service makes these applications perform as if they were connected directly to the Internet. ISA Server offers circuit-level filtering for both firewall and SecureNAT clients.

Circuit-level filtering enables support for virtually all standard and custom Internet applications on the Windows platform. These applications communicate on the network by using Winsock, and you can support them, unmodified, on client machines that have the Firewall client software installed.

Circuit-level filtering inspects sessions, rather than connections or packets. A session can include multiple connections, providing a number of important benefits for Windows-based clients running the Firewall client software.

PACKET FILTERING

The packet-filtering capability of ISA Server enables the administrator to control the flow of IP packets to and from ISA Server. When packet filtering is enabled, ISA Server drops all packets on the external interface unless they're explicitly allowed, statically, by IP packet filters, or dynamically, by access policy or publishing rules.

IP packet filtering intercepts and evaluates packets before they're passed to higher levels in the firewall engine or to an application filter. You can configure IP packet filters so that only specified packets will be passed through ISA Server. This practice provides a high level of security for the network. IP packet filtering can block packets originating in specific Internet hosts and can reject packets associated with many common attacks. IP packet filtering can also block packets destined to any service on an internal network, including the Web proxy, a Web server, an SMTP server, and others.

IP packets filters are static—communication through a given port is always either allowed or blocked. Allow-filters allow the traffic through, unconditionally, at the specified port. Block-filters always prevent the packets from passing through the ISA Server computer. ISA Server supports dynamic packet filtering, opening ports automatically only as required for communications, and closing the ports when the communication ends. This approach minimizes the number of exposed ports in either direction and provides a high level of security for a network. ISA Server supports inbound and outbound IP packet filtering. ISA Server's packet filtering also allows for blocking fragments and detecting packet-level attacks against the firewall.

APPLICATION-LEVEL FILTERING

The most sophisticated level of traffic inspection that the

ISA Server firewall provides is the application-level security. "Smart" application filters can analyse a data stream for a given application and provide application-specific processing, including inspecting, screening or blocking, redirecting, or even modifying the data as it passes through the firewall. This mechanism protects against known exploits such as unsafe SMTP commands or attacks against internal Domain Name System (DNS) servers. Third-party tools for content screening, including virus detection, lexical analysis, and site categorization, also use application and Web filters to further extend the firewall.

STATEFUL INSPECTION

Stateful inspection examines data crossing the firewall in the context of its protocol and the state of the connection. At the packet level, ISA Server inspects the source and destination of the traffic indicated in the IP header and the port in the TCP or UDP header identifying the network service or application used.

Dynamic packet filters enable the opening of a port only in response to a user's request and only for the duration required to satisfy that request, reducing the vulnerability associated with open ports. ISA Server can determine dynamically which packets can be passed through to the internal network's circuit- and application-layer services. Administrators can configure access-policy rules that open ports automatically only as allowed and then close the ports when the communication ends. This process, known as dynamic packet filtering, minimizes the number of exposed ports in either direction and provides a high level of problem-free security for the network.

INTEGRATED INTRUSION DETECTION

With the help of technology that a firm known as Internet Security Systems provides, ISA Server can help administrators identify and respond to common network attacks such as port scanning, WinNuke, and Ping of Death. This technology provides ISA Server with an integrated intrusion-detection mechanism that identifies these kinds of attacks. The alert also specifies what action ISA Server should take when an attack is recognized, action that might include sending an e-mail message or a page to the systems administrator, stopping the Firewall service, writing to the system event log, or running any programme or script.

HIGH-PERFORMANCE WEB CACHE

ISA Server has a completely redesigned Web cache that enables it to place cache into RAM. This high-performance Web cache provides greater scalability on the back end as well as a faster overall Web-client response time.

CACHE ARRAY ROUTING PROTOCOL

ISA Server uses the Cache Array Routing Protocol (CARP) to provide seamless scaling and high efficiency in an array of multiple ISA Server computers. CARP uses hash-based routing to provide a deterministic "request resolution path" through an array. Having a request resolution path, which is based on a hashing of array member identities and URLs, means that for any given URL request, the browser or downstream proxy server can know exactly where the requested information is stored in the array.

CHAINED-CONFIGURATION CACHE PLACEMENT

In this context, the term "chaining" refers to a hierarchical connection between individual ISA Server computers or arrays of ISA Server computers. With chaining, an ISA Server sends client requests upstream through the chain of cache servers until the requested object is found. During this process, each ISA Server caches the object as it is forwarded through each server to the client. Consequently, chaining becomes an effective means of distributing server load and fault tolerance.

ACTIVE CACHING

With a feature known as active caching, whereby you can configure ISA Server to automatically update objects in a cache, ISA Server can optimize bandwidth utilization by proactively refreshing content. With active caching, ISA Server proactively updates objects that a client accesses frequently during periods of low network traffic.

Active caching is a way to keep objects fresh in the cache by verifying them with the originating Web server before the objects expire and a client accesses them. The goal is to expedite those client accesses that would ordinarily require a round-trip to the originating server to revalidate the data. Because there's a cost associated with this (in both proxy processing and network bandwidth), the goal is to refresh only those objects that a client is likely to access in the future.

In contrast, object "popularity" isn't a useful criterion for this because many popular pages never expire. This is due to the fact that clients refresh the pages manually to keep the data fresh. In addition, an object might be popular for only a short time. The active-caching code tries to identify objects that follow precisely the pattern of accessed content that active refreshing would help—that is, objects that expire and which a client then touches again.

UNIFIED MANAGEMENT

ISA Server takes advantage of the Active Directory service, VPN, and MMC. All these capabilities, especially MMC, help to make administration easier because operations personnel are familiar with them and can manage both the firewall and Web cache from one console.

Using built-in reporting tools, ISA Server supports the running of scheduled standard reports that detail Web usage, application usage, network-traffic patterns, and security. ISA Server provides extensive support for reporting such matters as frequency of Internet access, what is being accessed, and by whom. By alerting and reporting such matters as out-of-boundary activity to administrators, ISA Server can help them to better understand how employees are using the Web. This is helpful for capacity planning and enforcing corporate policies.

For example, with modification to the AD schema and creation of policy, administrators can configure ISA Server to run in an array. Arrays allow administrators to apply policy, such as port configuration, at the enterprise level, thereby allowing them to apply a single change to every ISA Server within each array. AD multi master replication of ISA Server configuration ensures that each server in an array receives current and automatically updated configurations.

Administrators must control and enforce security policies while simultaneously supporting employees who need Internet access. Thanks to its integration with AD, ISA Server provides comprehensive support for controlling access by user, group, application, destination, content type, and schedule.

ENTERPRISE POLICY AND ACCESS CONTROL

ISA Server also supports the creation of enterprise-level and local array policies, for centralized or local enforcement. You can install ISA Server as a stand-alone server or as an array member. For easier management and administration, array members share the same configuration. When you modify the array configuration, you also modify all the ISA Server computers in the array, including all their access and cache policies.

Centralized administration can also mean greater security. Administrators can configure a single server, and apply that configuration to multiple ISA Servers. An enterprise can take this centralized management one step further, allowing administrators to implement one or more enterprise policies, which include site and content rules and protocol rules. Administrators can apply an enterprise policy to any array and augment it with the array's own policy. This approach enforces enterprise policies at branch and departmental levels while allowing local administrators to further restrict access.

NORTEL NETWORKS ALTE ON SWITCHED FIREWALL

One of Microsoft's internal networks uses Alteon hardware firewalls, and serves as an interesting study. It contains a high-speed security network designed to support enterprise-scale applications such as online transaction processing (OLTP) and business intelligence (BI). Nortel

Networks Alteon Switched Firewalls (ASFs) that are configured for high availability provide internal network security. Two separate ASFs provide stateful failover and deep packet inspection of all connections passing through them. The ASFs provide 3.2 gigabytes of data throughput and 32,000 sessions per second with 500,000 concurrent sessions. Microsoft's configuration consists of two Alteon Firewall Accelerators and two Alteon Firewall Directors. Environments with higher capacity requirements can expand this configuration up to twelve Alteon Firewall Directors; the ASF Plug and Play (PnP) configuration features provide the ability to scale network security with zero downtime.

From an operational perspective, the ASF runs Check Point Firewall-1 Next Generation software much the same as any server running Check Point software. Procedures for monitoring security events, handling security management, and so on are the same.

What's different is the scale and throughput of the firewalls. The increased scale introduces some operational differences in how you manage the system, including features unique to the characteristics of the ASF and some features in the Check Point Firewall-1 Next Generation software that are not in other versions of Check Point Firewall software. These unique differences are outlined below.

FIREWALL SCALE CONSIDERATIONS

The Nortel Networks ASF has some unique capabilities, notably DMZ partitioning and PnP scaling, that allow for both scale-up and scale-out of the firewall solution. Nortel Networks provides training on such capabilities as part of the system installation process. Details on the operational considerations of managing ASFs.

Large networks are typically very robust in design, and effective management can be difficult. Nortel Networks provides a single management solution for the ASFs by using the Check Point software management suite. When operating a large network, the firewalls must scale to take advantage of the capacity of the server and application requirements. The firewalls must be able to scale in bandwidth, and you must maintain a very secure environment for the traffic within the data centre while still providing access to external resources. This does impose some requirements on the security administrator; for example, the firewalls need to support and scale the number of add/drop sessions per second and concurrent number of sessions while maintaining adequate throughput. When running multiple firewalls, whether multiple instances of the same firewall or a number of different firewalls working together, the key requirement is that the firewalls not interfere with one another and maintain state between themselves for failover and failback purposes.

Nortel Networks provides a single image configuration for the Alteon Firewall Cluster that provides the security administrator with the ability to perform upgrades and other administrative tasks on a single firewall, while synchronization procedures populate the changes to the rest of the cluster.

ALTEON SWITCHED FIREWALL CONSIDERATIONS

The Alteon Switched Firewall contains a number of features, such as multilink trunking and VLAN tagging, that affect certain design aspects of the network. Nortel Networks provides installation support options that you can negotiate with a local Nortel Networks sales representative. For more information.

TOOLS

Check Point Enterprise Management Client is the suite of management tools that you need to manage the ASFs. Within the Check Point Management software, there are three main modules that deal with different operational aspects of the ASF:

- Check Point Policy Editor
- Check Point Log Viewer
- Check Point System Status Viewer

These modules are described in the following sections.

Check Point Policy Editor

The Check Point Policy Editor provides comprehensive

management of the Check Point Firewall engine that runs on the ASFs. The Policy Editor enables the security administrator to perform a wide range of functions, including:

- Create, delete, and edit security policies on the ASF cluster
- Create, delete, define, and edit objects, protocols, servers, and users within the firewalls
- Install and uninstall the security policies assigned to the ASF clusters
- Create, delete, and edit address translation rules from the ASF clusters

Check Point Log Viewer

The Log Viewer provides administrators a visual representation of the traffic flow through the ASFs. Security policies define which traffic to add to the Log Viewer, so communications that don't specify logging aren't logged. The Log Viewer is capable of displaying the following information for each communication:

- Date and time
- Interface on which the traffic entered
- The action taken on the communication
- The rule number
- Encryption and address translation details

The Log Viewer has the ability to filter on each of the information categories above to focus on any element of the logs. It has three modes: log, account, and active. The log mode shows each connection as it's created. The account mode shows information pertinent to accounting, such as the duration of the connection and the number of bytes transferred. The active mode lists all the connections currently open through the ASF. When the active mode is enabled, the administrator can block any connection (which can be very useful when policing the security domain).

Check Point System Status Viewer

The System Status Viewer gives a graphical view of the working state of each firewall, and provides information on how many packets have been accepted, logged, and dropped. You can also use this tool to summarize the policy for a particular firewall. In addition, the System Status Viewer is the system monitoring interface that allows the generation of alerts under security administrator–defined conditions.

DISTRIBUTED ENTERPRISE MANAGEMENT

Distributed Enterprise Management allows the ASF administrator to configure and support multiple firewalls from one workstation. The configuration of other activities is done through their respective GUIs and saved to a central management server.

The changes or actions applied to the required firewall are then downloaded from the management server, which allows for scale able management as the number of firewalls under the administrator's control increases. The management server holds a database that contains all the information needed to generate the required security policies.

OBJECT CREATION AND MANAGEMENT

After the installation of the ASFs and after the Check Point Management software is complete, the next step is to create and apply the rule-base of the security policy. The security of the ASF is centred on an object-oriented rule-base, which you manage through the Policy Editor's management menu and tool bars.

The utilities required to create and manage the different objects are in the following tools:

- Network Objects Manager
- Services Manager
- Resources Manager
- Servers Manager
- Users Manager
- Time Objects Manager

Depending on the size of a network, including subnets used, range of services provided, and number of resources and protocols, you can save a significant amount of time by defining each element in the Objects database. When building the Objects database, you should adopt standards for object creation.

Some standards to consider are the following:

- Naming convention
- Colour
- Groups

Assigning a short, intuitive name for an object can be a difficult task. Therefore, when truncating a name to a maximum of 10 characters or symbols, you should adopt a naming convention.

For example: WS31OWSEWA (WS=Web Server, 31=Thirty-one, OW=Outlook Web Access, SE=Seattle, WA=Washington) To many people the name WS31OWSEWA might seem meaningless, but to the security administrators it would make sense. The ability to assign a colour to an individual object is a powerful administrative feature. Colour can show certain characteristics of an object, such as the department it belongs to, or where it's located. Consider the following colour scheme:

- *Red*: Firewalls
- *Green*: Internal protected objects
- *Yellow*: External possibly harmful objects
- *Black:* Services

OPERATING

The following sections describe some of the software-specific operations tasks that you can perform on the ASF. Detailed documentation on how to perform these tasks is provided with the ASF and ASF training, and is not replicated here.

CONFIGURATION

You can configure the ASF as one or more "ASF offerings." An ASF offering is simply a set of hardware components you use together to create the ASF.

You can run the entire ASF as a single firewall, or you can split the system into multiple DMZ partitions, each with its own copy of the set of rules and policies. The Nortel Networks installation contract, documented and provided to the customer, covers all hardware configurations. You can configure the Policies, Objects, and Rules bases by using the Check Point Management Client software suite of tools.

MAINTENANCE

The only periodic maintenance required on the ASFs is replacement of the licenses for the Check Point firewall engines on the management station every 12 months, depending on environmental conditions within the data centre. In the event of any hardware problems, Nortel Networks provides maintenance under the terms of the applicable service and support agreement.

REAL-TIME MONITORING

The Check Point Management software suite provides security-log monitoring. This feature provides policy-based definition and event notification to monitor the security settings of the ASFs and Check Point Firewall-1 software environment. Monitoring is continuous and in real-time to provide rapid notification of fault conditions and to ensure that all critical rules and policies are operating within defined limits.

System health monitoring provides a real-time view of the ASF, which:

- Allows the security administrator to check policy configuration and status information via a graphical user interface.
- Offers a consolidated view of the rules and objects in the ASFs.
- Provides management wizards, which enable an administrator to implement system changes across all jASFs without having to make modifications multiple times on multiple firewalls.
- Provides a Security Logs status page, from which a security administrator can view a 24-hour history of all the logs the ASF has generated.

SUPPORTING

Incidents that affect a limited number of users might be

indicative of larger problems that can affect the overall functionality of a network. Troubleshooting is an important part of incident prevention and problem management. Troubleshooting guidance is provided to help operations personnel understand various incidents and problems that might occur. Nortel Networks provides support of the ASF hardware under the terms of a service agreement. There are various options, depending on the needs of the data centre.

CAPACITY MANAGEMENT

Whether you configure the firewall as one large DMZ or multiple DMZs, capacity management is important. Being an ASIC-based switch, the ASF can perform wire speed routing and intelligent decision making to provide the best performance for a given network. Nortel Networks offers extensive performance analysis and capacity planning services to ensure clients obtain the optimum throughput from ASFs. For more information. There are several other vendors for hardware firewalls that deserve investigating. Among these are SonicWALL, Nokia, Cisco, WatchGuard, NetScreen Technologies, Lucent, and Nortel, which all offer one or more models of hardware firewalls.

SUMMARY

Of all the choices presented here, the only one you can really go wrong with is choosing none of them. Don't make the mistake of thinking that no one will attack your network, because with the rise in automated attack tools, your network is as much at risk as every other network on the Internet. Unfortunately, there's a strong subculture that misaligns the bravado of a deep understanding of how networks and computer security works with digital breaking and entering. Because of the popularity and ease-of-use of always-on connections, small office networks provide easy targets. However, by taking some simple precautions, you can protect network and your data.

To take advantage of the networked world, organizations must prevent unauthorized users from accessing their networks, and at the same time, ensure that authorized users have access only to authorized assets. By providing advanced security technologies, common management, and lower cost through integrated solutions, Microsoft can enable businesses to take advantage of the network connectivity.

Security is one of the most important features of a business site. You can implement security at all levels: network, platform, application, and database. You need to implement security technologies and tools that are cost-effective and safe, and that don't adversely affect the performance of the site.

You must implement a DMZ in your site, and configure firewalls that prevent access to dangerous services. Network segregation, data encryption, and intrusion detection will provide further security for your network.

IP ADDRESS

IP ADDRESSING

An IP address is a network layer (Layer 3) address that uniquely identifies a host, including network components and devices, on a TCP/IP network. An IP address is composed of 32 binary bits and consists of two parts: a network ID and a host ID.

- The Network ID identifies the TCP/IP hosts that are located on the same physical network. All hosts on the same physical network must be assigned the same network ID to communicate with each other. If routers connect your networks, a unique network ID is required for each wide area connection.
- The Host ID identifies the individual hosts within a network. The host ID must be unique to the network designated by the network ID.

The boundary between the network ID and the host ID of the IP address is defined by the subnet mask, which is another 32-bit field. There is a bit-for-bit alignment between the IP address and the subnet mask. The subnet mask contains a continuous field of 1s followed by a continuous field of 0s. The contiguous 1s stop at the boundary between the network

ID and the host ID of the IP address. The network boundary can occur at any place after the eighth bit position from the left. Once the boundary between the network part and the host part of the IP address is known, all devices addressed in that network will have a common binary pattern in the network part that identifies the device as belonging to the specified network. There are a number of formats for referencing an IP address. These include binary, dotted decimal notation and Classless Interdomain Routing (CIDR) Notation.

A SHORT INTRODUCTION TO IP ADDRESSES

In order for systems to locate each other in a distributed environment, nodes are given explicit addresses that uniquely identify the particular network the system is on and uniquely identify the system to that particular network. When these two identifiers are combined, the result is a globally-unique address.

This address, known as "IP address", as "IP number", or merely as "IP" is a code made up of numbers separated by three dots that identifies a particular computer on the Internet. These addresses are actually 32-bit binary numbers, consisting of the two subaddresses (identifiers) mentioned above which, respectively, identify the network and the host to the network, with an imaginary boundary separating the two. An IP address is, as such, generally shown as 4 octets of numbers from 0-255 represented in decimal form instead of binary form.

For example, the address 168.212.226.204 represents the 32-bit binary number 10101000.11010100.11100010.11001100. The binary number is important because that will determine which class of network the IP address belongs to. The Class of the address determines which part belongs to the network address and which part belongs to the node address .

The location of the boundary between the network and host portions of an IP address is determined through the use of a subnet mask. This is another 32-bit binary number which acts like a filter when it is applied to the 32-bit IP address. By comparing a subnet mask with an IP address, systems can determine which portion of the IP address relates to the network and which portion relates to the host. Anywhere the subnet mask has a bit set to "1", the underlying bit in the IP address is part of the network address. Anywhere the subnet mask is set to "0", the related bit in the IP address is part of the host address.

The size of a network is a function of the number of bits used to identify the host portion of the address. If a subnet mask shows that 8 bits are used for the host portion of the address block, a maximum of 256 host addresses are available for that specific network. If a subnet mask shows that 16 bits are used for the host portion of the address block, a maximum of 65,536 possible host addresses are available for use on that network.

An Internet Service Provider (ISP) will generally assign either a static IP address (always the same) or a dynamic address (changes every time one logs on). ISPs and organizations usually apply to the InterNIC for a range of IP addresses so that all clients have similar addresses. There are about 4.3 billion IP addresses. The class-based, legacy addressing scheme places heavy restrictions on the distribution of these addresses. TCP/IP networks are inherently router-based, and it takes much less overhead to keep track of a few networks than millions of them.

IP CLASSES

Class A addresses always have the first bit of their IP addresses set to "0". Since Class A networks have an 8-bit network mask, the use of a leading zero leaves only 7 bits for the network portion of the address, allowing for a maximum of 128 possible network numbers, ranging from 0.0.0.0 – 127.0.0.0. Number 127.x.x.x is reserved for loopback, used for internal testing on the local machine.

Class B addresses always have the first bit set to "1" and their second bit set to "0". Since Class B addresses have a 16-bit network mask, the use of a leading "10" bit-pattern leaves 14 bits for the network portion of the address, allowing for a maximum of 16,384 networks, ranging from 128.0.0.0 – 181.255.0.0.

Class C addresses have their first two bits set to "1" and their third bit set to "0". Since Class C addresses have a 24-bit network mask, this leaves 21 bits for the network portion of the address, allowing for a maximum of 2,097,152 network addresses, ranging from 192.0.0.0 – 223.255.255.0.

Class D addresses are used for multicasting applications. Class D addresses have their first three bits set to "1" and their fourth bit set to "0". Class D addresses are 32-bit network addresses, meaning that all the values within the range of 224.0.0.0 – 239.255.255.255 are used to uniquely identify multicast groups. There are no host addresses within the Class D address space, since all the hosts within a group share the group's IP address for receiver purposes.

Class E addresses are defined as experimental and are reserved for future testing purposes. They have never been documented or utilized in a standard way.

The Paessler network monitoring products PRTG Traffic Grapher and PRTG Network Monitor use the IP address in order to connect to the respective machines they are intended to monitor/graph.

MAC-ADDRESS AND IP-ADDRESS RELATIONSHIP

MAC-addresses are used on local Ethernet networks.IP-addresses are more abstract and can be used on top of multiple types of networks.

WHERE DOES IP-ADDRESSES COME IN

Local networks like an Ethernet network sends all traffic to all computers that sits on the same network bus. Global networks like the Internet will not send all traffic to all of the connected computers. IP-communication (that is used on the Internet) have a much more sophisticated way to deal with sending and routing the data communication that we will not cover here. If you want to learn more about how the Internet communication works there is plenty of information on the Internet. However IP-communication is very useful on local networks as well but we have to separate the physical part of the network from the logical part.

The communication difference between the physical and the logical part of the networks goes within a grey area in software. To the physical (hardware) domain belongs cables and network cards.

Ones the data signals have been detected on the network card the low level software on the card and in the operating system takes on the task to process this data. That processing is divided in different levels. There are standard models for this leveling of software.

One such model is called the OSI modeland have 7 levels. When studying the IP-communication you will find that it doesn't comply fully with the OSI model but in general it works the same way. The OSI model will not be explained here. You will find plenty of information on the Internet about the OSI model.

On an Ethernet Network

You do not have to use IP-communication to communicate. Before the Internet become popular and dominating other protocols like NOVELL IPX was common on local networks.

Many companies already have working local networks when Internet and IP-communication become popular. However there is no problem running several different protocols at the same time on an Ethernet network as long as all "physical" (low level) communication uses the fundamental Ethernet rules using Ethernet frames with source and destination MAC-addresses. Today the majority of Ethernet networks only runs the IP-protocol.

Network Packets are Like Russian Dolls

An IP-packet resides within an Ethernet-packet. A TCP-packet resides within an IP-packet. A HTTP-packet resides within a TCP-packet.

The data part of an Ethernet packet can hold up to 1500 bytes. MAC-addresses (48bits) are 6 bytes wide each and the Number Of Bytes field is 2 byte wide. That gives the maximum size of an Ethernet frame to be 1514 bytes.

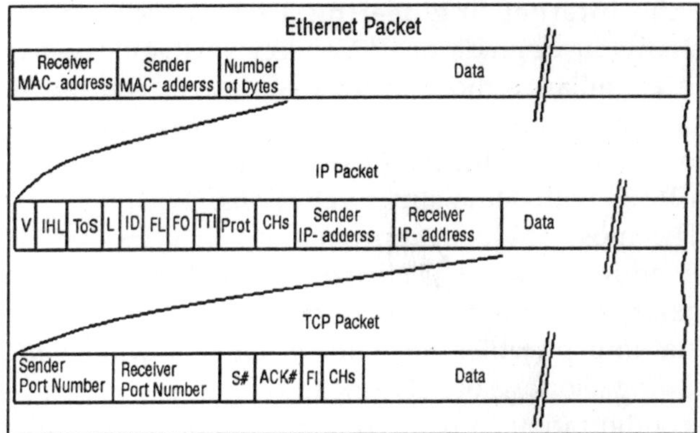

When introducing the IP-protocol on Ethernet the Number Of Bytes field is used to mark that the Ethernet frame holds an IP-packet by the number of 0x0800. By using a number that is greater than the maximum length an Ethernet frame can hold indicates that the Ethernet frame holds another protocol frame in the data part. The Ethernet standard says that if the Number Of Bytes field is greater than 0x0600 the Ethernet frame holds another protocol.

BENEFIT OF LAN EYE

LANeye detects devices by their MAC-address. As shown in the picture, IP-addresses in that perspective have no meaning to LANeye. This gives that LANeye will detect all devices on the network regardless of the device uses IP-protocol or any other protocol. This is because all devices that communicate on an Ethernet network have to use Ethernet frames. LANeye works on Ethernet level and not on protocol level.

However, LANeye make use of information on protocol level. LANeye will recognize IP-protocol packets and can extract information from IP-protocol packets like IP-addresses, Communication port number and higher level of protocols.

IPV6

DEFINITION

IPv6 (Internet Protocol Version 6) is a set of specifications from the Internet Engineering Task Force (IETF) that's essentially an upgrade of IP Version 4 (IPv4). The basics of IPv6 are similar to those of IPv4 — devices can use IPv6 as source and destination addresses to pass packets over a network, and tools like ping work for network testing as they do in IPv4, with some slight variations.

The most obvious improvement in IPv6 over IPv4 is that IP addresses are lengthened from 32 bits to 128 bits. This extension anticipates considerable future growth of the Internet and provides relief for what was perceived as an impending shortage of network addresses. IPv6 also supports auto-configuration to help correct most of the shortcomings in version 4, and it has integrated security and mobility features.

IPv6 features include:

- Supports source and destination addresses that are 128 bits (16 bytes) long.
- Requires IPSec support.
- Uses Flow Label field to identify packet flow for QoS handling by router.
- Allows the host to send fragments packets but not routers.
- Doesn't include a checksum in the header.
- Uses a link-local scope all-nodes multicast address.
- Does not require manual configuration or DHCP.
- Uses host address (AAAA) resource records in DNS to map host names to IPv6 addresses.
- Uses pointer (PTR) resource records in the IP6.ARPA DNS domain to map IPv6 addresses to host names.
- Supports a 1280-byte packet size (without fragmentation).

INTRODUCTION TO IPV6

The Internet Protocol (IP) is the most widely used communications protocol. Because it is the most pervasive communication technology, it is the focus of hundreds of thousands of IT professionals like you. Because so many people rely on the protocol, the safety of communications is top of mind. The security research that is performed on IP is conducted by both benevolent and malevolent people. All the security research has caused many patches and adjustments to IP, as it has been deployed internationally. In hindsight, it would have been better if deeper consideration were given to the security of the protocol before it was extensively deployed.

This book provides you with insight into the security ramifications of a new version of IP and provides guidance to avoid issues prior to deployment. This chapter provides a brief background on this next version of IP, IPv6. You learn why it is important to consider the security for IPv6 before its wide-scale deployment. A review of the current risks and industry knowledge of the vulnerabilities is provided, as well as the common ways that IPv6 can be secured.

Reintroduction to IPv6

The Internet Engineering Task Force (IETF) is the organization that is responsible for defining the Internet Protocol standards. When the IETF developed IPv4, the global expansion of the Internet and the current Internet security issues were not anticipated. In IPv4's original design, network security was only given minor consideration. In the 1980s, when IPv4 was developing, the "Internet" was constructed by a set of cooperative organizations. As IPv4 was developed and the Internet explosion took place in the 1990s, Internet threats became prolific. If the current environment of Internet threats could have been predicted when IPv4 was being developed, the protocol would have had more security measures incorporated into its design.

In the early 1990s, the IETF realised that a new version of IP would be needed, and the Task Force started by drafting the new protocol's requirements. IP Next Generation (IPng) was created, which then became IPv6 (RFC 1883). IPv6 is the second network layer standard protocol that follows IPv4 for computer communications across the Internet and other computer networks. IPv6 offers several compelling functions and is really the next step in the evolution of the Internet Protocol. These improvements came in the form of increased address size, a streamlined header format, extensible headers, and the ability to preserve the confidentiality and integrity of communications. The IPv6 protocol was then fully standardized at the end of 1998 in RFC 2460, which defines the header structure. IPv6 is now ready to overcome many of the deficiencies in the current IPv4 protocol and to create new ways of communicating that IPv4 cannot support. IPv6 provides several improvements over its predecessor. The advantages of IPv6 are detailed in many other books on IPv6.

However, the following list summarizes the characteristics of IPv6 and the improvements it can deliver:

- *Larger address space*: Increased address size from 32 bits to 128 bits
- *Streamlined protocol header*: Improves packet-forwarding efficiency
- *Stateless autoconfiguration*: The ability for nodes to determine their own address
- *Multicast*: Increased use of efficient one-to-many communications
- *Jumbograms*: The ability to have very large packet payloads for greater efficiency
- *Network layer security*: Encryption and authentication of communications
- *Quality of service (QoS) capabilities*: QoS markings of packets and flow labels that help identify priority traffic
- *Anycast*: Redundant services using nonunique addresses
- *Mobility*: Simpler handling of mobile or roaming nodes

Note: Remember the following IPv6 terminology:

- A *node* is any system (computer, router, and so on) that communicates IPv6.
- A *router* is any Layer 3 device capable of routing and forwarding IPv6 packets.
- A *host* is a node that is a computer or any other access device that is not a router.
- A *packet* is the Layer 3 message sourced from an IPv6 node destined for an IPv6 address.

During the development of IPv6, one of the requirements was that this new protocol must have flexible transition mechanisms. It should be easy to transition to this new protocol gradually, over many years. Because it was evident that IPv6 would become very popular, the transition would need to be slow and methodical.

Running both IPv4 and IPv6 at the same time, called *dual stack*, is one of the primary transition strategies. This concept describes the scenario in which a router supports two or more different routed protocols and forwards each type of traffic, independent of the behaviour of the other routed protocol. Seasoned network engineers will recall the concept of "ships-in-the-night routing." This term refers to the fact that packets from either protocol can pass by each other without affecting each other or having anything to do with each other. Because "dual stacking" can be a dominant migration strategy, running a network with both protocols can open that network to attacks on both protocols. Attacks can also evolve that leverage a combination of vulnerabilities in IPv4 and IPv6.

In addition to dual stack, the transition to IPv6 involves various types of tunneling approaches where IPv6 is carried over IPv4 networks that have yet to migrate to IPv6. There will likely be attacks on the transition mechanisms themselves to gain access to either the IPv4 or IPv6 portions of a network. The security of IPv6 systems must be assessed before IPv6 is permitted to be enabled on current and future networks and systems.

Because IPv6 and IPv4 are both network layer protocols, many of the network layer vulnerabilities are therefore similar. However, because the protocol layers above and below the IP layer remain the same for either IP version, many of those attacks will not change. Because the two protocols are related, the similarities between the protocols can create similar attack patterns. IPv6 could improve security in some areas, but in other areas, it could also open new threats.

IPv6 has continued to evolve since December 1998, when the IETF published RFC 2460. As the number of available IPv4 public addresses has reduced, IPv6 has become more attractive.

In fact, IPv6 is the only viable solution to this IP address depletion problem. Many of the problems in current IPv4 networks relate to address conservation. For example, perpetuating the use of Network Address Translation (NAT) and double-NAT is not a realistic long-term strategy for Internet expansion.

Today, the identity of users on the Internet is often unknown, and this has created an environment where attackers can easily operate. The use of anonymizer tools such as Tor and open proxies and the use of NAT allow users to hide their source IP addresses and allow hackers to operate without their targets knowing much about the source of the messages.

NAT is often misunderstood as a security protection measure because it hides the internal addresses and thus obfuscates the internal network topology. Many network administrators feel a false sense of security and put too much faith in NAT. NAT breaks the use of the full end-to-end communication model that IP Security (IPsec) needs to be fully effective. The firewalls that perform the NAT function have difficulty maintaining the NAT state during failover. Troubleshooting application traffic that flows through a NAT is often difficult. When using IPv6, the use of NAT is not necessary because of the large amount of addresses available. Each node has its own unique address, and it can use that address for internal and external communications.

After the core, distribution, and access layers are dual-stack enabled, the computer systems themselves can be IPv6 enabled. After this takes place, the system administrators can start to enable IPsec tunnels between IPv6-enabled nodes to provide confidentiality and the integrity of the communications between systems. This provides a greater level of security over current unencrypted IPv4 implementations. IPsec deployments utilizing both authentication and encryption are rarely used today for computer-to-computer communication. Today the common method of using IPsec only encrypts the payload in tunnel mode because the NATs that are in place prevent authenticating the header. However, communications between critical systems can optionally be secured with IPv6 IPsec, using both authentication and encryption.

IPv6 Update

IPv6 is becoming a reality. The many years of early protocol research have paid dividends with products that easily interoperate. Several early IPv6 research groups have disbanded because the protocol is starting to move into the transition phase. The 6BONE (phased out with RFC 3701) and the KAME IPv6 research and development projects have wound down and given way to more IPv6 products from a wide variety of vendors. Deployment of IPv6 is not a question of if but when. IPv6 is an eventuality.

The transition to IPv6 continues to take place around the world. The protocol is gaining popularity and is being integrated into more products. There are many IPv6-capable operating systems on the market today. Linux, BSD, Solaris, Microsoft Vista, and Microsoft Server 2008 operating systems all have their IPv6 stacks enabled by default, and IPv6 operates as the preferred protocol stack. Of course, Cisco equipment fully supports dual-stack configuration, and the number of IPv6 features within IOS devices continues to grow. However, the production use of IPv6 is still in the domain of the early adopters.

The rate of IPv6 adoption is growing but is also unpredictable. The timeline for the deployment of IPv6 is long and difficult to measure. Generally speaking, the transition to IPv6 has thus far been based on geography and politics. The Asian and European regions that did not have as many allocated IPv4 addresses have felt the pressure to transition to IPv6. While organizations in North America have more IPv4 addresses, the address-depletion effects are making the migration to IPv6 more urgent. The market segments that are focused on IPv6 are few and far between. There are few IPv6-specific applications that appeal to enterprises, service providers, and consumers that make them want to transition sooner. Some vertical markets such as government and defence, public sector, education, video distribution, and high tech are starting to see the benefits of IPv6 and are working on their transition plans.

There are still many areas of IPv6 where issues remain to be resolved. One of the remaining challenges for IPv6 is that few IPv6 service providers exist. Currently, Internet IPv6 traffic is still light compared to IPv4, but it continues to grow. This can be attributed to the lack of last-mile IPv6 access and customer premises equipment (CPE) that does not support IPv6. Multihoming, which is the concept of connecting to multiple service providers for redundancy, is an issue that will take some time to resolve, but it is doubtful that it is significantly holding back organizations from deploying IPv6. Hardware acceleration for IPv6 is not universal, and many applications lack IPv6 support. Just like the deployment of other networking technologies, network management and security are left to the end. The goal of this book is to raise awareness of the security issues related to IPv6 and to provide methods to secure the protocol before deployment.

IPv6 Vulnerabilities

IPv6 will eventually be just as popular as IPv4, if not more so. Over the next decade as IPv6 is deployed, the number of systems it is deployed on will surpass those on IPv4. While early adopters can help flesh out the bugs, there are still many issues to resolve. IPv6 implementations are relatively new to the market, and the software that has created these systems has not been field tested as thoroughly as their IPv4 counterparts.

There is likely to be a period of time where defects will be found, and vendors will need to respond quickly to patching their bugs. Many groups are performing extensive testing of IPv6, so they hopefully can find many of the issues before it is time to deploy IPv6. However, all the major vendors of IT equipment and software have published vulnerabilities in their IPv6 implementations. Microsoft, Juniper, Linux, Sun, BSD, and even Cisco all have published vulnerabilities in their software. As IPv6 has been noticed, it is evident that these major vendors have drawn the attention of the hackers.

The early adopters of IPv6 technology are encouraged to tread lightly and make sure that security is part of their transition plans. There are distinct threats of running IPv6 on a network without any security protection measures. Some operating systems can run both protocols at the same time without the user's intervention. These operating systems might also try to connect to the IPv6 Internet without explicit configuration by the user. If users are not aware of this fact and there is no security policy or IPv6 security protections implemented, they are running the risk of attack. IPv6 can be used as a "backdoor protocol" because many security systems only secure IPv4 and ignore IPv6 packets. For these reasons, it is important to secure IPv6 before it is widely deployed.

When you consider the ways that an IPv4 or IPv6 network can be compromised, there are many similarities. Attacks against networks typically fall within one of the following common attack vectors:

- Internet (DMZ, fragmentation, web pages, pop-ups)
- IP spoofing, protocol fuzzing, header manipulation, session hijacking, man-in-the-middle, sniffing
- Buffer overflows, SQL injection, cross-site scripting
- E-mail (attachments, phishing, hoaxes)
- Worms, viruses, distributed denial of service (DDoS)
- Macros, Trojan horses, spyware, malware, key loggers
- VPN, business-to-business (B2B)
- Chat, peer-to-peer (P2P)
- Malicious insider, physical security, rogue devices, dumpster diving

In 2007, The Computer Security Institute (CSI) 12th Annual Computer Crime and Security Survey stated that 59 per cent of all survey respondents suffered from insider abuse of network access. This percentage historically has been lower in the mid- to late 1990s and has risen steadily each year. So the percentage of internal attack sources is likely to be even higher today. Those internal sources of attacks could either be a legitimate hacker or an unknowing end user. The key issue is that most organizations do not spend 50 per cent of their security budget on mitigating inside threats. Therefore, external as well as internal devices must be hardened equally well but not necessarily against the same types of attacks.

One disadvantage of both IP versions is the fact that the signaling of network reachability information takes place in the same medium as the user traffic. Routing protocols perform their communication in-band, and that increases the risks to infrastructure destabilization attacks. The threat mentioned here is that user traffic can affect the protocol-signaling information to destabilize the network. Protections against these types of attacks involve securing the signaling communications between network devices. IPv6 routing protocols can use encryption and authentication to secure the signaling information, even if it is transported inside the data path. Domain Name System (DNS) is another key infrastructure component that provides important signaling functions for IPv4 and IPv6. As seen over the past ten years, there is an increase in the number of attacks that target the infrastructure and DNS of the Internet and private networks. The attacks aim to create a denial of service (DoS), which affects the usability of the entire network.

Attacks against network elements typically come from the Internet for perimetre-based devices, while attacks on intranet devices originate from malicious insiders. Most internal routers have simple protection mechanisms like simple passwords and Simple Network Management Protocol (SNMP) community strings. Ease of management typically outweighs security in most enterprise networks. Internet routers do not enjoy this friendly environment, and they are constantly susceptible to many different forms of attack.

Routers are not usually capable of running traditional server software or other applications that can have vulnerabilities. However, they can be the target of a buffer overflow, where the attacker attempts to send information to the router to overrun an internal memory buffer. The side effects can be anything from erratic behaviour to a software crash or gaining remote access. Any software that the router runs could be vulnerable, and any protocol supported and implemented within that software for communications to other devices is at risk for potential exploitation. Routers communicate over many different protocols, and each of those protocols is a potential target.

Hacker Experience

As mentioned before, there is a lack of IPv6 deployment experience in the industry. There is also a lack of experience in securing an IPv6 network. That is why it is important to understand the issues with IPv6 and prepare your defences. This should be done before IPv6 networks become a larger target for hackers. Not many IPv6 attacks exist or are publicly known, and there are few best practices for IPv6 security or reference security architectures for IPv6. However, a select few sophisticated hackers already use IPv6 for Internet Relay Chat (IRC) channels and back doors for their tools. Some DoS attacks are available and one IPv6 worm already exists, but there is little information available on new IPv6 attacks. It is fair to say that the current IPv6 Internet is not a big target for hackers. This is likely to change as the number of IPv6-connected organizations grows.

As IPv6 becomes more popular, it will continue to grow as a target of attacks, just as Microsoft software became more popular it became a larger target. Internet Explorer is a dominant web browser and experiences many attacks. As the Firefox web browser increased in popularity, so did the number of people working to find flaws in it. IPv6 will follow the same course as the number of deployments increases and it becomes a focus of new security research. The process of finding and correcting vulnerabilities will only make IPv6 stronger. However, because IPv6 has had so long to develop prior to mass adoption, the hope is that many of the early vulnerabilities have already been corrected.

The underground hacker community has started exploring IPv6. IPv6 is beginning to be well understood by these groups, and they are constructing tools that leverage weaknesses in the protocol and IPv6 stack implementations. Back doors that utilize IPv6 or IPv6 within IPv4 to obscure attacks and bypass firewalls are part of their repertoire. In fact, IPv6 capabilities have started to be added to several popular hacker tools. Many of these IPv6 attack tools are already available and relatively easy to install and operate. Tools such as Scapy6 and The Hacker's Choice IPv6 Toolkit come to mind.

Note: Throughout this book, you will see the terms *attacker, hacker,* and *miscreant* used interchangeably to refer to malevolent forces that try to take advantage of IPv6 vulnerabilities. Attacks can be initiated by an outsider such as a *malicious user* or some *malicious host* that has been compromised and is being remotely controlled. However, attacks also can be carried out by unknowing insiders who are not aware that they have just caused a problem.

IPv6 Security Mitigation Techniques

IPv6 security architectures are not substantially different from those for IPv4. Organizations can still have the same network topologies when they transition to IPv6 as they have today. The network can still support the organization's mission, and the network can still have data centres, remote sites, and Internet connectivity, regardless of what IP version is being used.

With IPv6, the perimetre design has the same relevance as for IPv4, and most organizations can continue to have the "hard, crunchy" exterior and the "soft, squishy" interior networks. The problem is that most organizations put most of their effort into securing the perimetre, and they overlook the internal security of their environments. If these organizations considered the malicious insider threat, they might rethink the perimetre model and move to a model that has an even layer of security spread throughout. Many of these classic security paradigms still apply to IPv6 networks. When it comes to securing IPv6 networks, the following areas of an IT environment needs to be protected:

- Perimetre protections from the Internet and external entities
- Secure remote-site connectivity with Virtual Private

Network (VPN) technologies
- Infrastructure protection measures to ensure a secure network foundation
- Server security to protect the critical IT assets and data
- Client security measures to mitigate the insider threat

Over time, there will be changes in the way systems communicate with IPv6. Traffic patterns can change from being primarily client/server to being more peer-to-peer in nature. The use of anycast communications can add redundancy to communications but also make them less deterministic. Mobile IPv6 and tunnels can change the perimetre concept because there needs to be trusted nodes outside the perimetre. This can transform the perimetre into a more fuzzy and nebulous concept. Greater use of end-to-end encryption is needed to secure the different communication flows. Therefore, over time, the security architectures for IPv6 networks will transform to keep up with the way people communicate.

Standard IT security principles still apply when thinking about the security of IPv6 networks. Organizations should utilize multiple defensive strategies that support each other. Organizations should also have diversity in their defences so that different types of protections help protect against multiple types of threats. Your defensive mechanisms are only as strong as the weakest link, so all parts of the protections should be fortified like a castle. A good example of this concept is to have a security architecture that has a perimetre and internal controls to not only mitigate the Internet threats but also the insider threats. Having both defence in depth and diversity of defence is like having "both a belt and suspenders" to prevent you from getting caught with your pants down. If you do not consider both for IPv6, you will have a network that is embarrassingly exposed to the elements.

The Cisco Self Defending Network (SDN) can also be a guide for protecting IPv6 networks. The SDN philosophies apply to IPv4 and IPv6 networks alike. The concepts of integration, collaboration, and adaptability are core capabilities of the self-defending network. Integrated security is the idea that security for networks should be inherent in the design and not added after the fact. This is very much the case with IPv6, where many devices have IPsec built in right from the start.

Collaboration between many diverse security solutions makes the security of the entire system more robust. IPv6 allows this form of collaboration because every node can have its own address and can easily communicate seamlessly across boundaries. Adaptability allows the security systems to respond dynamically to the situation at hand. IPv6 can provide the ability to communicate in new ways that can adapt to the needs of the users while providing security awareness. IPv6 can be the secure network platform that is the fundamental foundation of the Cisco Self Defending Network architecture.

The ways to protect IPv6 networks are much the same as those methods used to protect IPv4 networks. Concepts such as network perimetres, LAN security, remote-site communications and VPNs, infrastructure protection, server farm protection, and host/client security are all areas of focus for IPv6. The building blocks of a Self Defending Network include the following components:

- Endpoint protection
- Admission control
- Infection containment
- Intelligent correlation and incident response
- Inline Intrusion Prevention Systems (IPS) and anomaly detection
- Application security and anti-X defence

While not all of these technologies work seamlessly for IPv4 and IPv6, these are the types of components required for securing either IP version).

Few best practices exist for IPv6 deployment. As the Internet community continues to evolve IPv6 solutions, there will be solutions to the problems discovered through testing and trial deployments. IPv6 mailing lists, collaboration groups, the IETF v6ops working group, and interoperability testing organizations are deeply involved with gathering information on IPv6 deployment experiences. These organizations are experimenting with the early IPv6 solutions and documenting the best ways to implement IPv6. However, there are no current IETF Best Current Practices (BCP) for IPv6 security. As more is known about how IPv6 operates in live networks and more ways are found to secure it, the BCPs will develop.

Security risks can be mitigated through adequate training of the IT staff and the security administrators. Network professionals must understand the risks related to IPv6 and ensure that they are installing the correct protection mechanisms. Security policies need to be drafted or updated with the new security issues that IPv6 brings, and end users need security awareness training to help avoid unknowingly becoming insider threats.

Virtually all organizations rely heavily on their staff and their network security devices to protect their critical computer systems. Most organizations use firewalls, host-based and network-based intrusion prevention systems (IPS), antivirus software, and Security Information Management Systems (SIMS) to help monitor security events in this locked-down environment. Companies have spent a lot of money trying to secure their computer network infrastructure from invasion. This is primarily because there are weaknesses in the protocols and defects in applications used on computer networks that can be subverted by malicious individuals. While malicious individuals exploit weaknesses in protocols, unknowing individuals help propagate the threats by ignoring corporate security policy, guidelines, and standards.

IPv6 security devices need to be purchased when they are available and kept up to date so that when new IPv6 vulnerabilities are discovered, the computer systems are protected. Organizations are going to need IPv6-capable security products ahead of the deployment of IPv6. Firewalls are pervasive in today's networks, and there are several firewall solutions available for IPv6. However, in 2008, many IPSs and VPN concentrators do not support IPv6. The planning for the migration to IPv6 has been taking place for several years, but for now, much of the needed functionality does not exist. It can take a couple of years for there to be feature parity between IPv4 and IPv6 security products. Therefore, organizations should plan to upgrade their current security systems to achieve IPv6 functionality.

Instead of focusing on the theoretical security implications of IPv6, you should aim to implement the practical practices of securing a network based on the information that is available today.

No one can yet claim extensive experience deploying all the IPv6 security mitigation techniques. For now, we can only discuss what is known to be true, based on limited deployment experiences. However, there is some certainty that the techniques shown in this book are effective based on the current knowledge of IPv6, testing, and experience securing computer networks.

Summary

Effective security involves finding that perfect balance between protecting an asset and the handling the extra burden security adds to doing business. The implementation of security should match the value of your assets and the acceptable level of risk. You should craft a security strategy that matches your level of risk. When it comes to IPv6, this means adjusting the security measures to fit the changes related to using a new network layer protocol.

First you must understand the differences between IPv4 and IPv6 and know how those deltas have security implications. Next you must understand what vulnerabilities in IPv6 you must address. The final step is to implement security mitigation techniques to provide adequate coverage for your environment.

Even though the guidelines in this book are based on sound principles, they are not necessarily considered time-tested best practices. Just as IPv6 is in its early stages, the methods of securing IPv6 are rapidly changing. Because few IPv6 attacks exist, not all the future attacks are fully understood. Therefore, the guidelines in this book need to be customised to meet your organization's needs. Please do not just implement every command listed in this book. Rather, you should read the book, understand the threats, and then embark on using the correct techniques to secure your own IPv6 network.

4

Mobile Communication

In a mobile communication terminal for starting and simultaneously using a plurality of applications, one desired application starts fast to improve the operability when the number of started applications reaches a present limiting number of applications. An application start determining unit searches a list of started applications in response to the instruction of the start of application to obtain the number of started applications, and determines that the application cannot start when the number of started applications reaches a preset limiting number of applications.

An ending-application selecting unit selects, as an ending application to be ended, the application with the low priority from the start applications based on the preset priority of application when the application start determining unit determines that the application cannot start.

An application ending unit performs the ending processing of the ending application selected by the ending-application selecting unit and deletes the selected ending application from the list of started applications.

A mobile communication terminal for starting and simultaneously using a plurality of applications, comprising: application start determining means which compares the number of started applications with a preset numerical value that is a maximum number of simultaneously used applications, determines that the application can start when the number of started applications is less than the numerical value, and determines that the application cannot start when the number of started applications reaches the numerical value;

ending-priority list creating means which calculates values indicating the using situation of the started applications in response to the determination of the application start determining means that the application cannot start and creates a list of ending priority indicating the order of applications with low influence in the case of ending the application; ending-application selecting means which selects the ending application based on the list of ending priority in response to the determination of the application start determining means that the application cannot start and clears the list of ending priority; application ending means which performs the ending processing of the ending application selected by the ending-application selecting means; application starting means which starts the application instructed by a user in response to the determination of the application start determining means that the application starts; and wherein the ending-priority list creating means collects data on evaluation items indicating the using situations including the total time displayed after starting the application, the number of switching times for display operation, and the last display time, obtains the order of started applications every evaluated item, multiplies the order by a weighting coefficient preset every evaluated item and every type of application, adds the multiplied result every application, calculates the values indicating the using situations, sorts the applications in order of the larger values, and creates the list of ending priority.

An application starting control method of a mobile communication terminal for starting and simultaneously using a plurality of applications, comprising the steps of: presetting a numerical value that is a maximum number of simultaneously used applications; selecting, from started applications, an ending application to be ended based on a priority when the number of simultaneously used applications will exceed the numerical value; newly allowing to start an application after ending the selected ending application; and collecting data for the started applications, including a total time displayed after starting the application, the number of switching times for display operation, and the last display time, determining an order of the respective data for each of the started applications, multiplying each determined order by respective weighting coefficients for each of the started applications, adding the multiplied results for each of the started applications, and creating the priority by sorting the applications based on the added results.

A mobile communication terminal for starting and simultaneously using a plurality of applications, comprising: application start determining means which compares the number of started applications with a preset numerical value that is a maximum number of simultaneously used applications, determines that the application can start when the number of started applications is less than the numerical value, and determines that the application cannot start when the number of started applications reaches the numerical value; selecting means which selects an ending application to be ended on the basis of low priority from the started applications, in response to the determination of the application start determining means that the application cannot start; application ending means which performs ending processing of the ending application selected by the ending application selecting means; application starting means which starts the application instructed by a user in response to the determination of the application start determining means that the application can start; and ending-priority list creating means for collecting data on evaluation items indicating the using situations including the total time displayed after starting the application, the number of switching times for display operation, and the last display time, obtaining the order of started applications every evaluated item, multiplying the order by a weighting coefficient preset every evaluated item and every type of application, adding the multiplied result every application, calculating the values indicating the using situations, sorting the applications in order of the larger values, and creating a priority list.

INVENTION

The present invention relates to a mobile communication

terminal and an application starting control method thereof. More particularly, the present invention relates to a mobile communication terminal for starting and simultaneously using a plurality of applications and an application starting control method thereof.

Recently, one type of mobile phones is sold to start a plurality of applications and simultaneously use a plurality of functions similarly to a personal computer or the like, under the improvement of CPU processing capacity. Such a mobile phone terminal enables a user to send an e-mail while viewing a site screen on the Internet or to check the schedule by a scheduler while having a call. However, the mobile phone terminal does not have a sufficient memory capacity or power capacity. Therefore, if many applications simultaneously start similarly to the personal computer, a malfunction is caused in the communication function or the started application operation becomes unstable.

An unnecessary application must terminate without continuously staying resident in memory when the number of simultaneously-used applications reaches a predetermined limiting number. Preferably, the unnecessary application automatically ends. As disclosed in the above-mentioned publication, the degree of importance is set to the application so as to use the application with the high degree of importance for a long time when the remaining amount of battery is reduced while a plurality of applications start, and the application with the low degree of importance ends when the remaining amount of battery reduces. However, when the number of applications to be started is over a predetermined number, the application to be ended does not automatically end.

DETAILS

It is an object of the present invention to provide a mobile communication terminal and an application starting control method thereof, for fast starting a desired application and improving the operability by automatically selecting and ending the application to be ended when the number of started applications reaches a predetermined limiting number upon starting the application. According to the present invention, there is provided an application starting control method of a mobile communication terminal for starting and simultaneously using a plurality of applications, comprising the steps of presetting a limiting number of simultaneously used applications; selecting, from started applications, an ending application to be ended based on the priority when applications over a limiting number are going to be started; and newly allowing to start an application after ending the selected ending application. The priority may be preset or may be determined based on a using situation of the started application.

The selected ending application may be displayed on a screen in response to the selection of the ending application. In this case, the selected ending application is ended in response to the approval operation of a user. According to the present invention, there is also provided a mobile communication terminal for starting and simultaneously using a plurality of applications, comprising application start determining means which compares the number of started applications with a preset limiting number of simultaneously used applications, determines that the application can start when the number of started applications is less than the limiting number, and determines that the application cannot start when the number of started applications reaches the limiting number; selecting means which selects an ending application to be ended on the basis of low priority from the started applications in response to the determination of the application start determining means that the application cannot start; application ending means which performs ending processing of the ending application selected by the ending application selecting means; and application starting means which starts the application instructed by a user in response to the determination of the application start determining means that the application can start.

The application starting means may start the application instructed by the user in response to the ending processing of the application ending means. The application start determining means may determine whether or not the application starts in response to the instruction to start the application from the user.

The mobile communication terminal may have a list of started applications indicating the started applications. In this case, the application start determining means searches the list of started application to obtain the number of started applications. The application ending means deletes the selected ending application from the list of started applications. The application starting means starts the application determined as the start by the application start determining means and registers the started application to the list of started applications.

The mobile communication terminal may further comprises means for receiving the approval of the user before the ending processing of the ending application in response to the selection of the ending application by the ending application selecting means.

According to the present invention, there is also provided a mobile communication terminal for starting and simultaneously using a plurality of applications, comprising application start determining means which compares the number of started applications with a preset limiting number of simultaneously used applications, determines that the application can start when the number of started applications is less than the limiting number, and determines that the application cannot start when the number of started applications reaches the limiting number; ending-priority list creating means which calculates values indicating the using situation of the started applications in response to the determination of the application start determining means that the application cannot start and creates a list of ending priority indicating the order of applications with low influence in the case of ending the application; ending-application selecting means which selects the ending application based on the list of ending priority in response to the determination of the application start determining means that the application cannot start and clears the list of ending priority; application ending means which performs the ending processing of the ending application selected by the ending-application selecting means; and application starting means which starts the application instructed by a user in response to the determination of the application start determining means that the application starts.

The ending-priority list creating means may collect data on evaluation items indicating the using situations including the total time displayed after starting the application, the number of switching times for display operation, and the last display time, place a number to each of started applications in the order of their magnitude every evaluated item, multiply the number by a weighting coefficient preset every evaluated item and every type of application, add the multiplied results every application, calculate the values indicating the using situations, sort the applications in order of the larger values, and create the list of ending priority.

The mobile communication terminal may have a list of started applications indicating the started application. In this case, the application start determining means searches the list of started applications and obtains the number of started applications; the application ending means deletes the selected ending application from the list of started applications, and the application starting means starts the application determined as the start by the application start determining means and registers the started application to the list of started applications.

According to the present invention, the limiting number (maximum number) of applications for simultaneous use is set and when the start of a new application amounts to the number of applications over the limiting number, the application for ending is automatically determined and is ended in accordance with the priority from among the using applications. Thus, in case that the number of applications reaches the limiting number, the new application is started quickly and the operability upon starting the application is improved.

WIRELESS COMMUNICATIONS

Wireless communications is a rapidly growing segment of the communications industry, with the potential to provide high-speed high-quality information exchange between portable devices located anywhere in the world. Potential applications enabled by this technology include multimedia Internet-enabled cell phones, smart homes and appliances, automated highway systems, video teleconferencing and distance learning, and autonomous sensor networks, to name just a few. However, supporting these applications using wireless techniques poses a significant technical challenge.

This course will cover advanced topics in wireless communications for voice, data, and multimedia. We begin with a brief overview of current wireless systems and standards. We then characterize the wireless channel, including path loss for different environments, random log-normal shadowing due to signal attenuation, and the flat and frequency-selective properties of multipath fading. Next we examine the fundamental capacity limits of wireless channels and the characteristics of the capacity-achieving transmission strategies.

These strategies are typically not practical. Thus, our next focus will be on practical digital modulation techniques and their performance under wireless channel impairments, including flat and frequency selective fading. The next part of the course is spent investigating techniques to improve the speed and performance of wireless links. We will investigate the design and performance of adaptive modulation and diversity techniques to compensate for flat-fading. Three techniques to combat frequency-selective fading are then examined: adaptive equalization, multicarrier modulation, and spread spectrum. We will also study the multiple access capabilities of spread spectrum with multiuser detection. The course concludes with a brief overview of wireless networks, including multiple and random access techniques, WLANs, cellular system design, and ad-hoc network design. Applications for these systems, including the evolution of cell phones and PDAs, smart homes and appliances, sensor networks, and automated highways and skyways, will also be discussed. Presenting comprehensive coverage of this fast moving field, Wireless Communications and Mobile Computing provides the R&D communities working in academia and the telecommunications and networking industries with a forum for sharing research and ideas. The convergence of wireless communications and mobile computing is bringing together two areas of immense growth and innovation. This is reflected throughout the journal by strongly focusing on new trends, developments, emerging technologies and new industrial standards. Under the guidance of an international editorial and advisory board drawn from academia and industry, this high quality, peer-reviewed journal, provides leading edge coverage of the opportunities and challenges driving the research and development of mobile communication systems.

All you need to stay ahead:

- *High calibre survey papers*: Written by leading experts in the wireless and networking communities.
- *Rapid publication times*: Due to electronic review and submission of original research papers
- *Special Issues*: Addressing key topics of interest and managed by high profile editors
- An international forum for the sharing of research and ideas Key topics presented by leading individuals at the cutting edge of new technologies.

MOBILE INTERNET WML

WML (Wireless Markup Language) is the new web language for making sites on mobile phones. Over the past few months new WAP (Wireless Applications Protocol) phones have become extremely popular and many large websites have created special 'mobile' versions of their site. Many people predict that, over the next few years, WAP sites will become even morepopular and e-commerce over mobile phones will be widely available.

USING WML

Although you might not have any plans immediately for

creating a WAP version of your site, it is always a good idea to get involved in new technology. All you need to do is make a small site (even one page) which tells people a bit about your website. In the future you can develop the site further with things like e-mail and information for people to get directly off their phones.

The main sites which will benefit from WAP are ones providing a service like e-mail, live sports scores or a calendar service etc. but there are many other uses. For example, a site giving music reviews could put their reviews on a WAP site. People could then read the reviews on their mobile phone while browsing through the CDs in a shop.

HAVING WAP PHONE

To create a WAP site you don't need a WAP enabled phone. You can get a WAP simulator for a PC. This is a piece of software which will give you a WAP phone on your desktop. You can then type in the URLs of WAP sites and can view them on your PC. You can get a very good free WAP simulator from YourWAP

COMPARING SITES

WAP sites are not like standard web sites at all. As an example, you are looking at part of the Gowansnet web site. Here is a screenshot of the Gowansnet WAP site (http://gowansnet.waphosts.net):

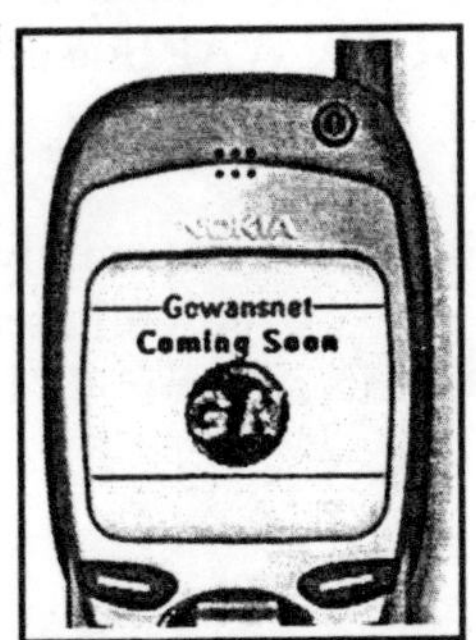

As you can see, sites written in WML are monochrome, very limited and there is very little screen space. Because of

this you must be very careful when you are designing a WAP site as it is nothing like a web site.

BEGINNING WAP SITE

After reading the introduction you should understand about WAP sites, WML and what you can do with them so I will go straight into how to create a site. Note that you should really either have a WAP phone or a WAP simulator so that you can view your site and a knowledge of HTML is useful.

Finding A WML Host

Unfortunately WML cannot be run on all web hosts. For WML content to be run, a web host must make some changes to the configuration of their web server. If your host cannot do this for you, you can try WAPHosts.net. They can provide you with a server which will support WML.

Declaring A WML Document

Cards

Instead of having pages, WAP sites have cards. These are what is displayed on the screen at one time, just like a page. More than one card can be inserted in each WML document. To declare a card, insert the following:

```
<card id="index" title="My WAP Site"
    newcontext="true">
```

This will make a card with the ID index (used for linking) and will display the text: My WAP Site at the top of the screen.

Closing Tags

Unlike with HTML, it is extremely important to close WML tags. If you do not, a page will certainly not work. You must close both the <card> and <wml> tags:

```
</card>
</wml>
```

ADDING TEXT

In the last part I showed you how to create the basic file

which will contain your WAP site. In this part I am going to show you how to insert text and how to format it.

The <p> Tag

Just like in HTML the <p> tag is used to show where a paragraph begins and ends. Unlike HTML, though, all text on a WML page must be inside these tags. You are not allowed to nest these tags either. One important thing to remember about WML is that, unlike HTML where a page will still display even if there is bad code, a WAP phone will just reject a page if there is and code it doesn't understand.

As with HTML you use the tags as follows:

```
<p>
information
</p>
```

Aligning Text

Aligning text in WML is nearly exactly the same as in HTML, except you can't use the centre tag. All aligning must be done using the following <p> tags:

Centre: <p align="centre">

Right: <p align="right">

The
 Tag

In WML (as mentioned earlier) all tags must be closed. This causes problems when using old HTML tags (like <Br>) which have no closing tag. To get around this, some tags have had a/put on the end e.g.

```
<Br/>
```

This, like in HTML will make a line break.

Text

In WML there is actually no font tag (as you can only display text in the phone's default font in black). To show text all you need to do is put it in between the <p> and </p> tags.

Here is an example of a full WML document:

```
<?xml version="1.0"?>
```

```
<!DOCTYPE wml PUBLIC "-//WAPFORUM//DTD WML 1.1/
    /EN" "http://www.wapforum.org/DTD/wml_
    1.1.xml">
<wml>
<card id="index" title="My WAP Site"
    newcontext="true">
<p align="centre">
```

Welcome to my new WAP site. You can view this on your mobile phone anywhere in the world!

It is amazing!

```
</p>
</card>
</wml>
```

HYPERLINKS AND IMAGES

In part 3 I showed you how to create a basic WAP site with one page and some text. This week I will show you how you can make this better by adding extra parts, linking to them (and other sites) and how to add images to your site.

More Cards

As I explained in the second part of this tutorial, WAP sites have cards instead of pages. They are really the same as pages except they can all be written in one file. To add another card, all you need to do is put in another <card> tag with a different ID to the others. For example:

```
<card title="About Me" id="about">
information
</card>
```

would be added below the first card but before the </wml> tag.

Linking

There are three ways to link to another WAP site, file or card. Just like in HTML these can either be the full path to a file or a relative link.

To link to a WAP site you use the following:

```
<a href="http://gowansnet.waphosts.net/">
```

```
Gowansnet</a>
```

in your text. To link to another file on your site you would use:

```
<a href="links.wml">My Links</a>
```

and to link to another card in the same page you use:

```
<a href="#about">About Me</a>
```

Images

Unfortunately, because WAP phones only have monochrome screens, images do not work very well on WML pages. They also use their own image format: WBMP. When you are creating an image to use on your site you will need to make it small (mobile phone screens are about 100x50 pixels).

The easiest way to get an image into the WBMP format is to create it as a GIF or JPG (it can be in colour if you want) and then visit Teraflops.com to convert it into a monochrome (black and white) WBMP image which you can then include on your site.

Images in WML are inserted using the <img> tag, just like in HTML:

```
<img src="logo.wbmp" alt="Logo"/>
```

Again, you can see that a/has been added at the end as the <img> tag has no closing tag. It is very important that you also include the alt text as it will be displayed while the image is being downloaded.

In part 3 I showed you how to create a basic WAP site with one page and some text. This week I will show you how you can make this better by adding extra parts, linking to them (and other sites) and how to add images to your site.

More Cards

As I explained in the second part of this tutorial, WAP sites have cards instead of pages. They are really the same as pages except they can all be written in one file. To add another card, all you need to do is put in another <card> tag with a different ID to the others. For example:

```
<card title="About Me" id="about">
information
</card>
```

would be added below the first card but before the </wml> tag.

Linking

There are three ways to link to another WAP site, file or card. Just like in HTML these can either be the full path to a file or a relative link.

To link to a WAP site you use the following:

```
<a href="http://gowansnet.waphosts.net/">
Gowansnet</a>
```

in your text. To link to another file on your site you would use:

```
<a href="links.wml">My Links</a>
```

and to link to another card in the same page you use:

```
<a href="#about">About Me</a>
```

Images

Unfortunately, because WAP phones only have monochrome screens, images do not work very well on WML pages. They also use their own image format: WBMP. When you are creating an image to use on your site you will need to make it small (mobile phone screens are about 100x50 pixels).

The easiest way to get an image into the WBMP format is to create it as a GIF or JPG (it can be in colour if you want) and then visit Teraflops.com to convert it into a monochrome (black and white) WBMP image which you can then include on your site.

Images in WML are inserted using the <img> tag, just like in HTML:

```
<img src="logo.wbmp" alt="Logo"/>
```

Again, you can see that a/has been added at the end as the <img> tag has no closing tag. It is very important that you also include the alt text as it will be displayed while the image is being downloaded.

5

Network Operating Systems

A network operating system (NOS) is a computer operating system system that is designed primarily to support workstation, personal computer, and, in some instances, older terminal that are connected on a local area network (LAN). Artisoft's LANtastic, Banyan VINES, Novell's NetWare, and Microsoft's LAN Manager are examples of network operating systems. In addition, some multi-purpose operating systems, such asWindows NT and Digital's OpenVMS come with capabilities that enable them to be described as a network operating system.

A network operating system provides printer sharing, common file system and database sharing, application sharing, and the ability to manage a network name directory, security, and other housekeeping aspects of a network.

A network operating system (NOS) is a software programme that controls other software and hardware that runs on a network. It also allows multiple computers, also known as network computers, to communicate with one main computer and each other, so as to share resources, run applications, and send messages, among other things. A computer network can consist of a wireless network, local area network (LAN), a wide area network (WAN), or even two or three computer networks. The heart of any of these networks, however, is the network operating system.

There are different types of operating systems. Most individual computer users run client operating systems, like Windows XP®, which run on a single computer. Personal computers that individuals use at home have a client operating system which manages the interactions and processes between the computer and its peripherals such as the keyboard, mouse, external monitor, and printer. In a sense, this is also a network, though it is different in scale than a network operating system which manages the interactions of many computers.

A network usually consists of many network computers that are connected to a central hub or router. The central hub, in turn, is connected to a larger, main computer. The network may also include other devices like printers, a tape-backup system, and a central storage facility. The main network computer runs all the connected computers and devices with the help of the operating system software.

A network administrator is the person who installs and manages the network and its operating system. He or she may configure the NOS to recognize a wireless network as well. If a WAN is involved, this would probably require more than one network administrator, as the network would likely be located offsite.

A network operating system has a menu-driven administration interface. From this interface, the network administrator may perform a variety of activities. He or she can use the interface to format hard drives, set up security restrictions, or establish log-in information for each user. The interface of a network operating system can also be used to attach shared printers to the network, or configure the system to automatically back data up on a daily basis.

An important component of a network is the file server. A file server is the device where data is stored for use by network computers. It can be a single computer or it can be a cluster of external hard drives hooked up in series to store data. A network operating system helps manage the flow of information between that file server and the network computers.

Examples of network operating systems include UNIX®, Windows 2000 Server ®, and Netware®. Each operating system runs differently, and as such has to be configured to perform the actions the network requires. A good knowledge of each operating system is necessary to work with them. Network administrators may need to be certified in order to manage particular network operating systems.

EXPLANATION

Network operating systems (NOS) typically are used to run computers that act as servers. They provide the capabilities required for network operation. Network operating systems are also designed for client computers and provide functions so the distinction between network operating systems and stand alone operating systems is not always obvious.

Network operating systems provide the following functions:

- File and print sharing.
- Account administration for users.
- Security.

INSTALLED COMPONENTS

- Client functionality
- Server functionality

FUNCTIONS PROVIDED

- Account Administration for users
- Security
- File and print sharing

NETWORK SERVICES

- File Sharing
- Print sharing
- User administration
- Backing up data

UNIX

DESCRIPTION

Is it possible for an Information Technology [IT] product to be both mature and state-of-the-art at the same time? In the case of the UNIX® system, the answer is an unqualified "Yes." The UNIX system has continued to develop over the past twenty-five years. In millions of installations running on nearly every hardware platform made, the UNIX system has earned its reputation for stability and scalability. Over the years, UNIX system suppliers have steadily assimilated new technologies so that UNIX systems today provide more functionality as any other operating system.

Perhaps the key to the continuing growth of the UNIX system is the free-market demands placed upon suppliers who produce and support software built to open standards. The "open systems" approach is in bold contrast to other operating environments that lock in their customers with resultant high switching costs. UNIX system suppliers, on the other hand, must constantly provide the highest quality systems in order to retain their customers. Those who become dissatisfied with one UNIX system implementation retain the ability to easily move to another UNIX system implementation.

The continuing success of the UNIX system should come as no surprise. No other operating environment enjoys the support of every major system supplier. Mention the UNIX system and IT professionals immediately think not only of the operating system itself, but also of the large family of application software that the UNIX system supports. In the IT marketplace, the UNIX system has been the catalyst for sweeping changes that have empowered consumers to seek the best-of-breed without the arbitrary constraints imposed by proprietary environments.

In a nutshell then, the UNIX system is the users' and suppliers' operating environment of choice. The UNIX system represents the best collective efforts of competing suppliers, the most refined standards in the public domain, and the rock-solid stability that comes from years of quality assurance testing, mission-critical use, and refinement.

This white paper examines the UNIX system with a special concern for both its extraordinary past and its equally extraordinary prospects for the future.

THE UNIX SYSTEM

The UNIX system has been around for a long time, and

many people may remember it as it existed in the previous decades. Many IT professionals who encountered UNIX systems in the past found it uncompromising. While its power was impressive, its command-line interface required technical competence, its syntax was not intuitive, and its interface was unfriendly.

Moreover, in the UNIX system's early days, security was virtually nonexistent. Subsequently, the UNIX system became the first operating system to suffer attacks mounted over the nascent Internet. As the UNIX system matured, however, the organization of security shifted from centralized to distributed authentication and authorization systems.

Now, a single Graphical User Interface is shipped and supported by all major vendors has replaced command-line syntax, and security systems, up to and including B1, provide appropriate controls over access to the UNIX system.

THE VALUE OF STANDARDS

The UNIX system's increasing popularity spawned the development of a number of variations of the UNIX operating system in the 1980s, and the existence of these caused a mid-life crisis. Standardization had progressed slowly and methodically in domains such as telecommunications and third-generation languages; yet no one had addressed standards at the operating system level.

For suppliers, the thought of a uniform operating environment was disconcerting. Consumer lock-in was woven tightly into the fabric of the industry. Individual consumers, particularly those with UNIX system experience, envisioned standardized environments, but had no way to pull the market in their direction.

However, for one category of consumer -governments- the standardization of the UNIX system was both desirable and within reach. Governments have clout and are the largest consumers of information technology products and services in the world. Driven by the need to improve commonality, both US and European governments endorsed a shift to the UNIX system. The Institute of Electrical and Electronic

Engineers POSIX family of standards, along with standards from ISO, ANSI and others, led the way. Consortia such as the X/Open Company (merged with the Open Software Foundation in 1995 to form The Open Group) hammered out draft standards to accelerate the process.

In 1994, the definitive specification of what constitutes a UNIX system was finalized through X/Open Company's consensus process. The Single UNIX Specification was born-not from a theoretical, ivory tower approach, but by analyzing the applications that were in use in businesses across the world.

With the active support of government and commercial buyers alike, vendors began to converge on products that implement the Single UNIX Specification, and now all major vendors have products labeled UNIX 95, which indicates that the vendor guarantees that the product conforms to the Single UNIX Specification.

Vendors continue to add value to the UNIX system, particularly in areas of new technology, however that value will always be built upon a single, consensus standard. Meanwhile, the functionality of the UNIX system was established and the mid-life crisis was resolved. Suppliers today provide UNIX systems that are built upon a single, consensus standard.

It is also important to remember that even when variance among UNIX systems was at its worst, IT professionals agreed that migration among UNIX system variants was far easier than migration among the proprietary alternatives.

Now with UNIX 95 branded products available from all major systems vendors, the buyer can for the first time buy systems from different manufacturers, safe in the knowledge that each one is guaranteed to implement the complete functionality of the Single UNIX Specification and will continue to do so.

UNIX system suppliers can assure customers that they own a standards-based system by registering them to use the Open Brand. Below is a list of suppliers who give users this guarantee.

UNIX 95 REGISTERED PRODUCTS

- *Digital*: Digital UNIX Version 4.0 running Digital's AlphaStations and Digital's Alpha Servers
- *Hitachi*: Hitachi 3050RX, 3500/3X, 3500/4XX running HI-UX/WE2 Version 06-01 and later HITACHI: Hitachi 3500 running HI-UX/WE2 Version 07-01 and later Hewlett-Packard: HP-UX Release 10.20 and later on all HP9000 Series 700 and 800
- HP-UX Release 11.00 or later (in both 32 and 64-bit configurations) on HP9000 Series (all models)
- *IBM*: IBM POWER, POWER2, and Power PCTM Systems with IBM AIX Version 4.2 or later IBM: OS/390 Version 1 Release 2 or later with OS/390 V1R2 or later Security Server and OS/390 V1R2 or later C/C++ Compiler on IBM System/390 Processors that support OS/390 Version 1 Release 2 NCR: NCR UNIX System V Release 4 MP-RAS Release 3.02 or later on NCR World Mark Series and System 3000 Series NEC: UX/4800 R12.3 and later on UP4800 and EWS4800 Series SCO: SCO UnixWare Family R2.1.1 and later for single and multiprocessor IntelTM 386/486 or Pentium® PCs conforming to PC/AT architectures
- *SGI*: IRIX 6.5 running on Silicon Graphics systems using the MIPS R4000, R5000, R8000 and R10,000 family of processors
- *SNI*: Business Servers running BS2000/OSD V3.0 and higher.
- *SNI*: Reliant UNIX V5.43 running on RM Server Family, all Models RM200/300/400/600
- *Siemens Pyramid*: Reliant UNIX Version 5.43 running on Reliant RM1000 Cluster Server
- *SUN*: Solaris 2.6 on SPARC based systems
- *SUN*: Solaris 2.6 on x86pc based systems

UNIX AND WINDOWS NT

It is common these days to read analysts' accounts and IS professionals' experiences that compare and contrast the

UNIX system with Microsoft Corporation's latest operating system, called Windows NT. Opinions vary, of course, but a number of common themes have emerged. The key differences between these operating environments are as follows:

The UNIX system today is more robust, reliable and scalable. Analysts say this observation, which is widely reported from many different viewpoints, makes practical sense. Engineers at Microsoft are retracing the steps that the UNIX system has completed. How else could it be?

In sharp contrast to the open standards that define the UNIX system, Windows NT technology remains fiercely proprietary. Microsoft remains ambivalent to the world of standards. Choosing NT entangles customers with nonstandard utilities, directories, and software tools that do not conform to any de jure or consensus standards. The UNIX system today is available on a wide spectrum of computer hardware. Particularly when high performance is at issue, hardware suppliers suggest the UNIX system, rather than Windows NT. The primary appeal of NT is for low-end, office-centred, departmental applications.

Unit shipment growth rates for Windows NT exceed the rates for the UNIX system, which is to be expected for a new product. However, revenue growth in UNIX systems sales is much higher than NT. It is reasonable to expect Windows NT to take a share in the operating systems market, along with other more specialized operating systems. There is no evidence today to indicate that NT will be dominant; in fact, most IT professionals predict that it will not.

Windows NT Server 4.0 is still not a full-function server operating system. While it does support multi-user computing via third-party add-on tools, it lacks certain fundamental features that the UNIX system is known for providing, such as directory services for managing user access and peripherals over a distributed enterprise network.

The presence of the UNIX system in the marketplace has been good for Windows NT. The UNIX system established the market for cross-platform client and server operating environments that NT seeks to address. In turn, NT will improve the market for UNIX systems in the future. That is, competition among UNIX system providers will be enhanced by competition with NT. The choice between open and proprietary products will be quite crisp.

TODAY'S UNIX SYSTEM

The key to the continuing growth of the UNIX system is the free-market demands placed upon suppliers who produce and support software built to public standards. The "open systems" approach is in bold contrast to other operating environments that lock in their customers with high switching costs. UNIX system suppliers, on the other hand, must constantly provide the highest quality systems in order to retain their customers. Those who become dissatisfied with one UNIX system implementation retain the ability to easily move to another UNIX system implementation.

The continuing success of the UNIX system should come as no surprise. No other operating environment enjoys the support of every major system supplier. Mention the UNIX system and IT professionals immediately think not only of the operating system itself, but also of the large family of hardware and application software that the UNIX system supports. In the IT marketplace, the UNIX system has been the catalyst for sweeping changes that have empowered consumers to seek the best-of-breed without the arbitrary constraints imposed by proprietary environments.

The market's pull for the UNIX system was amplified by other events as well. The availability of relational database management systems, the shift to the client/server architecture, and the introduction of low-cost UNIX system servers together set the stage for business applications to flourish. For client/server systems, the networking strengths of the UNIX system shine. Standardized relational database engines delivered on low-cost high-performance UNIX system servers offered substantial cost savings over proprietary alternatives.

UNIX SYSTEM EXISTENCE

For the last two and a half decades, the UNIX system has

upheld a tradition of providing its customers with early access to new technologies. For example:

- UNIX systems provided early access to RISC technology. Applications in CAD/CAM, multimedia, and large-scale publishing that demanded high performance workstations have always used the UNIX system platform.
- The UNIX system provided early access to symmetric multiprocessing [SMP] computers. UNIX system-based SMP parallel processors radically improved the price/performance of midsize and high-range servers.
- The UNIX system first enabled distributed transaction processing in conjunction with TP monitors from independent software suppliers. The server side of client/server technology was launched on the UNIX system.
- The UNIX system launched the Internet and the World Wide Web.

UNIX system suppliers also have a proud tradition of integration with legacy systems as well as innovation to uphold. No other system can ensure that disparate systems - usually proprietary systems - can be integrated, allowing the buyer's investment in data and information to be realised with minimal disruption and reinvestment. There is every reason to believe that the UNIX system will continue to be the platform of choice for innovative development. In the near term, for example, UNIX system vendors will define the scope of Java and provide the distributed computing environment into which the Network Computer terminal will fit and enable it to thrive and grow.

How will Java and the Network Computer terminal manifest themselves? The exact answer is unknown; however, in open computing, the process for finding that answer is well understood. The UNIX system community has set aside (via consensus standards) the wasteful task of developing arbitrary differences among computing environments. Rather than building proprietary traps, this community is actively seeking ways to add value to the UNIX system with improved scalability, reliability, price/performance, and customer service. Java and the Network Computer terminal offer several potential advantages for consumers. One key advantage is a smaller, lighter, standards-based client. A second advantage is a specification that is not controlled by one company, but is developed to the benefit of all by an open, consensus process. Thirdly, greater code reuse and a component software market based on Object technology, such as CORBA and Java. All of these options and more are being deployed first by members of the UNIX system community.

INDUSTRIAL STRENGTH UNIX SYSTEM

Today's UNIX system is robust, scalable, and it continues to provide uniform access to a wide variety of computing hardware. For these reasons the UNIX system continues to be the operating system of choice for mission-critical systems. The UNIX system is the key enabler for enterprises that wish to keep switching costs as low as possible. That is, the UNIX system remains the only open alternative to locking in on a proprietary operating system.

Scalability is here today, enabling application to run on small-scale systems through to the largest servers necessary. The UNIX system is available on hardware ranging from low-cost PC-class servers on through parallel architectures that harness together 60 or more processors. This range is wider and the choices of hardware more cost effective than any other system. The UNIX system is the only option for Massively Parallel Processing (MPP).

A robust operating system is tough enough to perform successfully under a variety of different operating conditions. By virtue of its worldwide deployment by an international community of system vendors, the UNIX system has earned the reputation for robustness.

Uniform operating system services are at the heart of the standardized UNIX system. Many enterprise systems are assembled with hardware from several different sources. Atop these different hardware platforms, the UNIX operating system provides a uniform platform for database management systems and application software. The market for the UNIX system continues to expand. IDC estimates the market at US$ 39 billion in 1996 and forecasts the market to be US$ 50 billion in the year 2000. In addition, the installed base of the UNIX system has an estimated value of US$ 122 billion. These market estimates lead to several conclusions about the UNIX system, as follows:

An annual market of US$ 39 billion is large enough to remain attractive to many suppliers and to provide sufficient revenue to fund continuing high levels of investment in support and product enhancement. The UNIX system's growth rates, which appear modest in comparison to the unit shipment growth of newer products, are anchored by an enormous installed base. High unit shipment growth rates are typical of new entries in a marketplace.

In key benchmarks and mission-critical applications, the UNIX system consistently performs better. The UNIX system is the dominant software platform for Relational Database Management Systems. Investment in developing and enhancing UNIX system products is significantly larger than in any other operating environment.

SINGLE UNIX SPECIFICATION

Today, The Open Group's UNIX 95 brand may be applied to any operating system product that is guaranteed to meet the Single UNIX Specification. The Single UNIX Specification is designed to give software developers a single set of APIs to be supported by every UNIX system. The most significant consequence of the Single UNIX Specification initiative is that it shifts the focus of attention away from incompatible UNIX system product implementations on to compliance with a single, agreed-upon set of APIs. If an operating system meets the specification, and commonly available applications can run on it, then it can reliable viewed as open.

So, the future looks as though it will be about a set of sturdy and dependable specifications standing as a firm foundation upon which many competing product implementations will be built.

By developing a single specification for the UNIX system, The Open Group and the computer industry have completed the foundation of open systems.

The next version of the Single UNIX Specification, known as Version 2 was announced in March 1997. Products guaranteed to conform to this specification will carry the label UNIX 98.

SINGLE UNIX SPECIFICATION

The Single UNIX Specification, Version 2 contains the following enhancements:

- *Year 2000 Alignment*: Changes to minimize the impact of the Millennium Rollover.
- *Threads*: POSIX 1003.1c-1995. The Threads extensions permit development of applications to make significant performance gains on multiprocessor hardware.
- Large File Summit extensions to permit UNIX systems to support files of arbitrary sizes, this is of particular relevance to database applications.
- *Networking Services*: The specifications are aligned with the POSIX 1003.1g standard.
- *MSE*: The Multibyte Support Extension is now aligned with ISO C amendment 1, 1995.
- Dynamic linking extensions to permit applications to share common code across many applications, and ease maintenance of bug fixes and performance enhancements for applications.
- N-bit cleanup (64 bit and beyond), to remove any architectural dependencies in the Single UNIX Specification. This is of particular relevance with the ongoing move to 64 bit CPUs.
- The real-time extensions are an optional feature group, allowing procurement of X/Open real-time systems with predictable, bounded behaviour.
- Inclusion of the existing specifications for the graphical user interface, CDE as an option in the UNIX 98 brand.

BENEFITS FOR APPLICATION DEVELOPERS

- Improved portability.
- Faster development through the increased number of standard interfaces.
- More innovation is possible, due to the reduced time spent porting applications.

BENEFITS FOR USERS

The Single UNIX Specification will evolve and develop in response to market needs protecting users investment in existing systems and applications. The availability of the UNIX system from multiple suppliers gives users freedom of choice rather than being locked in to a single supplier. And the wide range of applications - built on the UNIX system's strengths of scalability, availability and reliability - ensure that mission critical business needs can be met.

SUMMARY

When the history of the information age is written, the extraordinary dynamics of the UNIX system marketplace will be seen as playing an important role. The UNIX system was developed at just the right time and place to be the critical enabler for a revolution in information technology. Client/ server architectures, the Internet, object databases, heterogeneous transaction processing, and Web computing all emerged on the shoulders of the UNIX system.

Most importantly, the UNIX system continues to be a driving force for innovation because of its commitment to standards. When proprietary differences are set aside, and with the wide implementation of the Single UNIX Specification they are set aside, suppliers compete by adding value. This fundamental tenet is the reason that the UNIX system has thrived - and will continue to thrive in the years to come.

HISTORY OF UNIX

Unix was originally developed in the 1960s and 1970s by a group of AT&T employees at Bell Labs. Today, Unix systems are split into different branches which have developed over time by AT&T and by commercial vendors and non-profit organizations. Many variations (usually called "flavours") of Unix and Unix-like Operating Systems were released during the dot com boom of the 1990's. The dot com bust caused many of these to consolidate. As a result, of the dozens of commercial variations of Unix that were developed in the 1980s, only Solaris, HP-UX, and AIX are still doing relatively well in the market. Of these, Solaris currently holds the highest market share. A system is termed UNIX only if it complies fully with (and is certified by) the Single Unix Specification (SUS) standards. Similar systems that do not comply fully or are not certified are termed "Unix-like" operating systems. Examples of popular Unix-like systems include Linux and Xenix.

INTRODUCTION TO LINUX

Linux is quite possibly the most important free software achievement since the original Space War, or, more recently, Emacs. It has developed into an operating system for business, education, and personal productivity. Linux is no longer only for UNIX wizards who sit for hours in front of a glowing console (although we assure you that many users fall into this category). This book will help you get the most from Linux.

Linux (pronounced with a short i, as in LIH-nucks) is a UNIX operating system clone which runs on a variety of platforms, especially personal computers with Intel 80386 or better processors. It supports a wide range of software, from TeX, to the X Window System, to the GNU C/C++ compiler, to TCP/IP. It's a versatile, bona fide implementation of UNIX, freely distributed under the terms of the GNU General Public License.

Linux can turn any 80386 or better personal computer into a workstation that puts the full power of UNIX at your fingertips. Businesses install Linux on entire networks of machines, and use the operating system to manage financial and hospital records, distributed computing environments, and telecommunications. Universities worldwide use Linux to teach courses on operating system programming and design. Computing enthusiasts everywhere use Linux at home for programming, productivity, and all-around hacking.

What makes Linux so different is that it is a free implementation of UNIX. It was and still is developed cooperatively by a group of volunteers, primarily on the Internet, who exchange code, report bugs, and fix problems in an open-ended environment. Anyone is welcome to join the Linux development effort. All it takes is interest in hacking a free UNIX clone, and some programming know-how.

HISTORY OF LINUX

UNIX is one of the most popular operating systems worldwide because of its large support base and distribution. It was originally developed at AT&T as a multitasking system for minicomputers and mainframes in the 1970's, but has since grown to become one of the most widely-used operating systems anywhere, despite its sometimes confusing interface and lack of central standardization. Many hackers feel that UNIX is the Right Thing--the One True Operating System. Hence, the development of Linux by an expanding group of UNIX hackers who want to get their hands dirty with their own system.

Versions of UNIX exist for many systems, from personal computers to supercomputers like the Cray Y-MP. Most versions of UNIX for personal computers are expensive and cumbersome. At the time of this writing, a one-machine version of UNIX System V for the 386 runs about US$1500.

Linux is a free version of UNIX developed primarily by Linus Torvalds at the University of Helsinki in Finland, with the help of many UNIX programmers and wizards across the Internet. Anyone with enough know-how and gumption can develop and change the system. The Linux kernel uses no code from AT&T or any other proprietary source, and much of the software available for Linux was developed by the GNU project of the Free Software Foundation in Cambridge, Massachusetts, U.S.A. However, programmers from all over the world have contributed to the growing pool of Linux software. Linux was originally developed as a hobby project by Linus Torvalds. It was inspired by Minix, a small UNIX system developed by Andy Tanenbaum. The first discussions about Linux were on the Usenet newsgroup, comp.os.minix. These discussions were concerned mostly with the development of a small, academic UNIX system for Minix users who wanted more.

The very early development of Linux mostly dealt with the task-switching features of the 80386 protected-mode interface, all written in assembly code.

Linus writes,

- ``After that it was plain sailing: hairy coding still, but I had some devices, and debugging was easier. I started using C at this stage, and it certainly speeds up development. This is also when I started to get serious about my megalomaniac ideas to make `a better Minix than Minix.' I was hoping I'd be able to recompile gcc under Linux someday...
- ``Two months for basic setup, but then only slightly longer until I had a disk driver (seriously buggy, but it happened to work on my machine) and a small file system. That was about when I made 0.01 available (around late August of 1991): it wasn't pretty, it had no floppy driver, and it couldn't do much of anything. I don't think anybody ever compiled that version. But by then I was hooked, and didn't want to stop until I could chuck out Minix."

No announcement was ever made for Linux version 0.01. The 0.01 sources weren't even executable. They contained only the bare rudiments of the kernel source and assumed that you had access to a Minix machine to compile and experiment with them.

On October 5, 1991, Linus announced the first ``official" version of Linux, which was version 0.02. At that point, Linus was able to run bash (the GNU Bourne Again Shell) and gcc (the GNU C compiler), but not much else. Again, this was intended as a hacker's system. The primary focus was kernel development--user support, documentation, and distribution had not yet been addressed. Today, the Linux community still seems to treat these issues as secondary to ``real programming"--kernel development.

After version 0.03, Linus bumped up the version number to 0.10, as more people started to work on the system. After several further revisions, Linus increased the version number to 0.95 in March, 1992, to reflect his expectation that the system was ready for an ``official" release soon. (Generally, software is not assigned the version number 1.0 until it is theoretically complete or bug-free.). Almost a year and a half later, in late December of 1993, the Linux kernel was still at version 0.99.pl14--asymptotically approaching 1.0. At the time of this writing, the current stable kernel version is 2.0 patchlevel 33, and version 2.1 is under development.

Most of the major, free UNIX software packages have been ported to Linux, and commercial software is also available. More hardware is supported than in the original kernel versions. Many people have executed benchmarks on 80486 Linux systems and found them comparable with mid-range workstations from Sun Microsystems and Digital Equipment Corporation. Who would have ever guessed that this ``little" UNIX clone would have grown up to take on the entire world of personal computing?

Bibliography

Adkins, M.: *The Power of Language in Computer-Mediated Groups*, New York: Albany: State University of New York, 1997.

Balson, D.: *Telematics in the Third World: The IDRC Experience*, New York: Macmillan Publishing, 2002.

Edgar, S.: *The Information Utility*, New Jersey: AFIPS Press, 1999.

Herbert, S.: *The Emerging Network Marketplace*, New Jersey: Ablex Publishing, 2000.

Hiltz: *Online Communities: A Case Study of the Office of the Future*, New Jersey: Ablex, Norwood, 1999.

Johansen, R.: *Teleconferencing and Beyond*, New York: McGraw Hill, 1996.

Licklider, J.C.R.: *Social Prospects of Information Utilities*, New Jersey: AFIPS Press, 1999.

Lipnack, J.: *The Networking Book*, New York: McGraw Hill, 1999.

Masuda, Y.: *The Information Society*, Japan: Institute for the Information Society, 2002.

McConnell, J.: *Internetworking Computer Systems : Interconnecting Networks and Systems*, New Jersey: Prentice Hall, 2001.

McLuhan, M.: *The Native Computer Communications Network*, New York: McGraw-Hill Book Company, 2003.

Mosco: Vincent.: *Effective Moderation of Computer Conferences*, New Jersey: Pushbutton Fantasies, 1998.

Rice, R.: *The New Media*, Beverley Hills: Sage, 1999.

Rogers, E.: *Communication of Innovations: A Cross-Cultural Approach*,

New York: Free Press, 1997.

Stallings, W.: *Handbook of Computer-Communications Standards*, New York: Macmillan, 2003.

Stoll, C.: *The Cuckoo's Egg: Tracking a Spy through the Maze of Computer Espionage*, New York: Doubleday, 1999.

Tanenbaum, A.: *Computer Networks*, New Jersey: Prentice Hall,1999.

Vallee, J.: *The Network Revolution*, California: Press, Berkeley, 2005.

Welch, M.: *Networking*, New York: Harcourt Brace Janovich, 2003.

Index

A

Algorithms 11, 128
Ambiguous 6
Analogy 25
Anticlockwise 49
Asymmetrical 56, 57
Asynchronous 35, 69, 87, 113, 116, 123, 129, 134, 147, 163

B

Backbone Reliable 63

C

Coaxial Cables 4, 13, 28, 35
Competitors 3, 105
Congestion 28, 64, 140, 141, 142, 143, 166
Consequentl 43

D

Duplex 23, 32, 83, 102

E

Encapsulation 118, 130, 132, 150
Encrypted 155, 192
Enthusiasm 26
Equipment 4, 5, 7, 13, 49, 63, 66, 68, 80, 81, 83, 84, 110, 143, 241, 242, 284
Establish 27, 38, 80, 83, 158, 159
Establishment 31, 40, 87, 118, 159, 179
Execution 21

F

Far-sightedness 26
FTP 23, 27, 156, 178, 179, 207

H

Heterogeneous 24, 280
Hierarchical 20, 56, 57, 137, 158, 163, 164, 165, 220
Hierarchy 56, 57, 58, 63, 69, 158
Humanitarian 3

I

Illustrates 143, 147, 148, 149, 152, 156, 160, 161, 163, 165
Instantaneous 6

L

Limitations 48, 55, 56, 58, 74, 110, 111, 121

M

MAC 36, 37, 38, 90, 95, 100, 103, 107, 114, 116, 117, 118, 122, 139, 152, 153, 159, 160, 161,

162, 163, 165, 171, 233, 234
Mesh Topology 58
Metropolitan 8, 13, 66

N

Nationwide 12
Negligible 12, 13, 97
Noticeably 48
NSFNET 26

O

Omnipresent 5
OSI 21, 22, 27, 28, 31, 32, 33, 34, 38, 40, 69, 70, 71, 72, 74, 75, 117, 118, 120, 127, 145, 146, 147, 148, 149, 150, 151, 152, 153, 154, 155, 158, 159, 163, 167, 169, 170, 234

P

Peripherals 13, 52, 268, 274
Pharmacy 9
Phenomenon 4, 135
Priori 64
Protocols 1, 10, 21, 24, 27, 30, 31, 32, 33, 38, 39, 40, 41, 42, 43, 44, 64, 65, 70, 75, 78, 83, 91, 92, 93, 94, 95, 96, 97, 114, 116, 120, 121, 123, 124, 127, 148, 152, 153, 154, 157, 158, 163, 167, 170, 178, 180, 197, 213, 215, 217, 225, 226, 234, 235, 239, 243, 244, 245, 249
PSTN 8, 68
PVC 64

R

Redundancy 36. 48, 49, 59, 86, 118, 145, 167, 209, 242, 247
Reliability 39, 49, 59, 63, 107, 112, 121, 122, 144, 145, 277, 280
Restricted 8, 12, 28, 52, 119
Retransmits 29, 99, 167
Ring Topology 5, 48, 49, 50, 53, 65, 152
Robustness 20, 39, 277

S

Semiconductors 26
Simplistic 61
SMDS 10, 66, 157
SONET 48, 69
Suppliers 10, 270, 271, 272, 274, 275, 276, 278, 280
Synchronization 72, 73, 100, 116, 129, 224
Synchronizing 155

T

TCP 10, 21, 23, 24, 25, 27, 28, 33, 38, 39, 64, 65, 66, 70, 78, 121, 154, 159, 162, 163, 170, 171, 195, 196, 212, 213, 219, 230, 232, 234, 281
TIBCO 43
Topologies 11, 45, 47, 49, 54, 55, 57, 58, 59, 67, 201, 202, 246
Transit 26, 152
Transparency 1
Transudation 35

U

UDP 27, 39, 154, 179, 185, 187, 195, 196, 212, 219
Underpinnings 23, 25